The Authors

Ron Halliday is one of Scotland's best-known writers on crime, the supernatural and unexplained phenomena. A history graduate of the University of Edinburgh his best-selling books include *Evil Scotland*, *UFO Scotland* and *McX: Scotland's X-Files*. Halliday regularly contributes to television and radio programmes and his work has been serialised in several national newspapers. The *Evening Times* called him 'The real X-Files man . . . Scotland's answer to spooky Mulder', while *The Sun* described an earlier work as 'The most disturbing book of the year.'

Chris Terry has worked as a book editor for many years. A history graduate of the University of Manchester, he has a long-standing interest in true crime. Terry lives in Ayrshire.

SCOTLAND'S KILLERS:
FROM MANUEL TO MITCHELL

Ron Halliday and Chris Terry

Fort Publishing Ltd

First published in 2005 by Fort Publishing Ltd, Old Belmont House,
12 Robsland Avenue, Ayr, KA7 2RW

Cover illustration by Andy Bridge. Based on photographs:
left, Peter Manuel (courtesy of Mirrorpix); right, Luke Mitchell
(courtesy of Scotsman Publications Ltd)

Thanks to the staffs of the National Library of Scotland, Edinburgh and
the Mitchell Library, Glasgow.

Contact from copyright owners welcome

Graphic design by Mark Blackadder

Typeset by Senga Fairgrieve

Printed by Bell and Bain Ltd, Glasgow

ISBN 0-9547431-7-2

CONTENTS

INTRODUCTION

Scotland's murderers come from all age groups and every social class. They rarely stand out in a crowd and often appear like the man or woman next door. Dennis Nilsen was popular with his workmates. James Harkins, the 'Butcher of Gartnavel', was promoted shortly before he hacked his family to death. Gay slasher William Beggs was described as a 'good friend'. Iain Scoular came from a prosperous, middle-class background and had just got engaged.

More often than not murder is a solitary business. One killer, one victim. But occasionally killers form an exclusive 'club'. Two people become so close they don't just share each others fantasies, but want to turn those fantasies into reality. The bond is so intense that the relationship becomes the reality and anything outside becomes of less consequence. Stepping over the threshold becomes so much easier in those circumstances, as the cases of killer duos James Petrolini and Richard Elsey, and Rita Davidson and Edward Gallagher, show.

Many murderers have a long history of criminality. Both William Beggs and Angus Sinclair had murder convictions before killing again. Robert Black almost took the life of a young girl before he set out on his killing spree. Richard Coubrough, nicknamed 'The Cobra', perpetrated a string of sexual assaults before he finally murdered. Gavin McGuire had brutally raped a number of women before committing the ultimate crime. Donald Forbes cheated the gallows after his first murder but then killed again after being released; incredibly, even after serving a second life term, he became heavily involved in drug trafficking and was again incarcerated.

Have our courts been too lenient? Had Angus Sinclair been put away for life following his first murder, several women would still be alive today. The astonishing leniency shown to Gavin McGuire is an indelible stain on the face of Scotland's criminal justice system. And Brian Beattie was also the beneficiary of a system that seems to go out of its way to favour the wrongdoer.

But what is it that drives normally upright people with no obviously deviant trait to murder? Love is a strong motive. David Watt, the 'Casanova of the golf course', murdered to have his lover for his own. James Harkins wanted no one else to look after his little boy. Archie 'Mad Dog' McCafferty was driven over the edge by the death of his baby son. Teacher Grant Dunn, a middle-aged man, became obsessed with his beautiful young pupil. But what drove John Campbell and George Clelland – two teenagers from decent homes – to plan and carry out the vicious murder of a friend's mother? There is no obvious answer. It is acts like these, random events of madness, which suggest that the taboo of killing another human being will always be broken by someone, somewhere, sometime.

Then there are the 'Saturday night' killings. The murders that take place because young men have filled themselves with alcohol or drugs and lose control. Tragic deaths like those of 19-year-old Mark Ayton and brilliant student Robert Howie are the result. One thing seems clear. Murder won't just vanish from our streets. Its causes are too complex. Killers are too varied, as are their motives. Jealousy. Rage. Mental disturbance. Greed and arrogance. The list could easily be added to.

Monetary gain is another powerful motive. Men like David Donnell, Christopher Hutcheson, Robert Smith, Andrew Walker and Ricardo Blanco have no excuses. Murder was a means to an end. A way of advancing their criminal careers. The fact that in some cases they enjoyed killing was simply a bonus.

And what of police success in catching killers? Are there simply too many unsolved murders? Bible John, who spent hours with his victims and was seen by hundreds of witnesses, has remained free since his homicidal spree in the 1960s. In the same way the killers of Renee MacRae and Brenda Page have never had to face a jury. The saga of sex pervert Brian Beattie shows that even experienced police officers can become fixated with a suspect and ignore obvious evidence pointing to the real perpetrator. Angus Sinclair was never suspected of murdering adults because he was seen as a child killer and was only caught thanks to scientific advances in genetic fingerprinting. Pure detective work had got nowhere. In spite of an eight-year investigation, the biggest ever mounted, involving millions of pounds and tens of thousands of police hours, child killer Robert Black was caught by pure chance thanks to an observant member of the public. He wasn't even a suspect. For a short while detectives were suitably humbled though whether anything has been learned from these failures in police methods only time will tell. We have to remember though that our policemen are no different from the rest of us. Doing their best in difficult circumstances and, as in the case of Howard Wilson, giving their lives in our defence. If there are faults with the force, it lies in police methods and flawed procedures; not in the individuals themselves.

A last word should go to the fair sex. It is true that women murder far less than men, if we discount child killing. But when women do they can be just as calculating and vicious as men. Jealousy or a broken relationship is more often than not the driving force that sets a woman on the path to murder. But that hardly excuses Kim Galbraith's blasting of her husband as he slept. Or Sheila Garvie's involvement in the brutal murder of her partner.

There's no doubt that public attitudes to murder vary from outright horror to quiet sympathy. But everyone agrees that murder stands on its own as the ultimate attack on the values of our society. Killing another human being will always rank as the most evil crime.

Ron Halliday and Chris Terry, September 2005.

1. Owen Anderson

He killed to win back wife

As usual, the day started with a kiss. And as Gary Linn embraced his wife, Kathleen Linn gently warned him not to be late home. They were due to attend an engagement party for their niece that night and Kathleen knew that her conscientious husband was likely to put in extra hours. It was 31 August 2001.

But by seven o'clock that evening the 38-year-old had still not returned, which came as no surprise to his devoted wife or their three children at the family's home in Kilsyth. Her husband was dedicated to his work, so dedicated that he was the top salesman for his company, Snap-On Tools. But when another three hours elapsed – and calls to his mobile phone elicited no response – Mrs Linn was so worried that she called the police. Her fears were compounded when, twenty-four hours later, his Mercedes van was found burnt out at Edgelaw reservoir in Midlothian, fifty miles from his home. The tools that he carried in the van, worth £36,000, were missing. There was no sign of Gary Linn and no clue as to his whereabouts.

The police immediately suspected foul play and launched a major investigation involving more than one hundred officers from two police forces: Central Scotland and Lothian and Borders. They moved quickly to identify suspects. From mobile-phone records they established that the last call received by Mr Linn was made by Owen Anderson, a 30-year-old man from Stenhousemuir.

Detectives discovered that Anderson had had business dealings with Gary Linn; he had bought tools from him in the recent past and owed £145 for these purchases. Further investigation revealed more damning facts. It was established that Anderson had stolen Mr Linn's van and £36,000 worth of tools, and had subsequently sold the tools for just £2,000 to an acquaintance, garage owner Martin Birnie of Dalkeith in Midlothian. And then bloodstains were discovered seeping through the floorboards in Anderson's house. Feverish efforts by Anderson to remove the blood with bleach and to cover it with red paint failed to deceive forensic officers. But there was still one problem for the police: until a body was found there could be no murder charge; Gary Linn was still officially a missing person.

The search for a body intensified and, as is often the case, there was a number of false dawns, including fruitless searches of landfill sites, rubbish dumps and motorway verges. Kathleen Linn appeared on television to plead for help in locating her husband. The Linn family and Snap-On Tools offered a £10,000 reward to encourage anyone with information to come forward. In an interview with police, chief suspect Owen Anderson pledged to tell everything he knew about the case but never did. Months passed without a breakthrough but just when it seemed the case would never be cracked the police got lucky. On 17 May 2002, nearly nine months after Gary Linn disappeared, a man organising a group walk saw an old carpet on the banks of the river Esk next to Braidwood Bridge in Midlothian and, keen to preserve the environment, decided to take it away. But this upstanding citizen was to get a nasty shock: the carpet contained a corpse. He had found the remains of Gary Linn. Now, at last, Owen Anderson could be charged with murder.

At the trial in December 2002 in Glasgow's High Court the full story was revealed. Anderson had lured Gary Linn to his house on the pretext of repaying the money he owed for tools. Once in the house he felled the salesman with a single hammer-blow. He then put a bag over his victim's head and smashed the hammer on his skull a further eight times. Such was the force of the blows that Gary Linn's skull was broken into tiny pieces. After disposing of Mr Linn's van and selling the contents Anderson returned home, wrapped up the body and dumped it.

Anderson's defence was that he and Gary Linn had been involved in an insurance scam and that he had only disposed of the body. He claimed that it was a man called 'Stevie' from Edinburgh who had actually killed Mr Linn, and said he was unable to identify 'Stevie' because of worries about his family's safety. The defence team also tried to portray father-of-two Anderson as a devoted family man. But the prosecution argued that the insurance scam was simply a figment of Anderson's imagination and that 'Stevie' did not in fact exist. Despite the best efforts of the prosecution the waters may have been muddied somewhat by the defence because the jury, although it returned a guilty verdict on the murder charge, did so only on a majority basis. Anderson was also convicted of attempting to pervert the course of justice and theft. The judge, Lord Emslie, gave Anderson a life sentence for the murder with a recommendation that he should serve at least eighteen years before being considered for release. Martin Birnie and an accomplice also pleaded guilty to the reset of Mr Linn's tools.

The trial also brought out details of Anderson's background, personality and his motives for becoming a murderer. Far from having criminal genes he had a respectable trade as a mechanic and was the son of a prominent local politician, Maureen Anderson, the former deputy provost of Midlothian Council. But things had not been going his way. He was unemployed, had several convictions for dishonesty and his wife, Eloise, had left him only five months into their marriage. Their relationship had clearly been a stormy one; he was charged with threatening her, destroying her underwear and even killing her cat (charges that were later dropped). But he was still desperate to win her back and these feelings no doubt intensified as their first wedding anniversary approached on 1 September 2001. Maybe if he had money to clear his debts, and even buy her expensive presents, he could worm his way back into her affections. Indeed, so desperate was he to get back with his wife that in the weeks leading up to the murder he had actively been trying to arrange the sale of the tools carried by Gary Linn.

So for the sake of £2,000 a good man's life was snuffed out. A family man with a loving wife and three young children. The effect on Kathleen Linn and her family has been devastating. Shortly after the trial ended she said, 'We were always just very happy. The most frightening thing in all of this is being alone. I'm terrified of the future.' Her greatest wish was to have just one more minute with her late husband: 'I'd like a cuddle and a kiss.' And, like many family members in the same circumstances, she believes that the sentences passed on murderers are just not long enough. Life, in the view of Kathleen Linn, should mean life for cold, calculating killers like Owen Anderson.

2. Brian Beattie

An obvious suspect

Talented youngster Lawrence Haggart was over the moon: at just fifteen, he signed a contract with Celtic Football Club and then, on 14 March 1996, made his debut for the Scotland youth team in Belgium. Tragically, his potential was never to be realised. At 1.30 a.m. on Saturday, 16 March Lawrence's elder brother, John (17), woke at their home in Glenbervie Drive, Larbert to the smell of burning. He rushed downstairs to find Lawrence badly injured and the couch on which he was lying smouldering. The clothes that Lawrence had left in a heap beneath his feet had been set alight. The teenager was rushed to Falkirk infirmary but died the following day in the intensive care unit at the Western General in Edinburgh to which he had been transferred.

From the start police were in no doubt that Lawrence had been murdered. He had been savagely battered about the head and his shoulder deliberately mutilated. But to the detectives of the Central Scotland force it presented a mystery. One that officers, led by detective superintendent Jim Winning, struggled to solve. How had the killer managed to enter the house, attack Lawrence, start a fire and then escape without waking the rest of the family?

Police had an obvious suspect in convicted gay pervert, Brian Beattie (33), who was living nearby at the Evergreen trailer park in Denny. He was taken in for questioning on Sunday, 17 March, but released after he gave officers an alibi. Janet Haggart (38), Lawrence's mum, said that the police had told her that: 'There were three scenarios. The oldest brother had done it. The youngest was responsible, or someone had come off the street and done it. They said the third one was the most unlikely.' Having dismissed the random-attack theory, attention focused on Lawrence's family. Police knew that after returning home from an under-eighteen disco in Denny, Lawrence had rowed with youngest brother Dennis – who he shared a bedroom with – and settled down in the lounge for the night. Dennis, who was just twelve, came under scrutiny and was taken away for interrogation within hours of the murder.

It was the first of many visits to the police station, as Janet recalled:

Dennis and John were pulled in for questioning so often they didn't know if they'd be able to attend school each day. If it came to 8.15 and the police hadn't arrived, we knew the boys could go. I always got the impression the police thought I was lying. One day detectives warned my husband Larry and I that we could be charged if we were withholding evidence. I couldn't believe it. If I thought one of my sons was capable of this crime, then he needed help, and I wouldn't hide that. I never got time to grieve for Lawrence because of the frightening route the police were trying to go down. Until this we were an average family. We knew nothing about crime or the police.

Yet the bizarre aspect was that the police already had on record a series of attacks almost identical to the one on Lawrence Haggart. And the person responsible for these gay assaults was well known to Central Scotland police as a convicted arsonist and paedophile.

In August 1990, a 17-year-old youth sleeping in his home at Falkirk woke to find a man standing over him holding a pair of scissors to his stomach. The terrified youngster was ordered to lie face down. A pillow and duvet were pulled over his head and he was warned, 'If you look at my face I'll kill you.' The attacker then carried out a perverted gay assault on his victim.

Three weeks later, 23-year-old Lawrence Kane from Stenhousemuir woke up to find a stranger in his bedroom. 'I remember waking up and he had his hand over my privates and a knife in my belly. He said that if I moved he would slash me. I managed to push him off me and chased him out of the room. My room was never the same again after that.'

There is no doubt that Lawrence Kane had faced a dangerous individual. One prepared to take extreme risks in attacking a young man in his own home even though there were adults sleeping in adjacent rooms. He seemed to have an insatiable sexual appetite, carrying out two more attacks within a five-day period.

In October the attacker managed to get inside a house in Larbert, threatening to kill an 18-year-old with a screwdriver before sexually assaulting him. The same person then attacked a 14-year-old, the son of a well-known former footballer. The attacks would have gone on had the police not finally identified and arrested Brian Beattie. Just how dangerous he could be was shown when, having been released on bail, he attempted sexually to assault another young man.

Incredibly, this was the same Brian Beattie taken in for questioning after the attack on Lawrence Haggart and then released after he gave an alibi, claiming that on the night of the murder he had been having gay sex in an Edinburgh toilet. An alibi, it later turned out, detectives had never bothered to check.

Brian Beattie was a local man, a gay pervert with an extensive criminal past. He was brought up in the village of Airth, midway between Stirling and Falkirk, the youngest son of Thomas and Margaret Beattie. From an early age Beattie exhibited erratic behaviour and parts of his teenage years were spent in List D schools and similar institutions. When his parents' marriage broke up, Beattie moved with his mother and her lover to Redcar in Teesside. The job she took as a bus conductress was seized on by Beattie to further his criminal career. He travelled on bus routes and targeted vulnerable old people so that he could rob their homes. In March 1984 he appeared at Teesside Crown Court charged with four burglaries and two attempted arsons. While being held in prison awaiting trial, Beattie demonstrated his state of mind by setting his cell alight and attempting suicide by setting fire to himself.

After serving four years, Beattie was released from gaol and in 1988 moved back to Airth. It was then that his behaviour took a sinister turn and the sexually depraved crimes began. Beattie targeted victims by looking for a football lying in the garden, dirty trainers on the doorstep or sportswear hanging from a washing line. He would then find a way to break into the house. It was for these attacks that he was sent for trial to Edinburgh High Court in February 1991. In spite of his record, and a warning by the judge, Myrella Cohen, at Teesside, who told Beattie 'You are a danger to the public at large and also a danger to yourself', he received a sentence of only eighteen months. He was released in October of the same year having served only eight months. Within three days of stepping through the prison gates, Beattie was once more in trouble. In Stenhousemuir he threatened a 16-year-old at knifepoint and abducted him from his home. This time he received a five-year sentence and was taken to Peterhead prison. It was shortly after he had finished this sentence that the attack on Lawrence Haggart took place.

But as 1996 drew to a close Beattie was still not the prime suspect in Lawrence's murder, even though the attempt to pin the blame on young Dennis Haggart had taken the investigation up a dead end. In December 1996 detective superintendent Joe Holden was put in charge of a fresh inquiry. A new team of officers was brought in. But the breakthrough did not come till August 1997 when Beattie, who was in custody on fire-raising charges, confessed to the murder. Detective sergeant Graham Munro (41) described the moment Beattie – who had held to his alibi of having gay sex in Edinburgh on the night of Lawrence's death – burst wide open. 'It was about the most intense crying I have ever seen in my life', he said, 'Crying. Sobbing. Wailing. Noises like an animal struggling for breath.' But Beattie seemed sorrier about his own fate than that of Lawrence Haggart and kept protesting to the police: 'It was an accident.'

There is no doubt that Joe Holden saved the reputation of Central Scotland police. He commissioned a report by a psychologist that confirmed Lawrence's brothers could not have been responsible. He also ran a nationwide check of crimes similar to that which had led to Lawrence's death. The results all pointed to Beattie.

However, there was no forensic evidence linking Beattie to the murder and his previous record could not be introduced as evidence. It was all down to his confession. And his defence counsel at his trial at the High Court in Edinburgh argued that he had been bullied into admitting his involvement. The jury, however, found him guilty by a majority and he was sentenced to life imprisonment.

In October 2003 Central Scotland police formally apologised to the Haggart family and, in an out-of-court settlement, paid £20,000 damages to brothers Dennis and John. But the best news for the family came the following month when, in November 2003, Beattie lost his appeal against the murder conviction. Senior judges at a hearing in Edinburgh told Beattie's lawyers that they were satisfied that he had not suffered a miscarriage of justice. Lord Cullen said the court had fully considered Beattie's claim that his confession was all a fabrication, adding, 'It is clear that this issue was put to the jury.' It was also clear that the jury had believed the police version of events.

Larry Haggart, Lawrence's dad, told the media, 'We have been waiting seven years for this. We have been on tenterhooks. We were always on edge he would get out. I hope he stays where he is as long as possible and he is kept off the streets. We can get on and grieve for Lawrence in peace.'

But there remained one unsolved puzzle. Police could never get Beattie to reveal what the significance was of the number 110, written in ink on Lawrence's palms and gouged into his shoulder with a key. Only the twisted mind of Brian Beattie has the answer to that last mystery. One that may never be explained as he continues to protest his innocence.

3. William Beggs

The gay slasher

He was chubby, squat with his hair an unkempt mess. The sort of person who would avert his gaze rather than look you in the eye. But he could dress smartly and was very cunning. By the time he was living in Kilmarnock in 1991 he had already walked free from a murder charge. But, as often happens, his narrow escape from a lengthy sentence had not led him to rein in his activities. Rather it accelerated them, as it suggested to him that he could get away with anything. Including murder.

Kilmarnock is not the most picturesque town even on the sunniest day, but people know how to enjoy themselves, which is what 18-year-old Barry Wallace set out to do on the evening of Saturday, 4 December 1999. With Christmas approaching he had arranged a night out with workmates. As he set out he told his parents not to expect him back that night as he might stay with a friend. By the end of the night, he was in a pretty merry state. In fact, as far as Barry was concerned, the night was not yet over so he headed to a nightclub. At 1.45 a.m. a security camera caught him in the town centre. He was very drunk and in a confused state. He could have been heading for home but it was a distance of over two miles and, on that wintry night, it was unlikely that he would have welcomed the walk.

Barry Wallace did not return home on Sunday. Nor had he appeared by Monday. No one seemed to have any clue as to where he might have got to. His parents, understandably concerned, reported six feet two inches Barry as a missing person.

It was no more than a routine training session in Loch Lomond on that Monday, 6 December. A police unit was carrying out a practice dive when it made the unexpected find: a left arm. Further searches brought to the surface a severed leg. More finds were made: a right arm and then a right leg. A preliminary examination suggested that these four limbs belonged to the same person, but tests would be carried out to confirm it. Key parts of the corpse – the head and torso – had still to be located, but police trawled through the missing persons' files for any description that matched the victim. They believed that the limbs belonged to a white adult male, aged between eighteen and fifty, height between six feet two and six feet four. At this stage the police had made no clear link with Barry Wallace's disappearance.

But the next discovery suggested that the killer was either careless or so arrogant that he believed that nothing would link him to his victim. On 16 December a woman walking her dog along Barassie beach, near

Troon, made a horrific discovery. It was the dog that first drew her attention to it by sniffing at the object. As she later explained, 'it was a face inside a cream-coloured polythene bag. The bag had split.' The police quickly linked the find in Barassie with the discoveries at Loch Lomond. Analysis proved the parts belonged to the same person: Barry Wallace.

The police are very familiar with local criminals. So when the murder of a young man in Kilmarnock took place, detectives immediately turned out the files on local suspects. One name stood out like a sore thumb: William Beggs, who lived where he had been since he moved into Kilmarnock, at Doon Place. The first-floor flat was immediately put under police surveillance.

Beggs (36) was something of an enigma. He came originally from Northern Ireland and had grown up and gone to school there. Beggs came from a respectable home, but there may have been a less tolerant attitude towards sex. Most likely Beggs developed doubts about his sexuality at an early age, but could not admit to himself that it wasn't young women who aroused him. But he could not hide his true nature from classmates. One former pupil from the Quaker school Beggs attended in Lisburn claimed, 'Beggs was treated with almost blanket hostility. Nobody would sit near him, particularly women, because he made people very uneasy. He really was a creep.'

Even murderers have to start somewhere. And it usually isn't by killing. On a camping expedition, a young man sharing a tent with him woke during the night to find razor blades in his sleeping bag. Beggs was left to sleep on his own, thereafter. His unsavoury reputation intensified when he was seen hanging around secondary schools, trying to initiate conversations with male students. Around the same time he was attacked after exposing himself to young boys.

In 1982 he left Ireland to start a course at Teesside polytechnic in Middlesbrough. After graduation, he was free to focus on his sexual activities and these burst into life in various bizarre manifestations. Reports of cutting young men with a razor led to a police inquiry, but no charges. His victims were too anxious to avoid publicity. But these incidents only whetted Beggs's appetite. In May 1987 the body of 28-year-old Barry Oldham was found in a secluded country lane in North Yorkshire. His throat had been cut with a sharp implement and there had been an obvious attempt to dismember the body. The killer had either been disturbed in his work or had not been adequately prepared. His bungled efforts could most clearly be seen around Barry's head where his murderer had tried to separate it from the torso. Barry Oldham was a homosexual and had clearly gone willingly with his killer. Enquiries revealed that he met a man at a gay disco and returned with him to his flat. His partner was identified as William Beggs. Police digging brought out the earlier incidents in which gay lovers of Beggs had been slashed. In June 1987 he was charged with the murder of Barry Oldham and also faced five separate counts of wounding. Beggs denied the charges and, in Oldham's case, claimed that he had acted in self-defence. He was found guilty of murder and on two counts of wounding.

But due to a legal technicality Beggs's conviction was overturned and, after only eighteen months inside, he was set free. Beggs returned to Ireland, but did not stay there for long. It has been suggested that he was chased out by paramilitaries who resented his claimed association with them. But it is more likely that he was simply too well known to be able to carry on his clandestine activities. He needed a new hunting ground. Incredibly, he managed to obtain a white-collar job with Kilmarnock and Loudoun District Council.

Beggs may have avoided a jail sentence for his murderous activities, but he could not escape his impulses. In August 1991, back to his habit of cruising gay clubs, Beggs picked up Brian McQuillan at the Lorno disco in Glasgow. Once he had McQuillan safely in his private lair, Beggs's true nature burst into the open. McQuillan woke to find Beggs standing over him, slashing at his legs with a razor, shouting in a rage: 'things will be over soon. You have made me do this.' Blood was pouring from wounds on McQuillan's body and had splattered on the bedroom wall. He grasped that if he didn't get away immediately he would be killed and, though naked, dived through the window of the flat to escape.

Beggs was arrested, and later convicted. His sentence, however, was a comparatively light one of six years and he was released after only three. He returned to Kilmarnock in 1994, even choosing to live in the same flat where he had assaulted Brian McQuillan. Paisley University took him on and he eventually graduated with a master's degree in information technology, a qualification that helped him get a job at a call centre. His fellow students were less easily taken in by Beggs: they nicknamed him 'Fred West', after the notorious Gloucester killer. His neighbours too had had enough of Beggs and gangs targeted his car. It was known that he was regularly bringing young men back to his flat. Wild rumours circulated about what was going on inside.

By December 1999, however, perhaps even William Beggs was starting to wonder how long this carefree life could continue. There had been hints in the media that he was involved in some way in the murder of Barry Wallace. He was not aware, however, that the police had obtained a warrant to search his flat and, on the surface, appeared calm, even attending an office party on the evening of 16 December. The police broke into his house the following day while Beggs was on his way to work. Eventually over 5,000 items were taken away for further examination.

Interviewed by detectives, neighbours reported that they had heard the sound of sawing on the night that Barry Wallace disappeared.

As Beggs drove to work that morning he could not have realised that it was going to be his last day of freedom for some time. At some point during the afternoon he heard news that his flat had been raided. Having slipped the police net Beggs ended up in Amsterdam where he fought, unsuccessfully, against extradition. Meanwhile the search was continuing for Barry Wallace's torso and it was once again from Loch Lomond that the puzzle was solved. On 9 January a passer-by reported seeing a suspicious object floating in the water. When investigated it turned out to be the missing remains of Barry Wallace.

Piecing together the evidence, detectives believed that they had a clear idea of how Barry Wallace died. But it was not till the trial in October 2001 that the public heard the full extent of Beggs's behaviour. Encouraged to come back to the flat by the suggestion of a party or more drink, Barry was at some point handcuffed. Probably when he had fallen asleep or was drowsy. Or maybe Beggs tricked him into putting on the cuffs. The prosecution attempted to present a particular scenario: they suggested to the jury that Barry's hands had been handcuffed behind his back and that his ankles had also been bound. And that he had been kept in this position face down on the bed. It was claimed that the marks on Barry's limbs suggested that this was the position in which he had been held before death. It is possible that Beggs spiked his drink. In any event, he succeeded in getting Barry where he wanted: in a situation where he could not fight back. He was then repeatedly slashed with a razor and may have been choked to death. Or even have died of a heart attack overcome with fright. A forensic pathologist told the court that Barry had suffered injuries to his face before death, bruises that could have followed a punch or fall. But only Beggs himself could provide the answer and he was denying it all. Some facts are clear though. Barry's arms had been punctured by a hypodermic needle. He had been brutally sodomised causing severe internal injury. After Barry was dead, Beggs used a saw to dismember the body, finishing the job with a kitchen knife and snapping some bones with his bare hands. Beggs then wrapped the severed limbs in plastic bags, packed the body parts into his car and drove to Loch Lomond to dispose of them.

The police had gathered substantial evidence linking Beggs to the crime. On a bedside table lay a key to a set of handcuffs. In a cupboard outside, plastic bags had been stored. Some of the bags had the same logo, Scandinavian Seaways, as the one containing Barry's head. DNA from dried blood found in the flat matched the gene profile of Barry Wallace: there was only a one in a billion chance of it not belonging to the teenager. Just as significant was the revelation that DNA from two separate individuals had been found mixed together on the mattress. It came from Barry Wallace and William Beggs. A clinching factor was that blood on a kitchen knife also belonged to Barry. DNA from Barry was discovered in Beggs's car. It also turned out that Beggs was familiar with the area where the body had been dumped. The police could also point to a recent effort to redecorate Beggs's flat. He had been seen buying paint and other materials at a DIY store.

One unresolved question was the fate of Barry Wallace's head. Did Beggs dispose of it at the same time as the rest of the body? Or keep it in the fridge as some kind of sick trophy? The head wasn't found for ten days after the limbs were first discovered. People in Troon were of the opinion that the head had been placed on the beach as late as the night before it was found. Others suggested that Beggs could have thrown the head from a ferry during a crossing from Troon to Northern Ireland. Beggs might have used this trip to drop Barry's head into the sea or to dump it on Barassie beach.

At his trial Beggs continued to plead his innocence, although no defence witnesses were called. A different tactic was adopted. In a desperate attempt to defend his client, Beggs's advocate Donald Findlay presented Barry Wallace (who was not gay) as a willing partner in a sexual adventure that went wrong. As he reminded the jury, it is not a crime to dismember a dead body. Findlay also criticised what he considered was a campaign to 'demonise' Beggs. The jury did not agree with Findlay, preferring a more straightforward version: that Beggs, having somehow enticed Barry to Doon Place, had murdered him; and, afterwards, attempted to conceal his crime by dismembering the body and disposing of the parts. He was given a life sentence with a recommendation that he should serve at least twenty years.

4. The Bible John case

Still a mystery

On Thursday, 22 February 1968, at the Barrowland ballroom near Glasgow Cross, a man struck up a conversation with 25-year-old Patricia Docker. It must have been instant attraction. Several witnesses caught a good glimpse of him as he walked Patricia – a nurse at Glasgow's Victoria infirmary and married but separated from her soldier husband – back to her home in Langside Place, a stone's throw from the peaceful surroundings of Queen's Park. At some point in the early hours of Friday, 23 February, Patricia was strangled with her own tights in Carmichael Place just round the corner from the house that she shared with her parents. A few hours later, her naked body was discovered by Maurice Goodman as he made his way to his lockup garage. Patricia's grey duffel coat, yellow crochet mini-dress, brown shoes and matching handbag were missing and were never found. Patricia had been having her period and the sanitary towel she was using had been deliberately removed. It seemed an odd thing to do, even surprising experienced police officers who had seen more than their fair share of strange behaviour. The police jumped to the conclusion that the killer had been frustrated in his attempt to have intercourse and his passion had turned to violence.

At first, the police investigation hit a brick wall. No one remembered seeing Pat at the Majestic ballroom in Hope Street even though it had been packed that evening. Pat's parents were sure that the Majestic had been their daughter's destination. Detectives spent a fruitless two weeks interviewing patrons at the dance hall, and even attending in casual dress to scrutinise the regulars, before someone tipped them off that she must have met her killer at the Barrowlands. The place she had actually gone to. By the time police discovered their mistake the trail left by the man who came to be known as 'Bible John' was that bit harder to pick up.

At this stage police could not have been aware that they were dealing with a murderer willing to take incredible risks to get what he wanted. Even turning up at a dance hall on a Saturday night was taking a chance. In spite of the heaving crowd, if you were chatting to one of the women, you might easily be remembered by her pal. But 'John' didn't seem to worry too much. He had already chosen one victim from the Barrowlands. Now 32-year-old Jemima McDonald, a single mother of three, was unfortunate enough to be the next. Exactly why or how she got into conversation with 'John' is unknown. But around midnight on Saturday, 16 August 1969 Mima left the dance hall and set off for her tenement address in Mackeith Street about a twenty minute walk away. She wasn't alone. She felt safe enough in 'John's' company to allow him to walk her back to her flat. He kept his disturbed mind well hidden.

Several hours later, on Sunday, 17 August, Mima's body was discovered by her sister Margaret O'Brien lying in the bed recess of a ground-floor flat in a derelict tenement only thirty yards from her home. Detectives quickly noticed similarities with the murder of Patricia Docker some eighteen months before. Both had last been seen alive in the company of a man they had met at the Barrowlands. Both women had been strangled with their own tights and their handbag stolen. Both had been having their period and the murderer had carefully removed each woman's sanitary towel. It all seemed more than coincidence. The link between the deaths, though separated by eighteen months, suggested a serial killer. A shocking possibility that guaranteed Mima's death maximum publicity.

But the murderer either did not read the papers or didn't care. There were dozens of dance halls in 1960s Glasgow, but 'John' headed straight back to the Barrowlands in search of his next victim. As he moved across the dance floor he seemed unaware that his clothes marked him out from the crowd. According to Jean Langford, smartly dressed though he undoubtedly was, his clothes were certainly not in fashion. She chuckled at his well-tailored blue suit with three buttons, the white shirt and diagonally striped tie. 'John's' cutaway suede boots caused Jean real amusement and she overheard one of the dancers make a joke about them. Jean had made the trip to the Barrowlands that Thursday – 30 October 1969 – with her sister, 29-year-old Helen Puttock. They both enjoyed dancing and though Helen was married with two young children her husband had no objection to her evening out. And so Helen struck up a conversation with 'John' while Jean danced with another man, who also gave his name as John. Neither sister's dancing partner claimed to know the other.

As the two couples left the dance hall a strange incident occurred when the cigarette machine in the foyer jammed as Helen tried to buy a packet. According to Jean, Helen's 'John' suddenly exploded with anger, complaining furiously first to the manager and then to the assistant manager. He could hardly fail to notice that he was drawing attention to himself. As they headed for the exit, he commented, 'My father says that these places are dens of iniquity. They set fire to this place to get the insurance money and done it up with the money they got.' It struck Helen as a strange comment, but it was a foretaste of the more bizarre conversation 'John' was to make later.

Outside, 'John' calmed down and walked along the road with Jean, Helen and the other John to the taxi rank where they waited and chatted till a cab was free. The man who was with Jean now decided to leave, saying he would catch a bus in George Square. He had claimed he was a builder from Castlemilk, but was never heard from again. Bible John,

Helen and Jean clambered into the taxi. The driver, interviewed later, couldn't remember much about his passengers. He had only recently started the job and was concentrating on doing it properly. But Jean had already been in 'John's' company for two hours. Plenty of time to size him up and imprint a picture of the man in her head. 'John', meanwhile, seemed anxious to get Helen on her own so told the cabbie to let Jean off first even though she lived further down the road than her sister.

Jean was dropped off at the Kelso Street roundabout at around half-past midnight, said goodbye to Helen, and watched the taxi, with Helen waving through the rear window, turn back towards Earl Street, where Helen lived. A short while later the cab stopped to let 'John' and Helen out. They must have quickly headed for a back court not far from Helen's flat. By one o'clock Helen was dead and not a soul had heard her cry out.

Around seven in the morning, Archie McIntyre, taking his black Labrador for an early morning walk came across the body. Helen was lying face down in the open ground behind 95 Earl Street where she had taken 'John'. She still had on the ocelot fur coat and black woollen dress she had worn on the previous night's trip to the Barrowlands. But it was clear from the grass on her body and marks on the ground that Helen had made a frantic attempt to escape when 'John' began his attack. Like Patricia and Mima before her she had been strangled and sexually assaulted. There was a distinct bite mark on her neck.

The sisters' twenty minute journey in the taxi, during which Jean had spoken with Bible John, now became of key importance in the murder hunt. The killer had given clues about himself, but how far could they be relied on. He had told the women that he had a relative in Cumbernauld, played golf and that a cousin of his had recently managed a hole in one. He said he worked in a lab and knew the pubs in Yoker. He commented disapprovingly about married women going to the Barrowlands. He claimed that he prayed rather than drank at New Year. He quoted passages from the Bible, one of which seemed to be a reference to the story of Moses among the bulrushes. It was these snatches of conversation, linked to his 'dens of iniquity' remark at the Barrowlands, that led the press to dub the killer Bible John. It was also during the taxi ride that Jean believed she heard 'John' mutter something about his surname. She didn't quite catch what he said and thought it sounded like Templeton, Sempleton or Emerson.

Detectives now had plenty of clues and even a motive. In each case the sanitary towel that the victim was using was carefully removed and in Helen Puttock's case, the final murder, placed beneath the left armpit as if left as a clue. It seemed more than a coincidence that all three women were having their period when killed. 'John', his sexual urges aroused, found that his female companions would not allow him to go any further.

'John's' response, the police believed, was either one of sexual disgust or fury. But if 'John' was only attacking women who triggered his violence because of their period there must have been several women he had a normal relationship with between February 1968 and October 1969. Women who have never come forward.

Police, from Jean's description, and other witness statements, had an excellent description of Bible John. He appeared a distinctive individual. To the police it seemed that someone, somewhere would be bound to recognise him. An identikit of the man they wished to interview duly appeared with a volley of publicity and a detailed description of 'John'. He was, the public were told: 'aged 25-35, six feet to six feet two inches tall. Slim build with a thin pale face. He had reddish fair hair, cut short and brushed back. He was wearing a blue suit of good quality with hand-stitched lapels and a white shirt.' A final bit of evidence, police believed, must make him identifiable. The killer had distinctive front teeth with one crossing over the other.

As police know too well, serial killers do not stop because they have found something more 'interesting' to do. They just keep going till they get caught, die or are put in gaol for another crime. So if he was a man driven by a perverted obsession why did he slip away so abruptly and so successfully? Because, after Helen Puttock's murder, he disappeared as though he had never existed. Bible John vanished like a phantom into the night and has never, as far as is known, killed again.

But he has never escaped the attention of the police who are determined that one day Bible John will be caught. And scientific advances in DNA profiling have increased the chance that one day the killer, if still alive, will be identified. Semen stains on the brown nylon tights of Helen Puttock have provided enough material to enable scientists to produce a genetic profile of her killer.

In 1996 police, on the basis of this new evidence, exhumed the body of John McInnes (41) from a graveyard in the Lanarkshire town of Stonehouse. McInnes, a soldier, who resembled a photofit of Bible John and had been asked to attend identity parades at the time of the murders, committed suicide in 1980. Jean, Helen Puttock's sister, did not believe that he was the man she had shared a taxi with and was proved right. DNA tests revealed that McInnes was not Bible John.

The years that have passed since the events of 1968 and 1969 have spawned many theories and thousands of suspects. In 2000 a forensic psychologist suggested that, from evidence given to him, Bible John could be the son of a police officer who had moved to England. The lead petered out. As have the investigations into a host of names put forward to police as the likely killer.

Some detectives have even argued that the three murders are not linked, which would suggest that between 1968 and 1969 there were three different men picking up women at Glasgow dance halls then murdering them. Hardly reassuring or a testament to the police's power of detection. However, it is generally accepted that whilst there may be differences between the deaths there are obvious similarities which indicate that one man was responsible for all three murders.

By 2004 rapid advances in the use of DNA techniques led police to announce that a new clue had emerged in the hunt for Bible John. DNA evidence left at the scene of a crime in 2002 linked with that collected in 1969 from Helen Puttock. It was not Bible John, but a relative. It suggested that police were closing in on Scotland's most elusive killer. Detectives claimed, 'We are narrowing it down. Certain men have been targeted by our profilers and asked to provide DNA samples. Science will solve these killings, we have no doubt of that.'

5. Robert Black

He can never be released

'That's my daughter you bastard'. These angry words directed at the driver of a blue Ford Transit van marked the end of the hunt for Scotland's most prolific child killer. A search that had dragged on for eight years leaving detectives baffled and frustrated by their lack of success. The trail began with the abduction of 11-year-old Susan Maxwell from the village of Cornhill on 30 July 1982. Although at the time there had been nothing to suggest that her murder was other than a single disturbing event, that changed almost exactly a year later on 8 July 1983 when 5-year-old Caroline Hogg, having spent the afternoon at a friend's birthday party, was allowed, at around seven in the evening, a few minutes to play in the front garden of her terraced house before going to bed.

Caroline lived in Beach Lane, in the Portobello district of Edinburgh, only a few yards from the promenade which was always busy with visitors during the summer season. Caroline, ignoring her parents' instructions, or perhaps enticed away, left the front garden and wandered down to the beach. She was still proudly wearing her party clothes, a lilac-and-white gingham dress, white ankle socks, with her blonde hair tied in bunches. Caroline was seen that evening, by several people, perched on the side of the prom, a scruffy-looking man beside her. By 7.30 p.m. Caroline was on a ride at the amusement park, Fun City, only 500 yards from her home, sitting in a little bus, the fare of fifteen pence paid for by the same scruffy individual who had been talking to her earlier. The roundabout attendant, 17-year-old Derek Jackson, was the last person known to have seen Caroline alive as she walked towards the car park hand-in-hand with the unknown man.

On 18 July, ten days after her disappearance, Caroline Hogg's decomposing remains were found 308 miles from Portobello near a lay-by on the A444 close to the village of Twycross in Leicestershire. This discovery linked Caroline's murder to the abduction of 11-year-old Susan Maxwell. Her body had been left close to a lay-by on the A518 Uttoxeter to Stafford road within twenty miles of the spot where Caroline had been dumped. The fact that two young girls had been abducted from Scotland and their bodies left so close to one another seemed beyond coincidence. In both cases the motive appeared sexual. Susan Maxwell's pants had been removed and Caroline Hogg was naked except for her white ankle socks. There had been no serious attempt to conceal either body.

It had been a hot afternoon on 30 July 1982, a year before Caroline's disappearance, when Susan Maxwell – from the village of Cornhill which lies on the English side of the border – set off to play tennis with a friend in the nearby town of Coldstream. Susan was given a lift by a family friend to the Lennel tennis club, but planned to walk the mile or so back once the game was over. It was the first time she had been allowed to make the walk on her own. Her return route crossed the border into England over a bridge spanning the river Tweed along the busy A697 main road. Around four in the afternoon Susan's mother, Liz Maxwell, decided to drive to the tennis court to pick Susan up, but when she arrived the court was deserted. Liz had not seen Susan on the way along, and there was no sign of her as she made her way back to the farmhouse. So when Liz learnt that Susan's friend had arrived home, and Susan had last been seen heading for Cornhill, she was immediately concerned for her daughter's safety.

Susan would have cut a distinctive figure in her yellow terry-towelling T-shirt with a palm-tree motif, shorts, white ankle socks and tennis shoes. Susan's friend, Alison Raeburn, told police that after the game, which lasted an hour, they walked along the road together, separating at the end of the town at around ten past four. Several witnesses came forward to report that they had seen Susan walking back towards Cornhill. So it was possible to follow the route she had taken minute by minute and pinpoint the spot, a short distance after she had crossed the bridge over the Tweed, where she had been snatched.

However, in spite of a massive investigation, by the beginning of 1986 police were no nearer identifying the killer of Susan and Caroline. Then he struck once more.

Around 9.30 a.m. on 19 April 1986, 37-year-old David Moult, out walking his dog beside the river Trent at Wilford near Nottingham, made a shocking discovery. As he told police:

> I was walking along the bank when I spotted something floating in the water. I thought it was just a piece of sacking, then the current turned it round and I realised it was a body. Eventually, I managed to pull it to the bank. I could see then that it was a young person with fair, collar-length hair and a maroon-coloured top.

This turned out to be the body of 10-year-old Sarah Harper. A forensic examination revealed that she had been subjected to a savage sexual attack. Sarah had disappeared from her home town of Morley south of Leeds some three weeks before, on 24 March, after running an errand to the local store to buy a loaf of bread. A scruffy-looking man was seen acting suspiciously around the time Sarah was making her purchase. The location of Sarah's body, close to where Susan and Caroline had been found, linked the three deaths to the same individual. But, in spite of an intense investigation, by the start of 1990 the killer had still not been identified.

And it is a sobering thought that in spite of a police hunt stretching over eight years, the man who had murdered at least three young girls was not even on the list of suspects. But Robert Black's luck was about to run out. On 14 July 1990 Black entered the Borders village of Stow on the lookout for a victim. He spotted a 6-year-old walking alone and waited till she came level with the van door, then pounced, dragging her in to the driver's seat. Black drove to a lay-by where he sexually assaulted his young victim. After the attack he headed back towards Stow, supremely confident that, once again, he had got away with it. But this time he was wrong. David Herkes, a retired grocer, had witnessed the incident and alerted the police. Detectives had barely arrived on the scene when an astonished Herkes saw a blue vehicle approaching. 'That's the van', he shouted. The police brought the vehicle to a halt. The driver made no attempt to escape. The father of the missing girl dived into the van, describing the incident with raw emotion:

> The rear was almost empty. I reached out at what I first thought was a bundle of rags, but then realised that one of the items was a sleeping bag. I was calling out for her and the sleeping bag moved. Her face was very red with the heat and there was a look of absolute terror on her face. Her mouth was bound and gagged and her wrists were bound around her back.

The murder spree of Robert Black had been brought to an end.

The police investigation of 43-year-old Black revealed that he was a van driver living in London who drove all over England and Scotland delivering advertising posters. He regularly visited friends in the village of Donisthorpe close to the sites where the three murder victims had been left. Black was originally from Falkirk and had a troubled background. He had been convicted of sexual assault in the 1960s, but had kept out of police files since then. In his London flat, police found a collection of child pornography including videos. Black was a sick character who had even photographed himself inserting objects, including a table leg, into his anus.

Black was given a life sentence for the abduction of the girl in Stow. He also now became the chief suspect for the murders of Susan Maxwell, Caroline Hogg and Sarah Harper and, after intense police activity, was charged with these offences in 1994. During his five-week trial at Newcastle Crown Court, Black spoke only twice. On day one he confirmed his name and address and pled not guilty. After the jury returned a unanimous guilty verdict he looked towards police officers and murmured, 'Well done, boys'. Robert Black, Scotland's most prolific serial killer of children was sentenced to a minimum term of thirty-five years. Black is suspected of many more killings including the abduction of Devon teenager Genette Tate in August 1978. Unsolved child murders on the Continent have also been laid at his door. Black showed not a flicker of remorse nor offered to assist the police in their investigation of the killings of which he was suspected.

It is unlikely that this brutal killer will ever be released. Every parent will pray that he never is.

6. Ricardo Blanco

The hitman and the hooker

It was a routine deal for courier Paul Thorne; just another day at the office. The 27-year-old from Bristol had come to Glasgow in 1988 to sell £6,000-worth of drugs for his Rastafarian bosses. The buyers, the McFadyen family, were respected figures in the underworld with a web of criminal contacts that stretched from Florida to Spain and from London to Morocco. The McFadyens had bought many valuable consignments of narcotics from the Bristol connection in the past and the two gangs had established a good working relationship.

After a long journey, Thorne was tired and hungry and was pleased that his Scottish customers had arranged for him to stay in a country cottage on Fenwick moor to the south of Glasgow. He was accompanied by five members of the McFadyen team: John Paul 'Tough Tony' McFadyen (25), the son of gang leader, John Ross McFadyen; Ricardo Blanco (26); Thomas Collins (25); Thomas Currie; and Stephen Mitchell. On the road to Fenwick the gang members stopped and bought Thorne fish and chips. 'Tough Tony' said jokingly that it was his 'last supper'.

As they reached their destination on an isolated stretch of the moor, the group got out of their cars and walked through woodland towards the cottage. Then – in a scene reminiscent of the mafia movie *Goodfellas* – the unsuspecting Thorne was assassinated. He was blasted through the head with a shotgun by Ricardo 'the Hitman' Blanco, who then passed the gun on to McFadyen. Next – as Thorne screamed, 'Don't hurt me, man' – he was shot again by McFadyen. The gun was passed on and a third shot was fired by Collins and then a fourth, when Thorne was probably already dead, by Thomas Currie. McFadyen and Blanco laughed as they inspected the blood-soaked corpse and helped the others bury it in a shallow grave. The gang left the scene and travelled the short journey into Glasgow to look for drugs and hookers.

Thorne had paid a heavy price for his trust. But even he, a hardened criminal, did not realise the ruthless nature of the gang he was doing business with. John Ross McFadyen, originally from the East End of Glasgow, had built up a major drugs business from his semi-detached house in a rundown area of Rugby, Warwickshire. He had cocaine, cannabis, LSD and amphetamines smuggled in from sources in North Africa, America and Spain, and supplemented these supplies with wholesale purchases from the Yardie gangs of Bristol. The business was so lucrative that McFadyen boasted of depositing £10,000 a week in foreign bank accounts.

When he sought to expand McFadyen looked north, to his native Glasgow. He appointed Thomas Collins as his local manager and Collins was ably assisted by John Ross McFadyen's son, John Paul, and by Ricardo Blanco, who provided the muscle needed for a major drug-dealing operation. McFadyen and Blanco controlled the Glasgow dealers they supplied by violence and intimidation. They openly talked in pubs and at drug parties of murders and vicious assaults and built up a fearsome reputation as enforcers. Around this time two dealers – James Dougan of Glasgow and Wayne Lomas of Bristol – went missing and were never seen again; McFadyen and Blanco were questioned by police about their disappearance but never charged.

While 'Tough Tony' McFadyen was a genuine hard man it was Ricardo Blanco who was most feared by street-level drug-dealers. Born in Spain, Blanco joined the Foreign Legion but absconded and drifted across Europe before turning up in Scotland. He became embroiled in the drug scenes of Greenock and Clydebank and was quickly marked out as a capable enforcer. It is said that he killed a man with his bare hands when he escaped from the Foreign Legion. Another story has it that he literally ripped a German drug-mule apart to get at his consignment, which had been swallowed in condoms. The Scottish police also heard rumours that Blanco and 'Tough Tony' had shot dead two drugs couriers in Spain.

The trial of the McFadyen gang in October and November 1989 at Glasgow High Court took forty-six days and was one of the longest and most expensive in Scottish legal history. Despite the fact that Paul Thorne's body was never found three men were convicted of his murder and received life sentences: 'Tough Tony' McFadyen, Blanco and Thomas Collins. The charge against a fourth accused – Thomas Currie, who admitted in a police interview to firing the fourth shot – was found not proven. John Ross McFadyen, who was never charged with murder, was found guilty of drug dealing. The successful prosecution relied heavily on the evidence of gang member Stephen Mitchell, who had his murder charge dropped on the seventeenth day of the trial. Taking the witness box, Mitchell described in chilling detail the abduction and execution of Thorne, helping to persuade the jury of the guilt of his erstwhile partners in crime.

While little is heard today of McFadyen and Collins, Ricardo Blanco has become even more notorious during his time inside, and his misdeeds are covered extensively in the tabloids. Violent by nature, and with a hair-trigger temper, he found it impossible to cope with strict prison regimes and following a string of assaults had to be transferred from jail to jail. The worst incidents occurred in 1998, the first when he stabbed two prison officers, and the second when he attacked two inmates. (Despite his violent behaviour, Blanco has had the audacity to seek compensation in the courts for an alleged breach of his human rights. He claimed that a spell in solitary confinement was contrary to European law.)

But there was another story from Blanco's time in prison that caused even more media excitement. It all started when Blanco befriended William 'The Worm' Toye, a ruthless Clydebank gangster and drug baron who was serving life for the axe murder of a witness due to give evidence against his brother. Toye was himself killed in Perth prison in 1996 in a knife fight and Blanco later exacted bloody retribution on the two prisoners he believed were responsible for the death of his pal. As well as harbouring ambitions to take over Toye's criminal empire when he was released, Blanco also moved in on his late friend's common-law wife, Jacqui Wylie, a prostitute who worked Glasgow's many 'saunas' and 'massage parlours'. Romance blossomed between the hitman and the hooker and they were married at Greenock register office in 2001.

While Wylie tried to stay out of Glasgow's brothels after her wedding she could not resist the lure of easy money for long. She was back in the old routine after just a few days, offering a range of sex services to punters at prices ranging from £50 to £80. It was said that Blanco was enraged when he found out she was back on the game. Ironically he had been trying desperately to persuade the prison authorities to allow him a conjugal visit from Wylie to consummate the marriage; now his wife was selling sex to complete strangers. One of her prostitute colleagues thought it was a bad career choice: 'I doubt if anyone will want to go near her now – not with her husband being Blanco. You'd need to be mad or have a death wish.'

Blanco became even more newsworthy when he escaped from Gateside prison in Greenock. While on a home visit to see Wylie in July 2002 he got away, despite being escorted by a guard. Following a major police operation he was recaptured within twenty-four hours and charged with absconding and seriously assaulting a prison officer. Much to the disgust of the authorities, Blanco was acquitted on both counts. It was a strange move as he was on the Training for Freedom scheme at the time and eligible for parole in 2004. But then Ricardo Blanco is not a man who has ever lived by the rules.

7. Freddie Cairns

Murder in the BarL

Alexander Malcolmson was a petty thief from the Shettleston district of Glasgow but he earned a place in history. On 26 October 1965, eight days into a six-month sentence at Barlinnie prison, Malcolmson was stabbed in the back with a home-made knife and later died in Glasgow Royal Infirmary. The first serving prisoner to be murdered in a Scottish gaol. Twenty-five year old Freddie Cairns, doing time for housebreaking, but with no record of violence, was arrested that same night and charged with Malcomson's murder. It turned out that Cairns was a boyhood friend of Malcolmson.

The trial opened on 28 February 1966 in Glasgow High Court. Cairns claimed that though he had witnessed a scuffle around Malcolmson he had not been involved and had not stabbed him. However, two other witnesses, both prisoners, contradicted him testifying that they had seen Cairns attack Malcolmson. Events then took a bizarre twist when convict James Lindie admitted from the witness box, 'I stabbed Malcolmson. We were needling each other about tobacco.' The jury was left with the problem of which version of events to believe from people serving time for dishonest behaviour. As the trial judge, Lord Johnstone, put it: 'He may be telling the truth and he may be lying. It is for you to decide on the matter.' In the end the jury accepted neither side's story as a majority verdict of not proven was returned. Not exactly a clean slate, but it did mean that the murder charge against Cairns had fallen. He was returned to Barlinnie to serve out the rest of his eighteen-month sentence and was released a few weeks later. No action was taken against Lindie who was sent to a gaol in England to complete a term for an unrelated offence.

Events now took a further dramatic turn. On regaining his freedom in March 1966 Cairns went to the offices of the *Scottish Daily Express* newspaper and made an astonishing claim. He told reporters, 'I did murder Malcolmson' and said he had lied when he went into the witness box to claim that he was not involved in his death. According to Cairns he had decided to kill Malcolmson for two reasons: 'Four years ago I had a fight with him. He tried to smash a broken bottle in my face. I promised I would get him back for it some day. He also said something insulting about my sister.'

Cairns described to reporters how he had made a weapon from 'a wooden handle' and 'a mat needle' both of which he had been given by other prisoners. He added, 'I planned to stab him. I saw a friend of mine and asked for a knife.' Describing the murder Cairns recalled that Malcolmson 'was right in front of me so that's when I just pulled out the knife and put it in his back. I said to my friend I can't get the knife out and he replied, "Leave it in".' Cairns said the knife blade was about six inches long.

According to Cairns he had then schemed with cell mates to beat the legal system. They planned that one of the other prisoners would confess to the murder 'then once they found me not guilty I was to jump up and say "I am guilty".' This would, Cairns believed, force the judge to declare a mistrial.

His admission caused an outcry. It seemed that a self-confessed killer had got away with murder. No one can be tried twice for the same crime so Cairns could not be brought back for retrial. To the public it appeared that Cairns was making a mockery of the justice system. The matter was even raised in Parliament. Clearly, Cairns would have to be brought to book somehow.

Eventually, the Crown Office in Edinburgh charged Cairns with perjury. Telling lies on oath when he had been giving evidence at his trial. It was the first time that a person acquitted of one crime had been brought back to court for failing to tell the truth in his own defence. Just like his victim, Cairns was about to make history. And on the surface, it seemed a straightforward way of dealing with a brazen killer. But it was more complicated than it seemed at first glance. If Cairns was to be charged with perjury then any jury would have to hear once again all the evidence covering the murder of Alexander Malcolmson. It would, in fact, be a retrial in all but name.

Meanwhile, Cairns – alarmed at the impact of his story in the *Scottish Daily Express* with its dramatic headline 'I got away with murder' – began to backtrack. He claimed that the story he had given to reporters was made up simply to earn some money. It was not a true account of the events in Barlinnie and he was completely innocent of the charge of murder.

However, it was too late to retract such a public confession, especially as Scotland's senior judges had agreed that a trial could go ahead. It seemed though that fortune had again favoured Cairns as the main witness against him had been released from prison and disappeared. The trial was postponed while inquiries were made to discover the location of the key missing witness.

But the trial that might have established exactly who did kill Alexander Malcolmson never took place. Some days before it was due to start in May 1967 Cairns, who had been unwell for a few weeks, was taken in for a stomach operation, but his condition worsened and he died suddenly. Ironically, in the same Glasgow hospital that Alex Malcolmson had breathed his last. Cairns was only twenty-six. We will never know if he was innocent of the murder of Malcolmson, as he claimed to be. And as no one has ever been convicted of killing Alexander Malcolmson, someone may indeed have got away with murder right under the noses of the authorities, inside Scotland's most closely guarded prison.

8. Kenneth 'Kiddie' Calderwood

Killed for being middle class

It was one of the longest murder trials in Scotland's history. It also holds the record for the number of people in the dock accused of murder: in the summer of 1982, at the High Court in Glasgow, stood fifteen youths, charged with the brutal killing of Robert Howie. The trial attracted huge publicity, not only because of the number of people on trial but also because the victim was middle class and his assailants came from the other end of the social spectrum. The case, in many ways, was a microcosm of the divisions in the city.

Robert Howie came from an expensive home in a suburb that is synonymous with affluence: Newton Mearns, situated on the south side of the Glasgow conurbation. The apple of his family's eye, he lived with them in a beautiful detached villa. His father, also Robert, was an engineer; his mother, Margaret, a teacher; his older sister, Marjorie, was a postgraduate student at Strathclyde University. Robert had excelled at school, passing eight O grades and five Highers and had gone on to Glasgow University where he was studying dentistry. A popular, sports-loving 18-year-old, he had a multitude of interests and one overriding passion: motorbikes. It was in many ways a sheltered, even idyllic, upbringing. But there was another Glasgow, a Glasgow redolent of heavy drinking, low achievement, violence and gang warfare. A Glasgow that although not far away from Newton Mearns in geographical terms was a million miles away in its attitude to life. It was the clash of these two cultures that would lead to tragedy.

The name 'Cumbie' is attached to many gangs in Glasgow: the name comes from Cumberland Street in the Gorbals, an inner-city neighbourhood once associated with urban squalor and violence. It was used in the tough council estates close to Newton Mearns; most notably in Busby and Castlemilk, where the Castlemilk Young Young Cumbie and the Busby Young Cumbie – deadly rivals – fought pitched battles in places like Clarkston, a pleasant part of south Glasgow attractive to the young because of its many shops, restaurants and pubs. But, after the Castlemilk Cumbie found itself outnumbered in a pitched battle with its namesake from Busby in January 1982, the two branches of the Cumbie decided to stop fighting and join forces.

The alliance of the two Cumbies caused mayhem in the months that followed. The newly formed gang hung around the Buck's Head cafe near the Sheddens roundabout in Clarkston, fighting, drinking lager and sniffing glue. Many came from troubled backgrounds. Kenneth 'Kiddie' Calderwood (18), from a council estate in Busby, was the undisputed leader. The product of a broken home, he had been idolised by boys at school as a hard man, and by girls because of his good looks. One gang member said of him: 'He was mad, off his head. He picked on anybody he thought he could beat.' While fellow gang member Ronnie 'Boney' Scott (16) had had an equally difficult upbringing after his parents divorced; he was moody, surly and prone to violence, traits that were partly due to the heavy glue-sniffing that he and other gang members indulged in.

The events that led to tragedy started on the evening of Friday, 2 April 1982. Robert Howie met four male friends, mostly students, for a quiet drink in the Busby Hotel. After a couple of pints they walked to the Jasmine House Chinese restaurant at Sheddens roundabout. The first hint of trouble came when Robert left the Chinese with his takeaway. He and his pal Ewan McDonald were met with a tirade of abuse from Calderwood and his followers, who earlier that evening had assaulted two other youths. A bottle smashed on the pavement and a cry of, 'We are the Castlemilk Young Young Cumbie' rang out. In retaliation, Ewan McDonald shouted: 'Away you bunch of poofs'.

That was the catalyst for the cowardly and unjustified attack that followed. The gang had hidden weapons on the roofs and in the storage areas of the surrounding shops. They quickly retrieved the fearsome arsenal, which included a machete twenty-three-inches-long, two commando knives, a clothes pole, a chain and broken bottles. The degree of class enmity became clear when one of the gang shouted 'Get the punk – he's from Newton Mearns' and led by 'Kiddie' Calderwood the thugs charged. Physics student Stephen McIntyre – standing near his friend Robert Howie – was the first victim: dazed by a blow from a bottle the tendons of his hand were severed by the machete. Two others from the group of students were hit with bottles, including Ewan McDonald, who said it was the most frightening experience of his life.

But Robert Howie, perhaps because he was dressed, as usual, in motorbike leathers took the brunt of the attack: he desperately defended himself, swinging his belt as he furiously tried to fight off his assailants. But he fell under a hail of punches and kicks and was slashed with the machete and the commando knives. In a last-ditch attempt to escape, he ran up the nearby Greenwood Road chased by the jeering thugs, who were cheered on by a pack of female gang members. But there was no hiding place for the student as the mob, fuelled by an uncontrollable bloodlust, stabbed and hacked at him with their weapons. An ambulance was called shortly after the attack ended and Robert Howie was pronounced dead just before midnight. It was the first murder in leafy Clarkston in living memory.

The behaviour of the seven female gang-members was also reprehensible, although none were charged with any crime. They had, of course, egged on the males and in the aftermath of the attack helped by hiding weapons, cleaning off bloodstains and lending clothes to boyfriends with blood on their jackets and jumpers. Typical of them was 16-year-old Janice Lindsay, the boyfriend of gang member James McAllister. Lindsay – who had drunk seven cans of strong lager hours before the killing – admitted hiding a machete in Lewis's department store in the city centre because she thought McAllister had used it. All seven girls regularly visited the gang as they awaited trial and promised to stand by them no matter the outcome. It is clear that the boys' notoriety had done them no harm in the eyes of the opposite sex; indeed it gave them almost pop-star status. The public benches of the High Court were thronged by young girls through-out the proceedings and they would follow press photographers around and beg them for photos of the accused.

During the six weeks of the trial – as is often the way – murder charges were dropped against ten of the accused, although most of them still faced charges of assault. Three of the remaining teenagers were convicted of murder: Calderwood, Ronnie Scott and John 'Skeets' Sanders. All three got life sentences. Another two youths accused of murder – policeman's son Graham 'Plodder' Charlton and Allan 'Maxi' Maxwell – were cleared of the charge but found guilty of assault. All in all, ten youths not convicted of murder received sentences totalling seventeen years for assault and breach of the peace.

But the sentences meant little to the Howies, a respectable, hard-working family. As Mr Howie said: 'The verdicts don't really affect us. The sentences cannot change anything. They won't bring Robert back.' They were shattered by the murder and Robert's mother summed up the family's feelings perfectly: 'He meant the world to us. And losing him? I doubt if we will ever understand why we had to lose him. And how great that loss is we will never be able to put into words.'

9. Andrew Cameron

'I hope you catch the bastard'

It is every parent's worst nightmare. An argument with a temperamental teenager results in the young person storming out of the house and they are never on good terms again. Not because their relationship has broken down irretrievably, but because the youngster has come to harm. The anguish must be unbearable and, thankfully, such cases are extremely rare. Yet it happened in Ayrshire and the result was the most sensational murder case in the county's history.

The story begins one hot afternoon in July 1984. The scene is the Rise hotel in Ayr. A middle-aged man is unpacking, but he is not a resident. He is the owner of the hotel, which he had bought only seventy-seven days before when he moved back to Scotland after a career spent farming in Africa. The man comes across his teenage daughter's records and puts them to one side. At that moment his daughter comes in and starts to browse through her precious collection. Her father takes the view that she should be helping with the unpacking and tells her so. Homesick for her former life in South Africa, she is more highly-strung than usual. An argument ensues and the girl storms out. It was to be the last time they ever spoke.

The young woman was Kay Wyllie, an attractive 19-year-old who had returned to the town where, at the age of ten, she had spent two terms as a boarder at the exclusive Wellington School. Her father was Douglas Wyllie, who was born in Ayr and had decided to come home to the old country. Apart from family connections, one of the main reasons for moving back was the assurances friends had given them about the lack of crime in Scotland; a complete contrast with South Africa, where it was often dangerous to venture out.

Kay did come back home that day, but only to get ready to go out again. She saw her father but, stung by their earlier row, ignored him. She left the hotel and went instead to see her boyfriend, Russell Anderson, at his parents' pub near Kilmarnock. The couple stayed in the pub until closing time and then drove to the Andersons' luxury bungalow near Dundonald. Just after midnight, she left on her own to drive back to Ayr. Although he thought little of it at the time, Russell Anderson was sure she was going straight home.

Douglas Wyllie was also sure that she would be returning home that night. Despite their tiff, he left a light on for her. But when he woke at half-past-six the next morning he saw that the light was still on and knew that something was wrong. Overcome by worry he phoned friends, the police and local hospitals. He spent the rest of the day looking for clues. It was becoming clear that something was amiss, and it was time for the police to take a hand. Within forty-eight hours they found an abandoned car in a back street less than a quarter of a mile from the Rise hotel. It was Kay Wyllie's white Mini City.

Two days after the car was found, a farm labourer found Kay's half-naked body in a ditch next to a lovers' lane in Dunure, a fishing village outside Ayr. A forensic examination would later reveal that she had been strangled by her own white bra while being pinned down on rough gravel. The killer had then dumped her corpse in the ditch with her jacket and sweatshirt. There were no indications from under her nails that she had scratched her killer, nor were there any signs of sexual contact between them. To this day police have no idea how she met her killer. However, Kay's mother, Isabella Wyllie, later said that her daughter would never have stopped for a stranger in the middle of the night, much less have gone to Dunure with him.

At first Russell Anderson was the prime suspect, and he was interrogated before being eliminated from enquiries. The police now widened the net and compiled a list of twenty suspects. After eleven days of intensive investigation they got a break. From this point on their focus would be on an 18-year-old who, although he had racked up a considerable number of petty offences, did not have a reputation for violence. His name was Andrew Cameron.

It is unusual for people from Cameron's affluent background to be involved in crime. Born in Hartlepool in the north-east of England his father was an engineer and, reflecting the peripatetic nature of his work, the family moved several times during his formative years. Finally, in 1983, the Camerons settled in Troon where they bought a large detached house on a prestigious estate with fine views over Royal Troon golf course.

Yet Andrew Cameron was a troubled young man. By 1984 he had a lengthy record for breaking into, and stealing from, vehicles. His criminal tendencies must have been a source of anxiety for his parents, particularly his mother who often had to look after the family on her own as her husband frequently worked abroad. It may have been the stress caused by Andrew's constant lawbreaking that drove her to report him to the police for taking her car without permission. Little did she know this would implicate him in the murder of Kay Wyllie.

The police picked up Cameron on 17 July. They cautioned him for taking away his mother's car and, with nothing to lose, asked him about his whereabouts on the night Kay Wyllie was killed. His answers surprised them. He told them that he had been driving around breaking into cars. While driving past Wellington Lane in Ayr he said that he saw Kay's white Mini and a man walking away from it towards the beach. When the man disappeared from sight, he siphoned petrol from the car and stole other items, including a digital clock. Although he denied ever having met Kay, detectives were suspicious and carried out a range of forensic tests. The tests proved positive. Cameron's fingerprints were found on the inside of the driver's window. Police found the petrol cap from Kay's car in the front garden of Cameron's house. A fibre of clothing found in the back seat of the car matched the fibres on an anorak owned by Cameron.

This evidence pointed clearly to Andrew Cameron. But, on its own, it was not enough for a prosecution. Detectives racked their brains until, in September 1984, they decided to publish a photograph of the digital clock taken from Kay's car. The reasoning was that the murderer might either be using the clock or have tried to sell it. The picture of the clock was published in national and local newspapers, and it elicited an amazing response. The police received a letter that completely contradicted Cameron's story and convinced them that he had killed Kay Wyllie. It read:

> To whom it may concern,
> Last week as I read the article about the murder of Kay Wyllie in the *Ayrshire Post* I suddenly realised that you have got it all wrong. The murderer didn't take the clock. I did. I thought I had better put you in the picture. I hope you catch the bastard.

To prove it was not a sick hoax, the author also enclosed the keys to Kay's car. The police were jubilant, but they needed to speak to the thief and a second article appeared in the *Ayrshire Post* offering immunity from prosecution if the anonymous correspondent came forward. The offer did the trick: two boys contacted the police and confessed that they had broken into the car and stolen a number of items including the clock. More significantly the boys told police that they broke into the car a full sixteen hours before Andrew Cameron claimed he had stolen the clock and the other items. He was now revealed as a liar; a liar who wanted police to believe his fingerprints were found in the Mini because he was a thief, and not because he had killed Kay Wyllie.

By now there was no doubt in the minds of detectives: Cameron was their man. The only problem was the evidence, or lack of it. The Crown Office was not convinced that the case against Cameron was strong enough. It spent months weighing the evidence, but did not give the green light for a prosecution. It is easy to criticise the Crown Office for its inaction but it was concerned that, if he got off, he could not be retried for the same offence under the double-jeopardy rule. Meanwhile, police in Ayr had their own nightmare scenario. Cameron was free to kill again.

Nancy Nicol was a 19-year-old from Kilmarnock who, like many girls of her age, enjoyed dancing, a drink and the company of young men. She had a factory job and there must have been, from time to time, a temptation to give work a miss and to spend the time enjoying herself. This is exactly what happened on Friday, 2 May 1985 when she and a workmate decided on the bus to work that they would spend the day touring Troon's pubs and clubs. They later met other girlfriends, and it was clear to the newcomers that Nancy was already drunk. The girls continued to drink before moving on to other pubs. Eventually they ended up in Pebbles hotel in Troon, which Nancy left at 10.50 p.m. An hour later a taxi driver saw her chatting to a young man outside Greggs the bakers, a man she had first met five days before on another night out. It was Andrew Cameron.

Nancy was not the only woman Cameron had shown an interest in that day. Allison Bainbridge was staying with her sister in Troon and had been out for a meal with her husband. He was staying in a different house and walked back with his wife in the direction of her sister's house. In normal circumstances he would have taken her all the way home but on this occasion he left her to walk the last stage on her own. She was alone when a man holding a can of beer came out of a bus shelter and started to follow her. Mrs Bainbridge was understandably alarmed and hurried to her sister's house. She later picked out Andrew Cameron at an identity parade as the man who had followed her.

Nancy Nicol, an attractive blonde, did not return home that night. Nor did she turn up the next day. Her parents reported her missing. When police realised that Cameron was the last person seen with Nancy, there was fresh pressure for him to be arrested for the murder of Kay Wyllie. But, once again, the Crown Office decided there was insufficient evidence. It would now be up to the police to find more evidence.

Six days after Nancy Nicol disappeared, Andrew Cameron was again interviewed. His story contained many inconsistencies, just like the one he told police about Kay Wyllie. In one version he claimed he necked with Nancy in a phone box and then had intercourse with her in an alleyway. While in another he said that he took Nancy home and they had sex on a couch after eating supper and watching a video. He also claimed that he walked Nancy back into the centre of Troon where she got into a car with a man he did not recognise. At this point the interrogation was taken over by the top detective in the area: chief superintendent John Fleming. Although Cameron was well used to police procedures, this was of a different order: the police were under pressure to solve both cases and were prepared to use all the resources at their disposal to get a result.

After a day of questioning there was a breakthrough. According to police, Cameron confessed. In response to questions about Kay Wyllie's murder he is alleged to have said 'I remember arguing with her. I think

I punched her and then I choked her.' When Fleming asked why he had done this, Cameron replied: 'Because she argued. I can't remember about what. It was ten months ago.' Later the same day Cameron confessed to killing Nancy Nicol and dumping her body in the sea next to Royal Troon golf course. According to police he said:

> She's in the water. I remember waking up in the morning. My shoes were covered in sand my trousers were wet up to the knees I think. I think I can remember where I put her. I think I can show you where it happened. It was like the girl last year as well. It just happened. I don't know why it happens. I don't mean it. I just lose the head then I blank it out of my mind.

Cameron then went with officers to South Beach in Troon. According to them he was shaking with fear. Cameron asked for, and was given, a torch. After looking around to get his bearings he pointed out to the Firth of Clyde and said 'There – she's in there.' The police could see little in the dark, but marked the spot that Cameron had indicated. He was taken back to Troon police station and the next morning, with his solicitor present, charged with the murder of Kay Wyllie.

In the days after Cameron's confession the search for Nancy intensified. Police put all the resources they could spare into looking for what they now realised was a corpse and they even called in the Royal Navy to assist them. But, as with Kay Wyllie's body, it was a member of the public who made the ghastly discovery. Some weeks later, a man and his son were out whelking on the rocks near Troon when they saw something in the water. It was Nancy Nicol's body which, after a month in the sea, was in an advanced state of decomposition. Andrew Cameron could now be charged with a second count of murder.

Cameron spent five months on remand. He spent some of his time writing tender love letters to Kathleen Chisholm, his 18-year-old girlfriend. According to the young woman this was typical of him: 'Andrew was a very special boyfriend', she later said, 'I could never have believed he was capable of murder. He was gentle and kind. He never treated me badly in any way.' This view of Cameron was considered naive by the police, who believed that Kathleen Chisholm would have been his third victim.

Despite attempts by the defence to get the trial moved to Glasgow proceedings began at Ayr High Court on 2 September 1985. Public interest was unprecedented and people queued from seven in the morning to get a seat. The prosecution was headed by the highest law officer in the land, Peter Fraser QC, the solicitor general. The defence team was no less formidable and was led by Nicholas Fairbairn QC, the colourful veteran of many high-profile murder trials.

Cameron pleaded not guilty to both murder charges – and to the breach-of-the-peace charge relating to Allison Bainbridge – and lodged a special defence of alibi. Much of the prosecution's case rested on his alleged confessions. This was a time before the landmark Police and Criminal Evidence Act, which stipulates that interviews have to be taped, and that accused persons are entitled to have their solicitor present. It was argued by Fairbairn that the police simply wore him down to such an extent that he would admit to anything, even murder. In the witness box, Cameron said that police had punched him to extract a confession.

At the end of the trial, on 18 September 1985, the jury must have been in two minds about Cameron's guilt, as it was by no means an open-and-shut case. There were no witnesses to either murder. There was limited forensic evidence in the case of Kay Wyllie, and none at all in respect of Nancy Nicol. There was no apparent motive for either murder. While Cameron had criminal tendencies, he had never been violent before. Understandably the jury took time to reach a conclusion, emerging after four hours to deliver its verdict: guilty, on both counts of murder. But the members were far from unanimous; in fact Nicholas Fairbairn believed that the split may have been only eight to seven in favour of the guilty verdict.

The trial judge, Lord Ross, imposed a life sentence on Cameron with a recommendation that he should spend at least twenty years behind bars. As he was led away Cameron sobbed loudly and shouted that the CID 'are all liars'. But there was one more dramatic twist. The defence team produced a witness who had not been heard at the trial – a witness whose evidence may have swayed some members of the jury. Mrs Ruby Steed of Prestwick claimed that she had seen Kay Wyllie in a car with a man only a short time before the teenager was murdered. And it was not Andrew Cameron. The official reason for her not being called was that she had come forward too late and could not be cited three days before the trial started. Nicholas Fairbairn believed the real reason was that she would have contradicted the other witnesses. He argued that if the jury had been able to hear her evidence his client would not have been convicted, and he gave notice of Cameron's intention to appeal.

An appeal was considered in 1987, but was rejected. Cameron suffered another hammer blow in June 2002 when his sentence was increased to a minimum term of thirty years. The reason for this was that courts were obliged to review the punishment element of sentences under human rights legislation and the judge took the view that his sentence should be set at the higher end of the tariff. Andrew Cameron will be in prison until 2015 at the earliest.

10. John Campbell and George Clelland
The bored killers

It seemed an innocent photograph, typical of the thousands of school snaps that had appeared on the *Friends Reunited* website. But it hid a chilling secret. One of those in the photo was a convicted killer and had murdered the mother of the classmate pictured standing beside him. The snap outraged fellow classmates and was quickly withdrawn once the truth was revealed. A school friend from the time commented, 'I couldn't believe it when I saw the picture of John Campbell staring back at me. It brought back a lot of memories from my schooldays.'

Memories of a spring day that the residents of Glasgow's Castlemilk estate are unlikely to forget. On the afternoon of Wednesday, 9 April 1975 10-year-old Craig Finlayson arrived home from school and knocked on the front door of his house at 107 Glenacre Drive. When his mum didn't come to let him in, he bent down to look through the letterbox and was confronted by the shocking sight of her body lying in a pool of blood in the hallway. Craig ran to a neighbour's house for help.

Detective sergeant Robert McKillop began door-to-door inquiries starting at those addresses closest to the murder scene. A few doors down McKillop came across George Clelland and John Campbell, who claimed to be visiting a school friend. The teenagers appeared nervous and admitted they had been to Mrs Finlayson's house at lunchtime when they had called in for her son Ronnie. Taken to Castlemilk police station for questioning, 15-year-old Clelland, an active Boys Brigade member, tore his BB badge from his jersey and threw it on the floor, screaming 'I'm not fit to wear it.' A hysterical Clelland then admitted:

> John knocked on the door and the two of us went in. I shoved her out of the road and she fell down. I knifed her first then John knifed her with my knife. We both stole some money. It was John who pulled her zip down. I got rid of the knife at my granny's under the mattress in my room. I couldnae stop myself. John and I were kidding on if we had the guts to kill somebody and it got serious.

Clelland knew there was cash in the house as he had been invited inside on a previous visit by Jean's eldest son, 15-year-old Ronnie Finlayson, a classmate.

John Campbell admitted, when confronted by his father, that he had gone with Clelland to 107 Glenacre Drive, but denied any part in the murder. In his statement to detectives he claimed that he thought that he was only taking part in a robbery for cash. He was aware that Clelland was carrying a knife but claimed that, as far as he knew, the knife was not going to be used. On arriving at the flat he had been the one to knock on the door. Jean Finlayson (38) knew John Campbell and George Clelland as they both attended the local church-run youth fellowship and Bible class where she did voluntary work as a teacher. So, on opening the door, she had no reason to be alarmed and asked Clelland: 'What is it, George?' Clelland had his knife in his hand by this time. Campbell had seen him take it out of his pocket and unfold the blade, but made no attempt to walk away believing, as he claimed, 'I thought the knife was only to be used as a threat.' When Jean had glimpsed the knife she had started to scream. It was at this moment that Clelland launched his attack.

Detectives established that Jean Finlayson had been murdered for less than £40 stolen from her purse. Her two attackers had split the proceeds. Clelland had hidden his share, £20, in his shoe and still had it secreted there when police arrested him. Campbell had put £19.85 inside a box that he had stored in the hallway cupboard of his house at 82 Drakemire Drive.

During the trial held at Glasgow High Court in July 1975 more details emerged of how the two teenagers had inexplicably transformed into juvenile killers. The court learned that Clelland and Campbell called at the Finlayson home to meet Ronnie and another chum to go back to school together after the dinner break. But Clelland and Campbell doubled back, leaving the other two, making the excuse that they had lost a key. Following the attack, they washed their hands and clothes to remove the blood and calmly returned late to school, Glenwood secondary, arriving halfway through an English class. However, a classmate noticed a spot of blood on Clelland's thigh when he changed for a physical-education lesson and later reported what he had seen to the police.

The calm manner displayed during the trial by the two 'baby-faced killers', as the press dubbed them, was in stark contrast to the vicious manner in which their victim had met her death. Medical expert Dr William McLay gave evidence that 'Mrs Finlayson had been stabbed more than twenty times on the face and body. One four-inch-deep wound punctured her heart and another nicked the main artery in her neck.' One had penetrated her brain.

The court also heard the youths blame each other for the wounds that killed Jean Finlayson and deny any sexual motive for the attack. Clelland, however, admitted under questioning that he had attacked Mrs Finlayson without any provocation. 'She opened the door and when she did I stabbed her and she said "Oh my God, what have I done to deserve this?"' This had no effect on Clelland whose blood lust now turned into a frenzy. He claimed, 'I couldnae stop myself after this. John got the knife next and stabbed her.' Clelland said that he stabbed Mrs Finlayson only twice. He knifed her in the stomach after she screamed then stabbed her again. After receiving this second wound she fell down clutching her stomach. He told the court that the other wounds on her arms, body and face had been inflicted by John Campbell. Clelland also claimed that he had taken no part in a sexual assault and said that Campbell had been responsible. Clelland said 'we were just going out of the house and John said "wait a minute". He lifted her body up and I pulled down her trousers. I don't know why.' Clelland denied that he had touched her sexually and said that Campbell had touched the top part of Mrs Finlayson's clothing 'just to see if she was still alive'.

John Campbell, in his evidence, not only denied involvement in a sexual assault, but also having any responsibility for her death. He accused Clelland of having inflicted every one of the stab wounds on Jean Finlayson. He could not deny the forensic evidence that his finger-prints were on the bloodstained knife, but had an innocent explanation as to how they had come to be there.

After Mrs Finlayson asked, 'What is it, George?' Clelland stabbed her, Campbell told the court, adding: 'The first time she was still on her feet, but after the second time she fell down. After that I could not bear what was happening and went into the kitchen. At the same time I got the purse and took the money.' Campbell said he turned off the washing machine because it was flooding then saw Clelland throwing the knife at Mrs Finlayson as she lay on the floor. The knife missed and bounced off the wall, landing in a pool of their victim's blood. He took it and washed it before passing it back to Clelland. He claimed that this accounted for the fact that his fingerprints were all over the knife. Campbell consistently denied stabbing Mrs Finlayson, claiming that he did not run away after Clelland knifed her because he was afraid that Clelland would attack him too.

Campbell, an assistant patrol leader in the Boy Scouts, who had known Clelland since primary school, claimed that it was Clelland who had first suggested robbing Mrs Finlayson. Campbell claimed that his pal needed money to take out his girlfriend, money he believed his father would not give him. He added that the plan was to dodge school and carry out the robbery. The day before the robbery Clelland had shown him the knife. Campbell told the court, 'I didn't know it was going to be used. I thought he was just going to threaten her if she didn't give up the money.' On the way to Mrs Finlayson's, Clelland had asked him, 'Do you have the guts to kill anyone?' and Campbell had answered 'no'.

Campbell had no previous convictions and there was no obvious reason to explain why he had become involved in the crime particularly as he was the son of a serving police officer. His dad, detective inspector John

Campbell (41), was on duty at a football match at Hampden Park when he was asked to go to the police station at Castlemilk where his son had been taken for interview. John readily admitted to his father that he had agreed with Clelland that they would rob the Finlayson home.

At his trial Clelland changed his plea of not guilty and admitted murder. Clelland lived just a few doors down from his victim at 86 Glenacre Drive and was a classmate of her eldest son, 15-year-old Ronnie Finlayson. Campbell continued to protest his innocence, but the jury took only forty minutes to find him guilty of murder. Both Campbell and Clelland were cleared of the charge that they had indecently assaulted Mrs Finlayson.

The only motive that emerged for what seemed a senseless attack was boredom. The two youths told police at the time of their interrogation at Castlemilk police station that they were fed up with sitting through lessons in school. At his trial Clelland repeated his explanation, saying from the witness box: 'It was just that we did not like the periods at school.' When the prosecuting counsel asked, 'So you did not like the periods at school so you decided to carry out a robbery just for something to do?', Clelland nodded his head in agreement. Jean Finlayson had died simply because two teenagers were bored with their teachers, apparently. It was a sickening thought.

Sentencing Campbell and Clelland to be detained during her majesty's pleasure, the presiding judge Lord Robertson told them that in the murder of Jean Finlayson 'the level of depravity and wickedness shown had reached a new low'. Clelland and Campbell had the dubious distinction of becoming part of a select group. Up to 1975 only three other youths under the age of sixteen had been convicted of murder in Scotland and been ordered to be detained at her majesty's pleasure. However, by the time of the *Friends Reunited* scandal in 2003, Campbell had long been free and made a new life for himself, but the memory of Jean Finlayson's savage death will not easily be forgotten by the residents of the Castlemilk estate no matter how many years go by.

11. Mark Clark

The smirking fiend

The pathologist who examined the body of 3-year-old Chloe Highley found that the little girl had suffered unimaginable agonies before her death. No less than fifty-three separate injuries were found on her body, many of them inflicted by hard punches to the head and torso. There was evidence that she had been thrown against a wall and that considerable pressure had been applied to her neck. He also discovered that she had been tortured by her assailant, who had burnt her skin with the wheel of a cigarette lighter. The cause of death was blunt-force trauma caused by the punches or by being hurled against the wall.

The savagery involved in these assaults on an innocent and helpless child is hard to come to terms with. That the attacker responsible for the fatal injuries was a close relative makes them all the more inexplicable. Chloe's killer was her uncle, Mark Clark, a 20-year-old from Clermiston in Edinburgh. The fatal attacks took place when he was babysitting for his half-sister, Geraldine Smith, and her husband, James Smith, at their home in Restalrig Road, Edinburgh on 6 February 2002 while Mrs Smith went to play bingo. Geraldine Smith's decision to leave Chloe (the daughter she had with former partner, David Highley) and her three other children in Clark's care was a surprising one: she had noticed bruises and bite marks on Chloe's body after Clark had been in the child's company. In fact she was so concerned that she had arranged for Chloe to have a medical check-up; an appointment that was never kept due to her death.

In February 2003 Mark Clark was put on trial for murder in Edinburgh's High Court, and pleaded not guilty. Clark lodged a special defence blaming Geraldine and James Smith for Chloe's death, an allegation that they vehemently denied. As Mrs Smith told the court: 'The only people in the house before I left were me, Mark Clark and my four children. When I left, my children were alive and in their beds. Nothing happened to Chloe before I left.' She only heard that something was wrong when police arrived at the bingo hall and took her to the Royal Hospital for Sick Children, where a consultant told her that her daughter was dead.

But there was yet more compelling evidence against Clark. The Smiths' next-door neighbour in Restalrig Road recalled that she heard several thuds through the wall at ten past six on the night Chloe died, followed by knocking on the wall an hour later. But the most shocking evidence led by the prosecution was a 999 call made by Clark at 7.35 p.m. During the call – which was recorded and played back to the court – Clark said that Chloe was making 'funny noises' and on the tape the little girl could clearly be heard gasping and choking. Clark called her name and said to the ambulance controller: 'She is not breathing . . . her lips are going purple . . . Chloe, c'mon baby, Uncle Mark needs to talk to you. She looks like she is dying in front of me . . . you will need to hurry.' The emergency call was also overheard by the same neighbour.

With evidence like this it was clear that Clark had to be the killer. But was it strong enough to secure a guilty verdict on a charge of murder? The prosecution plainly did not believe that it was. In a dramatic development, ten days after the trial started, it was announced that Mark Clark had pleaded guilty to a lesser charge of culpable homicide. The Crown, effectively, had entered into a plea bargain with the defence (a decision that was heavily criticised in the aftermath of the trial). It was accepted by prosecutors that the precise circumstances leading up to Chloe's death would never be known for certain and that the 'wicked recklessness' necessary to make a murder charge stick was absent. The prosecution also took into account Clark's limited intelligence and his 'significant emotional problems'. Allegations that he had sexually assaulted Chloe were dropped.

Mark Clark returned to the High Court in Edinburgh for sentencing on 20 March 2003. Despite the fact that he came up with a new excuse – that his drink had been spiked with LSD – temporary judge Roderick Macdonald dismissed it for the fiction it undoubtedly was. In his judgement he said, 'It almost defies belief that anyone could do such a cruel thing to a three-year-old girl' and handed down a sentence of fifteen years. Throughout the proceedings Clark had not shown any remorse for his crime, and was even seen to smirk as he left the court. This further enraged Chloe Highley's family, who were already aggrieved that he had avoided a life sentence.

But given the attitude of his fellow cons to people who have harmed children it may well be that Clark will never leave jail alive. After he had been in Edinburgh's Saughton prison for only a few weeks it was reported that he had been bombarded with death threats. A search of his cell revealed a number of handwritten notes, one of which said he was going to get a thousand slashes and another that promised he would be murdered. Warders were continually asked by inmates to turn a blind eye to allow time for Clark to be stabbed. It seems that even hardened criminals feel the same sense of outrage towards child killers as their law-abiding fellow citizens.

12. Richard Coubrough

The cobra strikes

The cigarette packet had a strange message written on the back. It read, 'Mr Polis. I have killed that woman in cold blood. Bible John.' The police did not take the Bible John connection seriously, but they did suspect that the evidence had been deliberately planted to throw them off the scent. And they also guessed that it had a connection with a gruesome discovery made on 14 April 1971. That afternoon three boys – Gordon Cherrie (10), Walter Howard (8) and Alistair Buckley (10) – catching bees near the former Renfrew South railway station, walked along the disused railway track and found themselves at a site where three old railway carriages had been converted to use as bothies. Wandering behind one of the huts Gordon Cherrie came across the naked body of a woman, lying face down under catkin bushes. The corpse had been partially covered by leaves and branches and an old bit of carpet. The boys alerted workmen who in turn contacted the police.

Uniformed officers cordoned off the area, photographs of the crime scene were taken and the site combed for clues. A tracker dog was brought in to search two miles of railway line and several items were taken away for investigation. The body, that of a slimly built woman, five feet two inches in height with dark, auburn hair cut short, was soon identified as that of 37-year-old part-time nurse and mother of two Mrs Dorothea Meechan, who had last been seen alive on Saturday, 28 February. Forensic examination established that she had been stripped and raped before being brutally strangled.

The last person to see Dorothea alive had been her mother, Mrs Sarah Cunningham (64), who told detectives that she and Dorothea 'had been visiting the home of a relation in Renfrew on the last Saturday in February to see slides of friends and relatives in Australia. It was the first Saturday night Dorothea had been out for ages.' They had walked back together till they were near to Mrs Cunningham's house in the Moorpark district of Renfrew where the pair separated. Dorothea still had a way to go to reach her own home in the nearby Kirklandneuk estate. Mrs Cunningham recalled: 'We reached Moorpark Square about 12.30. I said to Dorothea to wait and I would get her brother Tony to walk back with her. But she laughed and said, "Don't worry mum I'll be all right. I have my umbrella and shoes to protect me. There'll be plenty of people about because of the dance in the town." ' They then waved each other goodbye.

Having left her mother at the junction of Maitland Place and Moorpark Square, Mrs Meechan would have taken a route that criss-crossed several streets till she reached the last well-lit spot at Clerk Street. From here her journey took her down a badly lit lane leading to an iron railway-foot-bridge which linked the Porterfield estate to Kirklandneuk housing scheme where she lived. It was at a spot overlooked by the footbridge that her body was discovered.

When Mrs Meechan had first disappeared six weeks earlier neither the police who had conducted a search nor her family had suspected that she had been the victim of a crime. Mrs Cunningham believed there was a straightforward explanation, 'We had a lot of trouble recently. Her father, a brother and a cousin all died within a few weeks. We thought her mind had gone, she had become depressed and so decided to run away.'

The truth, however, was that Dorothea Meechan had met her death at the hands of Scotland's most notorious sexual psychopath. A man who, police believed, was responsible for more attacks than he was ever brought to trial for, and whose criminal record marked him out as a danger to any woman unlucky enough to come across him when his sexual desire was ready to explode.

And detectives had a lead. A man had, in the weeks leading up to the discovery of the murder, attempted to sexually assault a woman very close to the spot where Dorothea Meechan's body was found. The publicity surrounding the murder encouraged the victim to come forward and she gave the police a description of the incident and of the individual who had confronted her. The 40-year-old mother of two related how, as she was walking home, a man approached her and took hold of her. She instinct-ively knew that he was out to rape her. Her screams of terror attracted the attention of two other women and frightened her assailant, who ran off. She was later to tell the High Court in Glasgow, 'This man tried to do some-thing to me. I felt he was actually going to kill me.'

From the descriptions given by the women involved in this incident, and by witnesses who had seen a man hanging around the footbridge Dorothea had been heading for on the way home, police thought they knew the identity of the suspect. Ex-slaughterman Richard Joseph Coubrough. Nicknamed 'Snake' or 'Cobra' from the pronunciation of his name 'Coo-bra', he had a fearsome reputation. Short and stocky with a swarthy complexion, his arms were adorned with tattoos including a slave girl, a heart with a dagger and a swallow. The last out of keeping with the character of this Glasgow-born criminal who had eleven convic-tions for rape, theft, housebreaking and assault by 1971. In 1962 he was sentenced to four years' imprisonment at the High Court in Glasgow. While serving the sentence at Inverness prison and having been granted trustee status and allowed outside to help with painting jobs, he sneaked into the house of a prison officer, grabbed the man's wife from behind, bound and gagged her, dragged her to an upstairs bedroom and then raped her. True to his nickname, the Snake claimed, in his defence, that the woman had enticed him to her bedroom and that he had kissed and cuddled her on an earlier visit. The jury weren't taken in by Coubrough's story and returned a guilty verdict. In January 1964 he was sentenced at the High Court in Inverness to six years for the attack.

Events at Inverness were in keeping with Coubrough's previous criminal record. He first came to police attention in 1957 in Edinburgh following a series of attacks on six women. He was given a two-year sentence. In 1958 he escaped from Glasgow Sheriff Court while awaiting trial. He was recaptured eight days' later and faced fresh charges of breaking into the Strathclyde nursing home in Clairemont Street, Glasgow while on the run and raping a 26-year-old patient terminally ill with cancer. She died three weeks later from her illness and the charges against Coubrough were dropped.

By 1969, having completed his Inverness rape sentence, Coubrough was living in Aberdeen and back to his criminal activities. He was charged with the attempted rape of a school teacher in a street near her home. But the charges were dropped because of lack of evidence. The Snake, however, was gaoled for eighteen months on arson and theft charges. So dangerous was Coubrough judged to be that, at the end of this sentence, police forces across Scotland were alerted to the fact that he was once again free. On his release he moved to Cardwell Road in Gourock. It was shortly after his arrival in the area that Dorothea Meechan disappeared.

But although the police believed they had identified the man responsible for Dorothea's murder, Coubrough had no intention of surrendering easily. Detective sergeant Frank Duncan told the High Court in Glasgow that he was on patrol with constable Alec Pollock when he saw a man whose description matched that of the suspect in the attempted-rape incident. A case that seemed closely linked to the murder of Dorothea Meechan. The man was Richard Coubrough. Duncan chased him into a close, but Coubrough threw a whisky bottle at him which shattered on a wall nearby. Duncan was later to describe to the jury the struggle he had to arrest Coubrough. 'I banged his head against one of the doors to try and get some help. He was very strong and at the time I knew I would never hold him. I have never experienced anything like this before. He went wild.' Coubrough fought so ferociously that he managed to escape.

But the message to the court was clear. Few women would be able to fight off unaided the assault of a man with Coubrough's physical strength and vicious temperament. Dorothea Meechan, a slimly built figure of five feet two inches, would have been little match for the Snake.

Although he had evaded Frank Duncan's brave attempt to arrest him, Coubrough's freedom was short lived. The police discovered his address, where he was staying with his mistress, and on 18 April 1971 he was arrested at his lodgings. After he was taken into custody, detectives searching his flat found pornographic magazines and books, including one with the title, *I the Rapist*. Coubrough had underlined certain passages, and police believed he had imitated events in the book in his sex attacks on women.

Taken by officers to the police station, Coubrough told detectives, 'I have been thinking it over and I just want to say that I did not murder the woman. It was an accident. She screamed and I didn't steal the clothing. I panicked and only took them to get rid of them.' This admission was later contested in court by Coubrough, who claimed, 'During the course of the night the police were at me every ten minutes. If I did not reply they came in and shook me.' He described his alleged confession as 'pure fabrication' by the police, and claimed that on the night of 28 February he was in a bingo hall and then went to a pub. He also denied that he had left the Bible John message on the cigarette packet.

In spite of the Snake's protestations of innocence, the jury took less than half an hour to find him guilty. The presiding judge, Lord Migdale, told Coubrough: 'By our law as it stands, there is only one sentence I can pronounce – imprisonment for life.'

Incredibly, in 2005, thirty-four years after he was gaoled, Coubrough, now a 72-year-old, and still protesting his innocence, was given leave to appeal against his conviction for Dorothea Meechan's murder.

13. Graham Coutts
The Internet pervert

Murderers commit the ultimate crime for a whole range of reasons. Many are ordinary people driven to the act by extraordinary circumstances; others are motivated by baser instincts like jealousy, greed and revenge. Few are moved to kill by a need to satisfy their perverted urges. But then few have the sexual preferences of a man like Graham Coutts.

Coutts was born in Leven, Fife in 1968 and attended primary school in Glenrothes before moving to Cheltenham with his parents, Frank and Elizabeth, at the age of eleven. Highly intelligent, he won a place at grammar school and later went on to South Cheshire College of Further Education in Crewe. But he lacked the self-discipline necessary to succeed academically and left after two years. After a number of menial jobs he drifted south to the trendy seaside resort of Brighton where he made a living as a salesman and part-time musician. Attractive to women he had several relationships before meeting the first real love of his life in 1988. She was a divorced mother of five named Sandra Gates who, at thirty-one, was ten years his senior.

From his schooldays Coutts had a fascination with women's necks and strangulation and, during his six-year relationship with Sandra Gates, his sexual deviations became more and more pronounced. At first the couple had normal, missionary-position sex. But after about a year – by which time they were living together – Coutts's behaviour had become increasingly bizarre. He had a powerful sex drive and demanded sex every day. One of his peccadilloes was deliberately to upset Sandra as this seemed to arouse him even more; another was to masturbate in front of her. She naively thought these behavioural patterns were common to all young men.

But things soon got even worse. Coutts pressurised Gates into taking part in sex games. Worried that she would lose her young lover – and at the same time afraid of his violent rages – she reluctantly agreed. The games followed a familiar pattern: he was always first into bed and would lie in the dark waiting for her. Then he demanded: 'Put on your white panties and stockings babe', before telling her to kneel on the floor. Coutts would then creep up behind her and start stroking her neck as they had intercourse. The sex became even more bizarre as Sandra Gates later recalled: 'Then he moved on to putting his hands around my neck . . . He used to like the lights off and for me to be silent . . . I never lost consciousness but feared I would. He told me asphyxiation would improve my orgasms but it did nothing for me.' In a variation on this game, Coutts would tie tights and white cotton knickers around her neck in a clear attempt to intimidate: 'He knew how to frighten me. Once he put a pillow over my face during sex and I really struggled and panicked.'

Other aspects of his behaviour also worried Gates. Coutts would hide in a wardrobe to watch her daughters getting undressed and even drilled a hole in the bathroom ceiling to watch them bathe. But it was while Coutts was on one of his many absences from the house in 1995 that she made the most disturbing discovery of all. Gates forced open a locked briefcase that he kept under the bed and found photographs of naked girls trussed up. He had also drawn ligatures around the neck of a girl he worked with. It was when she confronted him about the porn that he made the most stunning prediction she had ever heard: 'He said he had the most awful feeling he was going to rape, strangle and kill a girl.' It was a prediction that was to have tragic consequences.

The relationship between Graham Coutts and Sandra Gates ended in 1996. It followed a family tragedy: Sandra's 18-year-old son Daniel – who despised Coutts – had drifted into crime and had fallen to his death during a burglary; Gates was distraught and told Coutts to leave, which he did without any fuss. He then had a relationship with a woman called Nicola – with whom he claimed to have had asphyxial sex more than one hundred times – before that too ended in 1998. But Coutts soon had a new love: Lisa Stephens, an attractive and highly intelligent young woman who had an English degree from Bath University and worked as a teacher. At first Stephens was prepared to experiment with kinky sex: she allowed Coutts to put his hands around her neck and squeeze while they were having intercourse; on another occasion he used a dressing-gown cord. But she did not enjoy the experience and told him not to try it again.

On the surface Coutts appeared to have settled down to a life of quiet domesticity with Lisa Stephens. He was working regularly: during the day as a Kleeneze salesman and at night as a guitarist with 17 Black, a 1960s-style 'mod' band. They had a number of close friends and enjoyed a busy social life. Then, in early 2003, the couple were thrilled to learn that, after having had fertility treatment, they were expecting twin boys. But Coutts needed an outlet for his perverted longings; longings that Lisa Stephens was unwilling to accommodate. And he found that outlet on the Internet.

He used his credit card to subscribe to vile websites with names like 'Necro Babes', 'Rape Passion', 'Violent Pleasure' and 'Shrink Wrap Bitch'; websites that are all too readily available in cyberspace. One site offered stomach-churning images of dead bodies. Another featured pictures of women being hanged, strangled and electrocuted. And, when he was not online, Coutts avidly read his huge collection of hard-core porn magazines.

This material undoubtedly fuelled his unhealthy obsessions; obsessions that he would later admit had haunted him since childhood. He was an accident waiting to happen.

In their social circle, Lisa Stephens and Graham Coutts counted Malcolm Sentance and Jane Longhurst as particularly close friends. The couples frequently socialised together, as often as not in their own homes. Lisa had first met Jane at Oakmeeds community college in Burgess Hill, West Sussex where they were both teachers and the two women grew closer together when they moved to new jobs in Brighton. Jane Longhurst (31) was a daughter any mother could be proud of. She had grown up in Reading before going on to Liverpool University, where she studied music. Bright, charming and popular, she doted on the special-needs children she taught. She was also an outstanding musician and loved nothing better than playing her antique viola at home and in a local orchestra.

Despite the fact that Jane Longhurst believed Coutts was unstable she got on well with him. He was friendly and attentive to her and she would often visit him at home when Lisa Stephens was out at work. This did not make Lisa jealous, as she would later explain: 'I had no reason to mistrust either of them. . . . She was a classically trained musician and he was in a band, so they had something in common. She used to come to the flat to see him when I was at work. He told me she wasn't his type but she thought he was attractive. I was flattered. Nobody wants to go out with an ugly bloke.'

So when, on 14 March 2003, Jane Longhurst phoned her friend Lisa only to find she was at work it was the most natural thing in the world for her to have a friendly chat with Coutts. And it was also quite normal for them to arrange to go for a dip together at the beach; they had been swimming together several times before. But only Coutts knows what happened after their swim. His story is that Jane was upset and they went to his place for tea; that, he said, led to consensual, asphyxial sex. The police, however, believe that Coutts attacked her moments after they arrived at the flat. Whatever the truth, the end result was that Jane Longhurst met her end in the flat, strangled to death by a pair of tights while Coutts was having sex with her. He would later insist that her death was completely accidental.

It was more than a month before the body was discovered. Coutts hid the corpse behind his flat for eleven days and then moved it to a six-feet-by-four-feet lock-up he had rented from a Brighton storage company using a false name. He kept the body there for almost a month, visiting seven times for – detectives believed – further sexual gratification. When staff at the storage company began to complain about the smell, Coutts retrieved Jane's naked body and took it to a remote nature reserve near Pulborough, West Sussex where he covered it with petrol and set it alight.

The burning corpse was found later the same day; a tightly knotted pair of tights was still embedded in the neck.

Information supplied by workers at the storage company quickly led police to Coutts. He had been captured on closed-circuit television taking away a large cardboard box. A search of the lock-up revealed not only Jane Longhurst's clothes and personal effects but also her, and Coutts's, DNA. Then police found hundreds of downloaded photographs of necrophilia, rape and violence against women on his home computer; detectives said the material was truly sickening.

Despite pleading not guilty at his trial in early 2004, the jury at Lewes Crown Court found him guilty of murder after deliberating for nine hours. As the verdict was delivered, members of the Longhurst family shouted 'yes' and punched the air with delight. Judge Richard Brown sentenced Coutts to life imprisonment, stipulating that he should spend at least thirty years inside. And as Coutts was led away cries of 'pervert' and 'pig' rang out from the public benches.

14. Rita Davidson and Edward Gallagher

Scotland's Bonnie and Clyde

'Right dear', were the last words ever spoken by 56-year-old postmistress Mrs Mary Ridgway. Moments later she was dead, throttled by a couple who were branded Scotland's 'Bonnie and Clyde'. But when the chips were down the murderous pair tried to escape justice by blaming each other for the crime and claimed to be innocent spectators of their victim's last seconds.

It was in 1964, at a dance in Dalkeith, Midlothian, that 24-year-old Rita Davidson first met Edward Gallagher (26), a native of Donegal, who had emigrated to Scotland several years earlier to find work as a farm labourer. The two hit it off from the start and Rita soon left her mother's home in the village of Arniston to move in with 'Eddie', as she liked to call him. For the next eight months they lived together in a caravan at Middleton farm near Dalkeith before moving into a cottage at Cammerlaws farm, Westruther where Edward had got a job, and stayed there for the next year. But then things went drastically wrong. Gallagher was sacked and, by August 1966, desperately short of money, and unwilling or unable to find work, the couple hatched a plan to carry out a robbery in a nearby village.

The combined shop and post office at Westruther near Duns was owned by 56-year-old Mrs Mary Ridgway who had taken over the premises eight years' previously. She was a native of the village, but had spent her married life at Ashton in the Wirral district of Cheshire where her husband had worked as a chauffeur. After her husband's death she retired to Westruther and used her savings to buy the village general store with its post office. The living premises were conveniently situated right next door. Although childless and living on her own, she had the comfort of knowing that her sister, Mrs Isabella Wood, lived nearby. A quiet person, Mary Ridgway kept herself to herself and took no part in village activities. It seemed that she had never really got over the premature death of her husband. Her only constant companion was her adored pet cat, Whitie.

On the morning of Thursday, 1 September 1966 gravedigger John McCallum, a neighbour of Mrs Ridgway, went to the shop for his morning paper and found it still locked. He noted that Whitie was pawing at the door trying to get in. Mr McCallum alerted Isabella Wood who, finding her sister's house empty and the post office locked, contacted the police. Jim Wood, Isabella's husband, helped police to force the shop door. Inside they discovered the body of Mary Ridgway, fully clothed, lying on the floor with a stocking round her neck. Police searching the house noticed that a cup of Ovaltine had not been drunk and Mrs Ridgway's bed had not been slept in. Detectives immediately set out to narrow down her movements to fix the time of death. A vital clue in the hunt for the killer. Jim Wood told police that he had last seen Mary at five the previous evening. A youth came forward to say that he had seen her about ten o'clock on the Wednesday putting her cat into a shed for the night. Isabella told police that when her sister went to put the cat into the shed she never locked her door, but just left it on the latch. She speculated that someone might have entered the house while she was round at the shed at the back. It was common gossip in the village that she kept large sums of money in her home.

Meanwhile detectives called in the fire brigade to search the village wishing-well for the missing shop-door key as it was believed the killer might have dumped it there as he fled. At the same time, police with mine detectors searched the length of the village in the hunt for clues. Door-to-door inquiries were organised to find out if any of Westruther's 150 inhabitants had noticed anything suspicious.

Random killings are the hardest of all crimes to solve and detectives anticipated a long inquiry. But they had a stroke of luck. A man and woman travelling together had hitched a lift from the main road close by Westruther to Edinburgh in the early hours of Thursday morning. By following their trail officers soon had them in their sights. On Sunday, 4 September 1966, police – at their headquarters in Hawick – announced that a man and woman had been arrested in Midlothian and charged with the murder of Mrs Mary Ridgway. The pair were Rita Davidson and her lover Edward Gallagher.

At first Gallagher seemed quite willing to admit responsibility for the night's events and revelled in the Bonnie and Clyde tag. He confessed to the police:

Me and Rita had that planned for a fortnight before it happened. We went down that night to do it. The woman was getting some things behind the counter where we were standing and she said 'Right, dear'. I got hold of the woman, struck her on the chin and knocked her down. I put my hands on her throat. Rita was in the lobby peeping in and she told me I was taking a hell of a long time. She thought I was interfering with the woman which I was not. She then handed me the stocking. We went back into the shop about two o'clock and there were some pennies in the drawer. We took them and some money which was in a tin box and then went back into the room again. We had a look round upstairs, but didn't take nothing. Rita took a tin of corned beef and a packet of biscuits and a wee cake. I took sixty cigarettes, I think. After that we sat in the room for about ten minutes and we left the place about ten past two. We went on the Lauder road from Westruther and I threw the shop key away on the left hand side going to Lauder, about one or two miles down the road. That's all. We got a lift in a lorry to Edinburgh.

But the brutal side to Rita Davidson and Edward Gallagher only fully emerged at the trial when each blamed the other for Mary Ridgway's death and denied their own involvement. In the time since his arrest Gallagher had experienced a dramatic change of heart. He now claimed that the statement he gave to police after the arrest had been made to protect Davidson. According to Gallagher she had told him that he 'wouldn't be much of a fellow if he did not stand up for her and take the whole blame for the murder.' Gallagher told the court that after robbing the till he went into Mrs Ridgway's house to count the money leaving Davidson with Mrs Ridgway. When he returned to the post office, Mrs Ridgway was dead. He asked Rita what had happened and she replied that she had 'got nervous'. In a dramatic gesture in court Gallagher leant forward in the dock and looking directly at Davidson exclaimed, 'You did it. You know fine you did it.'

Rita Davidson gave the jury a radically different version, claiming that when they set out to rob the post office, Gallagher had said to her: 'To keep the woman from talking, the best thing to do is to kill her.' She also claimed that Gallagher had 'asked me earlier for a nylon stocking. He wanted the stocking to choke her.' Davidson admitted that they decided to rob the post office because they had no money, but played down her own involvement.

In her version of events:

We left about 8.30. We went down to the shop. Mrs Ridgway opened the shop which was locked and we went in. We ordered some messages. I ordered something from the back of the counter – a necklace I think. Before I knew where I was I was closing the shop door. I sat and waited and I never saw anything happening. The shop door was closed and Eddie was inside with the woman and I was outside and I never saw anything. I was in the room where the television was and sitting in a chair. Edward called on me and asked for the stocking which I brought out of my bag. I gave it to Edward and closed the door and went back through into the room and we sat down. I couldn't do anything else.

She heard 'the woman's screams', but ignored them. Afterwards, she said, Gallagher joined her in the house and told her with a laugh, 'She will be all right for a long, long time.' Davidson claimed, 'I was going to telephone the police but he had threatened me before and I was frightened.' She added, 'Edward put the light and television off. We sat on the settee together. We just waited there till half past one in the morning because there were some people coming from the pub. We didn't want to do anything sudden because the woman was dead.' Davidson told her former lover's defence counsel, 'You should all know that it was Mr Gallagher who killed Mrs Ridgway because anyone would know from the fingerprints on her throat. You all know Mr Gallagher did it.'

Ignoring their protestations of innocence, the jury at the High Court in Jedburgh took less than an hour to find both Davidson and Gallagher guilty by a unanimous verdict of the murder of postmistress Mary Ridgway. As prosecuting counsel Ewan Stewart had told the jury, 'It doesn't really matter which hand was the strangler because they were both in it.'

But why had Mrs Ridgway been killed? Isabella Wood who last saw her sister at 4 p.m. on the day she was murdered said that Mary was well aware of the danger of keeping a sub post-office with money on the premises. She had often talked about the possibility of being robbed or held up and she used to say that she would always tell anyone who threatened her to take the money rather than risk violence. In fact she was killed for £5 and a few packets of cigarettes. Items that she would have undoubtedly handed over had Gallagher not set about her from the start.

So what had triggered the Irishman's murderous attack? In trying to throw the blame on Davidson, Gallagher's defence counsel had claimed that, 'Seeing Mrs Ridgway's clothing in disarray Rita took her spite out in a moment of insane jealousy by tying the stocking round Mrs Ridgway's neck instead of round her hands and feet.' The sexual aspect of the crime was played down at the time, but detectives claimed that Gallagher had told a fellow farm worker that he was interested sexually in Mrs Ridgway. Davidson certainly believed that he was interfering with Mary Ridgway, telling the court, 'He was a man like that.' She had left him on a previous occasion when she believed he was having an affair.

We may never know whose hands throttled the life from Mary Ridgway. But it seems likely that Rita Davidson's jealousy of her former lover turned her mind against him. And though her evidence confirmed his guilt, it linked her intimately to the murder so that Scotland's 'Bonnie and Clyde' each found themselves with a life sentence for a brutal but senseless crime which Davidson admitted to Gallagher, 'Simply was not worth it.'

15. David Donnell

The beast of Linwood

'Why me?' Those were the last words uttered by Billy Fargher as he lay dying on a busy street in Linwood, Renfrewshire on 9 October 2002. It is little wonder that he was confused. His killers, local gangsters, had shot the wrong man. An entirely innocent man.

In common with many towns and cities in Britain there was an ongoing turf war in Linwood for control of the drugs trade. One of the leading protagonists was David Donnell (39), nicknamed the 'Beast'. Although small in stature – he was barely five feet tall – Donnell was one of the most feared criminals in the area and had a police record longer than his diminutive arms. And his thirteen convictions were probably just the tip of the iceberg: he was suspected of involvement in a raft of other crimes. Extreme violence was a feature of many of his run-ins with the law. In 1989 he was accused of murdering a man in a pub knife-attack but walked free from court when his brother took the blame. Four years' later he was charged with attempted murder when he fired a shotgun at a couple through their window. Once again he was acquitted. But his run of luck had to end sometime and, in 1996, he was given a seven-year sentence for attempted murder when he rammed his car into another vehicle in a road-rage incident.

Donnell was clearly someone who bought into the whole ethos of the gangster. He named his two pistols Reggie and Ronnie after the notorious Kray twins and had a group of accomplices keen to carry out his nefarious orders. Another trait he shared with the so-called 'brothers Grim' was a need to control all the criminal activity on his own turf. This led him to plot the murder of one Sammy Quigg, a landscape gardener and alleged drug dealer (allegations that Quigg has always denied). The plan that Donnell hatched involved luring Quigg to a house in Linwood on the pretext of getting an estimate for laying slabs. He would then be ambushed by the Donnell team.

Everything seemed to be going to plan. A white Vauxhall Astra van, the make and model used by Quigg, drove up to the house and a man matching Quigg's description got out. Lookouts posted by Donnell alerted him to this development and he quickly drove two of his gang, James Campbell and Colin Garrett, to the scene. Campbell and Garrett ran up behind their target and pistol-whipped him. Campbell then blasted him in the chest with a shotgun at point-blank range. But it wasn't Sammy Quigg. The man attacked by Donnell's accomplices was 38-year-old Billy Fargher, the manager of a fast-food outlet and someone with no links to either crime or drugs. Mr Fargher was simply in the wrong place at the wrong time. By a terrible coincidence he drove an Astra similar to Quigg's and also bore a passable resemblance to him. As he lay in the road Billy Fargher begged passing motorists who had stopped to help him to tell his girlfriend, Paula Young, what had happened.

David Donnell, who left the scene before the hit was carried out, got a text message from his friend, Isabella 'Hot Lips' Calderwood to say that Quigg was dead. The 'Beast' was ecstatic: 'The power has just gone out in Linwood. The grasscutter's power went out' was his reply to 'Hot Lips'. Of course it was the unfortunate Billy Fargher who was dead. Quigg, for reasons that are unclear, had not turned up as planned and the gangsters proceeded to make a fatal error. When Donnell found out the truth he exploded with rage, screaming 'I can't believe it' and smashed a mirror with his mobile phone. But he showed no remorse for the death of an innocent man.

The scenes at the end of the eight-week trial in Glasgow's High Court on 15 October 2003 were a further illustration of the depravity of the Donnell gang. Donnell and Campbell were both given life sentences with a recommendation that they should serve at least twenty-five years; Garrett was also handed a life sentence with a twenty-year minimum term. A fourth man, Shaun O'Neill, was cleared of the murder on a not-proven verdict. But during the sentencing process there were scenes that one lawyer present said were the worst he had witnessed for twenty-five years. Garrett, who refused to stand to hear his sentence, spat at the judge, Lord McEwan, and boasted, 'I'm proud of it'. He then turned to Billy Fargher's sister, bowed and made obscene gestures to her. When Campbell was told by the judge it was clear that he was the one who shot Billy Fargher he replied, 'So fucking what. It won't make any differ-ence.' He then ranted at the jury, 'Fucking hang your heads in shame. I hope you can sleep tonight.' And he ended by calling the jury foreman a 'fucking specky prick'. By contrast, David Donnell, their boss, sat in silence as he was sentenced.

As Billy Fargher's sister said after the trial the murder of her brother gives the lie to the belief that gangsters only harm other members of the underworld. And she paid a heartfelt tribute to the happy-go-lucky brother who never did anyone any harm: 'We came here for justice for Billy. He would never have been involved with these people. He was a kind caring man who would help anyone who asked. The people who murdered him had no idea of what kind of man they destroyed.'

But the devastation caused by the Donnell family was far from over. In a clear case of 'like father like son' David Donnell junior was found guilty in April 2005 of savagely stabbing a workmate to death. Ironically

Donnell (23) had moved from his native Paisley to Aberdeen because of the notoriety caused by his father's crimes. Although he had managed to hold down a steady job in a distribution depot in the city his violent nature was never far from the surface. And it only needed a futile argument over a £30 car stereo for it to boil over. He had bought the stereo from Roddy Mitchell, a 24-year-old father of one. But when it was returned with missing wires the two men fell out. After a wrestling match as they left work, a frantic car chase – with Donnell in hot pursuit of Mitchell and his brother Daniel – ended in a supermarket car park. Then, in a frenzied attack, Donnell plunged a knife into his colleague's heart and proceeded to stab him five more times. Despite the best efforts of the emergency services they were unable to save Roddy Mitchell. Although he claimed self-defence Donnell was found guilty of culpable homicide at the High Court in Glasgow. In another twist of fate his trial was held in the same courtroom where his father had been found guilty of murder.

16. Gary Dougan and Craig Houston
The railway killers

In some cases we can understand the reasons for a killer acting in the way he, or she, did without condoning the act. Greed, revenge, jealousy, lust, despair, anger; these emotions – in their most extreme form – can often lead to the ultimate crime being committed. But from time to time there are cases so pointless that they defy rational explanation. Cases motivated only by stupidity and thoughtlessness. One such case occurred in Greenock on 25 June 1994.

It was a fine night when the Wemyss Bay to Glasgow train pulled out of Branchton station in Greenock. One of those typically Scottish summer evenings when it is still light until close to midnight. It was eleven o'clock and there were only four passengers left on board, along with two railwaymen: driver Arthur McKee (35) and ticket examiner Brian McGuire (26). Then, as the train approached Whinhill station in Greenock, all hell broke loose. Brian McGuire recalled what happened after hearing what he described as a 'clanky' bang:

> We were just picking up speed out of Branchton with myself, the driver and four passengers. The train started decelerating, shuddering violently and throwing us about. Eventually it came to a stop. There was a scrunching noise. I threw myself to the ground. I was hoping for the best that we had not crashed. There were two girls and another male passenger, John Madden. The girls were shouting and distressed and the lights were flickering. There was mayhem at this stage. I thought we had collided with another train.

Realising that his colleague must have been hurt, McGuire quickly made for the cab at the front of the train. But it had been completely demolished and Arthur McKee was lying on his back about twelve feet from the driver's position. He tried to resuscitate the driver but was pulled back by Madden. It was no use, as McGuire later recalled: 'It was obvious the driver was no longer with us at this stage.'

Then they turned their attention to the other male passenger – Alan Nicol, a 21-year-old student – who had been waiting to get off at Whinhill station. Once again it was to no avail. Mr Nicol was lying face down on an embankment a few feet from the train. He too was dead; he had died instantly after being thrown from the first carriage. The two female passengers, teenagers Suzanne McNeill and Jane Fry, were luckier; they had moved to the middle of the train because they were afraid of a daddy longlegs that appeared in the front carriage, a decision that almost certainly saved their lives. They got away with a few cuts and bruises.

Thanks to the efforts of Brian McGuire and John Madden the four survivors managed to open the doors of the carriage and scramble out, enabling them to raise the alarm. It was then that the full impact of the accident became clear. After the train had derailed it plunged into the Peat Road overbridge at a speed of fifty miles per hour. The crash had been so violent that large pieces of masonry from the bridge had been displaced and had lodged in the train. It would be a week before the line was finally cleared of debris and services restored.

In the immediate aftermath, the authorities were understandably anxious to find the cause of the crash. A £10,000 reward was offered by Railtrack, the owners of the track, and Scotrail, the train operators. Initially it was thought that the train had hit trespassers. Another theory was that the driver had lost control after being hit by a stone thrown by a youngster, a common occurrence on that part of the line. But then an investigation by specialist investigators revealed the truth: the train had been derailed by up to eight concrete blocks on the tracks, heavy blocks that weighed forty kilos each (about 100 pounds). They could not have got there by accident. It was now a murder investigation.

The finger of suspicion soon fell on two Greenock youths: Gary Dougan and Craig Houston, both aged seventeen and members of the Young Overton Boys, a name abbreviated to the highly appropriate 'Yob Mob'. On the night of the crash they had been at a teenage drinking party and had moved on with two girlfriends to a bench near the Peat Road bridge. When interviewed by police they admitted going under the bridge and onto the line but said they had only done so to 'do the toilet'. But there were inconsistencies in their stories; inconsistencies so marked that police felt able to bring murder charges against them both.

At their trial in the High Court in Glasgow in December 1994, the prosecution admitted there was only circumstantial evidence against the teenage duo; no one had actually seen them put the concrete blocks on the line. But advocate depute Colin Boyd argued that when the evidence was pieced together it was compelling. The boys did not deny being on the line just before the train crashed. Dougan had told police, in the presence of his lawyer, that he had seen Houston put the blocks in place, an account that the police had on tape and which was played in court. Dougan changed this story when he gave evidence, saying that the police 'wanted him to' and had told him repeatedly that Houston was blaming him for the derailment.

There was also compelling testimony from Gary Dougan's girlfriend, Michelle Low (16). She confirmed that both youths had been on the track before the crash and that when they came back up the embankment

Dougan said: 'Wait and see a train crash.' Although Low said he was 'only joking' it must have made an impression on the jury.

The jury took three hours to find both youths guilty of culpable homicide on majority verdicts, a lesser charge than the original indictment of murder. But there was a sting in the tail for Dougan and Houston. To gasps from the public benches, the judge, Lord Murray, sentenced them to fifteen years, a sentence he indicated that was designed not only to punish their wicked deed but also to deter others from mindless vandalism on the railways. As he was led away Dougan blew a kiss to his girlfriend, while a woman shouted from the public gallery, 'We'll stand by you son.'

There was one person who did not think the punishment was too severe: Tricia Darrah, the 22-year-old fiancée of Alan Nicol. Alan had bought her a beautiful diamond-and-ruby ring to seal their engagement, a ring which, she said, 'I am still proud to wear'. She punched the air in delight when she heard Lord Murray's sentences and said: 'These sentences are the best Christmas gifts I could ever get. They deserved it. I wish they could have hanged.'

Appeals were lodged by Dougan and Houston against the convictions and the sentences, which their lawyers argued were too severe. Both were rejected by the Court of Criminal Appeal.

17. Ernst Dumoulin

Bride was thrown from the crags

On Saturday, 24 June 1972 an advertisement appeared in the lonely hearts column of the *Rhein Zeitung* newspaper published in Koblenz, Germany. It read, 'Young man because of lack of opportunity is seeking to get to know a nice girl in this way with a view to later marriage.' The notice caught the eye of 18-year-old Helga Konrad who lived with her parents on a sixty-acre farm high above the Rhine valley near the village of Schwerbach. A remote spot with a population of less than fifty people. Helga was looking for more than life in the country had to offer and so the advert, placed by 21-year-old Ernst Dumoulin, triggered a ready response. It seemed to offer a passport to adventure. After an exchange of letters, Helga and Ernst arranged to meet.

Unfortunately, Helga was not aware that Dumoulin had recently been sacked from his job in a bank, where he was a trainee on probation, because of his 'unreliability'. If she had known, she might have thought twice about making a blind date to meet him at the Golden Anker dance hall in the nearby town of Rhaunen. On this first date, Helga fell in love with Ernst. She was impressed by his sophisticated manners and charm. Over the next few weeks, Dumoulin wined and dined Helga. It must have seemed as if she had entered a different world. So it's little wonder she was spellbound by the life Dumoulin had introduced her to. But how pure were Ernst's intentions towards Helga? A smooth-talking, aspiring city slicker who was going out of his way to court an inexperienced teenager from the German backwoods. It seemed completely out of character. Dumoulin was desperate to make a name, and fortune, for himself. As his boss at the bank put it, 'He wanted to be manager at 21, board member at 25 and managing director at 30.' Ernst envied his 26-year-old elder brother, Gerard, who was making a fortune as a financial adviser. Ernst's problem was that he did not want to graft for money and wanted it now.

However, in his pursuit of Helga, Ernst was pushing at an open door. Even though her parents threw him out of the house when Helga brought him round, she still doted on Ernst and continued to see him secretly. On 16 September 1972 Dumoulin drove up to the Konrad farm in a new Fiat 850 sports coupé. Helga's father agreed that she could go for a short drive with Ernst. They never returned. The couple had secretly hatched a plan to elope. Ernst had promised to marry Helga and now flew her to Edinburgh for a romantic wedding. To Helga it must have seemed like a dream come true. On Tuesday, 19 September 1972 they arrived at a guest house at 19 Torphichen Street in the Haymarket area of the capital. Here they booked a twin-bedded room. Three weeks later on Friday, 13 October Helga and Ernst were married at Haymarket register office. The two witnesses were Mr and Mrs Wood, the owners of the guest house where the couple were staying. Afterwards all four went for a drink and a meal. By late afternoon Ernst and Helga were back in their room.

A little while later the newlyweds left the guest house. Hand in hand they wandered through the historic streets of Edinburgh's Old Town heading for Arthur's Seat, the extinct volcanic rock that overlooks the city. Here, at the top of a steep cliff known as Salisbury Crags, Helga and Ernst could enjoy a panoramic view of the capital and anticipate a fulfilling life together. But Dumoulin had quite a different future planned for his bride. Only he knows exactly what happened next, but whatever the actual course of events it ended with Helga lying ninety-six feet below the cliff top with a fractured skull. Only a few hours after her dream wedding, 18-year-old Helga Konrad was dead. Around 8.30 p.m., Ernst came stumbling out of the dark to bang on the door of a parked car screaming in broken English that an ambulance be called.

At first the police took the view that it was little more than a bizarre accident. There was no suspicion of Ernst Dumoulin, who tearfully explained to detectives that Helga must have accidentally slipped while his back was turned. Brought back to Torphichen Street, he lay weeping on his bed while he played the theme from the hit film of the time, *Love Story*, over and over again on a record player.

Detectives began having second thoughts when a phone call was received informing them that Helga had been insured by Dumoulin, in the event of accidental death, for the huge sum of £400,000 – over £1 million at today's value. Police, in cooperation with their German counterparts, immediately started to investigate Ernst's background. From Koblenz came the news that he had falsified the details of his bank account. On the strength of this forgery he borrowed 700 marks (about £1,000) to buy a Fiat 124. Then he traded it in for the more expensive 850cc coupe which he'd used to run off with Helga. He paid the balance, several thousand marks, by cheque. It bounced. In reality, Ernst Dumoulin, for all his smooth talk and upmarket manners, was flat broke.

Police now learnt that Dumoulin, who had been portraying himself as the grieving husband, had gone to the offices of Hambro Life, on the morning after Helga's death, and tried to claim on the insurance. He was shocked to learn that the policy did not cover accidental death on a mountain and immediately suggested that the document be destroyed on the grounds that no one needed to know about it.

On 15 October Dumoulin rang Helmut Konrad from Edinburgh and told him, 'Helga and I are married. May I call you father-in-law.' Mr

Konrad asked: 'Where is Helga?' Dumoulin replied, 'She is in heaven. She is dead.' It was to be some time before Helmut Konrad learnt the details of his daughter's death and the extent of Dumoulin's evil. By the time Helmut Konrad arrived in the capital, hoping to discover that Ernst had been lying and his daughter was still alive, Dumoulin had been charged with murder.

At his trial, held in the High Court in Edinburgh, Dumoulin's credibility took a severe dent when he tried to claim that Helga had, in fact, attacked him on the Crags that evening. According to Ernst, they had concocted a joint plan to defraud the insurance company taking out policies of £200,000 on each other's life. He was going to 'disappear' leaving his wife to collect the cash. From the witness box, Dumoulin now suggested that Helga had intended to kill him and collect the payout for herself. Dumoulin explained that during a passionate first kiss, Helga had suddenly made a move to push him over the cliff edge. He had fought back. It was during this struggle that Helga had fallen to her death.

It was a defence born of desperation. And in sharp contrast to his initial statement to the police that Helga's death had been a tragic accident. Some members of the jury, however, made up of eight women and seven men, still gave Dumoulin the benefit of the doubt. The vote was eleven to four for conviction. Had Ernst's charm worked some of its magic? Perhaps. But not enough to save him. He was sentenced to life imprisonment. But even the judge, Lord Wheatley, seemed anxious to reassure Ernst, explaining to him that life did not necessarily mean life and that he could be released on licence after a few years if he behaved himself. In spite of Helga's terrible death, Ernst Dumoulin, for some strange reason, found it easy to win sympathy.

When Ernst ran down from Salisbury Crags that evening, hammering on a stranger's car, calling for help, the driver's view was that if he was acting he was putting on a good performance. But that, of course, was the key to Ernst Dumoulin's character. He was above all else a very good actor and an inspired con man. The simple truth was that greed, and a love of the high life, had got the better of him. But what of poor Helga Konrad? As she plunged to her death did she at last realise the cruel deception that her 'dream lover' had inflicted on her? Or did she live the lie to the end, refusing to believe that behind the mask Ernst Dumoulin was simply a monster?

18. Grant Dunn

The love-crazed teacher

Love can do strange things, even to the most intelligent and apparently rational people. So it proved with Grant Dunn, a 38-year-old teacher from Oban who was working in the Italian town of Pinerolo, near Turin. Dunn became obsessed with a younger woman, a 19-year-old beauty called Emanuela Ferro. He had been introduced to Emanuela by his wife Cristina – Emanuela's teacher – and arranged to give her English lessons. But, during their time together, his feelings for Emanuela grew stronger and he bombarded her with love letters, which he often left on the windscreen of her car. Dunn even fantasised that he was having an affair with his young pupil, despite the fact that she had a steady boyfriend and wanted nothing to do with him. Understandably Emanuela became concerned by his behaviour and stopped going to his house for lessons.

Although Dunn continued to send her letters, declaring his love, for almost two years no one was unduly worried by his behaviour. Emanuela told her boyfriend that he was trying to court her but otherwise seemed unconcerned. Nor was Cristina Dunn alarmed: 'I never suspected there was anything between her and my husband. Emanuela was my student. She was lovely and I will remember her with affection.' But Emanuela's continued rejection of his advances was clearly taking its toll on the Scot.

Matters came to a head one morning in May 2001 when Grant Dunn left home saying that he had to pop into town to run an errand. His wife later recalled that he was his usual self and even laughed and joked with family members before he left the house. But, armed with two Browning automatic pistols, he drove instead to Emanuela's school where he found her sitting in her Fiat Punto. Dunn threw open the car door and, despite Emanuela's desperate attempt to get away, he pumped two bullets into her head and three into her back at point-blank range. Dunn then put the gun to his temple and shot himself, dying instantly. The victim's father, Piergiorgio Ferro, rushed to the scene and had to be treated for shock by the medics who were trying to save his daughter.

In his final letter – which he gave to Emanuela's best friend just before the shooting – Dunn outlined the reasons for his actions: 'She was going away forever, leaving me alone. But now we will be together forever in heaven. Don't cry because we will be happier.' It was the final delusion of a man who seemed sane and rational to those around him. His wife said he was an 'exceptional man, generous and reserved'; others described him as quiet and polite. And his life to that point seemed to confirm these descriptions of his character. Dunn came from a respectable family and had been an outstanding pupil at Oban High School. He had gone on to study at Glasgow University, where he took a degree in languages, before becoming a teacher in Italy where he had lived for ten years before committing the first, and only, crime of his life. He had no history of mental illness; nor did anyone in his immediate family.

Yet there was another side to Grant Dunn. He had an obsession with the Nazis from the age of five and hoarded books about the Third Reich. He suggested school trips to Hitler's mountain retreat at Berchtesgaden and would bring daggers, swastikas and other Nazi memorabilia to school to show pupils. His politics were also disturbing and were described as 'extremely right wing, bordering on the fanatical' by one colleague. Although he had once been a respected teacher, his headmaster said that his attitude had deteriorated in the two years since he had met Emanuela. In this period, Dunn's attitude to pupils often bordered on the sinister and he would wink at the girls he taught and insult them if they wore short skirts or smoked. Indeed, his conduct had become so bad that the head was planning to sack him.

It is a tragic story: of a rather pathetic middle-aged man and a beautiful young girl. It was obsession and lust, not love, that drove Grant Dunn. As Emanuela's heartbroken father said: 'If that man had really loved her he would never have done this. Only a madman could have done such a thing. He tormented her with poetry and it wasn't love. That bastard just fancied her, that's all.'

19. Donald Forbes

Scotland's most dangerous man

Some criminals seem destined never to learn or welcome the opportunity of a second chance. Donald Forbes escaped the gallows only to commit a second murder and then, released after serving twenty-eight years, attempted in his sixties to become a Glasgow drug baron. The criminal career of Donald Ferguson Forbes, a former trawlerman, began on 2 June 1958, when he set out to rob the offices of Thomas L. Devlin Ltd, a trawling firm, situated in Lower Granton Road, Edinburgh. Forbes was in debt and desperate for money when he went to the premises at midnight, planning to break into the upstairs office. He was, however, caught in the act by a 67-year-old nightwatchman, Allan Fisher. Forbes claimed that Fisher took hold of him then threatened him with an iron bolt. Twenty-three-year old Forbes reacted in a way that was to become his trademark. 'I was already in a panic', he later explained, 'and I just lost my head. I know I grabbed the bolt out of his hands and just went berserk.'

Allan Fisher was left lying badly battered on the office floor. As he left the office Forbes callously emptied Fisher's wallet and picked up his cigarette case and lighter, which were lying on a shelf.

A short time later, at around 2.45 a.m. on 3 June, Forbes met up with 24-year-old Robert Henry, in an all-night cafe. Henry noticed that there were bloodstains on Forbes's coat and trousers. A nervous-looking Forbes told Henry, 'I got £10, but I ought to have got £100', adding 'I could be taken up for murder tonight.' Forbes and Henry then booked into a lodging house, Forbes giving a false name. Later Henry noticed Forbes trying to wash the bloodstains off his clothes.

Having rested, Forbes went 'up town' buying a fresh pair of trousers and a jacket, which he changed into in a public toilet, taking his old clothes to a cleaners, where he gave his name as Robert Henry. For the rest of the day Forbes and Henry toured local pubs and cafes. Flush with cash, Forbes paid for everything. At one pub, Forbes handed Henry a cigarette case and lighter as a present. Eventually the pair found themselves in Frederick Street where they saw a newspaper bill stating that there had been a murder. According to Henry, Forbes 'went white' and told him, 'I did not mean it'. Henry immediately gave him back the lighter and cigarette case.

The pair headed to the Stockbridge district where Forbes threw the objects into the Water of Leith. Visiting another public house, Forbes flushed the receipts for the bloodstained jacket and trousers down the lavatory. However, the police were already on their trail and they were arrested when they came out of the pub toilet.

The evidence against Forbes at his trial in September 1958 was overwhelming, which probably explains why he made no effort to hide his involvement in Allan Fisher's death. Forbes, however, claimed that it had not been murder, but the lesser crime of culpable homicide, in that he had not meant to kill the nightwatchman and was not responsible for his actions. But he failed to convince the jury. Perhaps the evidence of forensic scientist Dr Fiddes and his description of Mr Fisher's 'twenty-four wounds to the head and face with corresponding fractures to the skull . . . a fractured nose, a fractured jaw, a broken finger . . . a broken elbow and three fractured ribs . . . there were not less than thirty blows . . . by an iron bolt', which persuaded them to find Forbes guilty of murder, a crime which then carried the death penalty.

The nightwatchman had put up little resistance and Forbes admitted that he had been uninjured in the struggle. But in spite of the brutal nature of Mr Fisher's death the jury was still willing unanimously to recommend mercy. They may have been swayed by the evidence that Forbes 'as a child had a period of three and a half years' psychiatric treatment' and when he was in his twenties 'was involved in a motorcycle accident and suffered head injuries as a result of which he was unconscious for two days'. Consultant psychiatrist Dr Margaret Methven told the court she had treated Forbes as a boy, but that when she visited him in prison, 'he was rather more disturbed than when she had known him originally'. She thought he might be a psychopath.

The judge, however, handed out the only sentence allowed, one of death. It proved traumatic for the jury, several of whom broke down in tears. Just two weeks before the execution date of 16 October, Forbes made history when he was given permission by the secretary of state for Scotland to marry his pregnant girlfriend, 21-year-old Rita McLean, which he did on 2 October on the first floor of the hospital block at Saughton prison. Rita told the press: 'I love Don and have stood by him from the first. I wouldn't desert him now.' A Glasgow millionaire, A. E. Pickard, caused controversy by presenting the couple with a cheque for £1,000. The marriage, however, was to last less than a year. Meanwhile, a campaign was launched to save Forbes, and it succeeded in having his death sentence commuted to life imprisonment.

Forbes served only twelve years and in May 1970 was released on parole. Less than eight weeks' later, he was back in prison facing a second murder charge after he stabbed 25-year-old father of two Charlie Gilroy, a former soldier, in a knife attack outside the Duke's Head pub – owned by Raith Rovers manager and former Rangers player Jimmy Millar – situated in the Leith district of Edinburgh.

Robert Gilroy (21), Charlie's brother, told the court that on 2 July 1970 he was walking back to the pub after fighting with a man outside when

Forbes suddenly came up and stabbed him in the groin. James Carse (27), a painter, said that moments later he saw Forbes walk up to Charlie Gilroy and stab him several times in the chest and side. Carse described how, 'Forbes went to speak to a girl across the street. They walked back to the pub talking and laughing. It was as if nothing had happened.'

The woman in question was Forbes's girlfriend, 35-year-old divorcee Mrs Alice Noble. She told the court, 'There was a fight, but Donnie wasn't involved. Then a girl rushed in and said there were three men kicking a friend of his, Jackie Dick. I held on to Donnie and told him not to bother. But he said, "I'll have to go. He's my mate."' Mrs Noble added, 'I will never recognise him as a killer. He was always good to me. He had a nice personality, kind and helpful, and was never moody.' In September 1970, after a trial lasting less than five hours, Forbes was sentenced to life imprisonment, the first man in Scottish legal history to murder again after serving a life sentence.

But Forbes was not planning a quiet life. In August 1971 he escaped from the maximum security wing at Peterhead prison where he was being held, but was recaptured within days after a car chase in Edinburgh. The media branded him 'Scotland's most dangerous man'. Forbes revelled in it and in 1973 attempted a second gaol break, using a hacksaw to open his cell door. He was on the loose for ten hours before being caught. Forbes again hit the headlines when, in 1980, he married his second wife, Alison Grierson, in a register office. She later gave birth to a son James, claiming she got pregnant when they were left alone after the wedding ceremony.

By the mid 1990s, Forbes, largely forgotten by the public, was being held at Penningham open prison, near Newton Stewart. However, he could not escape the tag of 'double killer' and when he was granted home leave in November 1996, the press soon got wind of it. A spokesman for the prison service explained: 'Forbes is a category D prisoner and is now eligible for home leave.' From a council estate in Greenock, his wife Alison said: 'We have kids and they will be affected by anything we say. I've nothing to say about our relationship.'

Despite a campaign led by William Gilroy – the brother of Forbes's second victim who delivered a petition signed by 400,000 to Downing Street opposing freedom for the killer – he was released on licence in 1998. Forbes was recalled in December 2000, but avoided police until the beginning of 2003. Police received a tip-off that he was dealing in drugs from home. They already had reason to suspect him as a search of a car owned by Forbes had revealed cocaine worth £27,000 hidden under the front seat. A raid on his flat in Ryehill Road, Royston, Glasgow uncovered a cache of cocaine and cannabis worth nearly half a million pounds, along with an industrial press to cut and package the drugs.

At his trial in the High Court in Edinburgh in June 2003, Forbes admitted his involvement in supplying drugs. His defence counsel, Barry Divers, argued that Forbes was a vulnerable man who had been used by others. However, the judge, Lord Menzies, commenting that the equipment found at his flat suggested that he 'was not at the bottom of the drug-dealing hierarchy', gaoled Forbes for twelve years. Forbes, who will be eighty when released, will have plenty of time to watch his favourite soap. According to former inmate Walter Norval, who knew Forbes at Peterhead prison, 'We'd sit around and play cards or walk in the yard for a bit, but we were always back in front of the television in time for Donald to make coffee before settling down to watch *Coronation Street.*'

20. Nat Fraser

Downfall of a Jack-the-lad

There's one in every small town. The loveable rogue: charming, cocky, with an eye for the ladies and the main chance. In Elgin, Nat Fraser was that man. By day he was the owner of a small, but thriving, business; by night the guitarist in a band. Playing the pubs and clubs gave Nat the perfect opportunity to meet women, and it was an opportunity he grasped with both hands. He was attractive to the opposite sex and had notched up a string of conquests in Morayshire.

Then, in 1985, at the age of twenty-six he met Arlene McInnes, a pretty 18-year-old from Elgin. Although popular, Arlene was a very ordinary teenager; she had failed to shine academically and left school at sixteen with no qualifications. She then drifted through a number of menial jobs in a chip shop, a baker's and a pub before becoming a sales assistant in a local boutique. This seemed to suit her; she had a passionate interest in clothes and make-up. Arlene's only other real interest was in the opposite sex, and she had already had several boyfriends by the time she first encountered Nat Fraser at one of his gigs.

Arlene must have been flattered when Nat sidled over during a break and began to chat her up. He was not only smooth and good looking but also a successful businessman who owned his own house. Many women considered him quite a catch and would undoubtedly have been jealous when she and Nat started going out together. Before long Arlene was head over heels in love.

Her family were not so sure about Nat Fraser. Although they considered the smooth-talking businessman to be good company they worried about his reputation as a womaniser. But this did not stop the relationship from becoming serious and, in September 1986, the couple got engaged. Arlene moved into Fraser's bungalow at 2 Smith Street, New Elgin and, happier than she had ever been, began to make plans for their wedding.

The road to the altar would be a rocky one. One night Arlene picked up her downstairs phone and caught Nat having an intimate conversation with a woman. With the help of her family she packed her belongings and moved back in with her mother. But in a matter of days she was back; Fraser was nothing if not persuasive and he managed to talk her round. The wedding went ahead as planned on 9 May 1987 and the bride's beautiful white dress hid the fact that she was already six months' pregnant. Arlene got another clue to Nat's character when she walked up the aisle; he was sporting a black eye, a souvenir of his stag night. The moment when she first saw the eye is captured on the wedding video; for a split second she looked shocked and seemed to be wondering what she was letting herself in for. But the thought passed quickly; she was besotted with Nat and her father said he had never seen her looking so happy as on the day of the wedding.

In many ways the marriage was a traditional one. Nat worked hard to build up his fruit-and-vegetable wholesaler's and continued to play in the band at night. Another lucrative – and illegal – sideline was selling illicit booze, using his legitimate business as cover. Arlene stayed at home, devoting herself to looking after the house, a job that became more time-consuming when the couple's two children, Jamie and Natalie, were born. But it would not be long before this domestic bliss was shattered. Like many women, Arlene thought she could tame her husband. She was to be quickly disabused of this notion.

Nat went back to his old ways. Indeed, he became a serial adulterer. During the day he met women while on his rounds delivering fruit and vegetables. At night, playing with his band – The Minesweepers – he met even more potential conquests. And, with his easy charm, he quickly got them into bed. He told friends that being in a band was the best way 'to get the knickers off a girl'. He was well known for his virility: Hector Dick, a local farmer and Nat's best pal, revealed that his nickname was 'Horse-hung', a reference to his huge penis.

His tastes became kinkier. He had set up a secret love nest above his company warehouse, complete with bed, heater and a well-stocked bar. There was also a range of sex toys including handcuffs and belts. He was so proud of his sexual prowess that he even committed his performances to film. In a home-made porn video he is seen romping with one woman in a bath and then with three more in bed. The tape did the rounds of Elgin's pubs and clubs, something that Fraser would have relished, according to Hector Dick: 'He wasn't in the slightest bit bothered by the thought of other people watching him in action. He would have loved it.' But Nat was developing a more sinister habit – he was turning into a wife-beater.

If Nat thought that Arlene would meekly accept his behaviour he was to be disappointed. She had a wilful, independent streak. At first she was resentful of his late nights, rightly suspecting that he was having affairs. The violence inflicted on her by Nat was an even more serious bone of contention. She was also annoyed that while she was stuck at home he was enjoying life to the full. So when, in 1988, the opportunity arose she had an affair; with a 17-year-old toy boy, Dougie Green, who worked for the fruit-wholesaling firm jointly owned by her husband and his business partner, Ian 'Pedro' Taylor.

The affair lasted only three weeks. Arlene still loved Nat and, despite the constant rows about his womanising – one of which ended with him almost breaking her jaw – she hoped he would return to the straight and narrow. To make herself more attractive to him she saved £4,000 and had an operation to enlarge her breasts. But it did not work and the marriage plunged even deeper into trouble, resulting in at least one trial separation. Arlene became depressed and began to realise that she had to make a life for herself. She enrolled on a business studies course and started going out more with her female friends. Despite his own philandering Nat resented his wife's greater independence; in fact he was consumed by jealousy. The result was yet more violence.

Things came to a head on 22 March 1998 – ironically it was Mother's Day – after Arlene came home at half past five in the morning after a girl's night out. Fraser had stayed up and, when she walked in the door, a furious row erupted. Nat grabbed Arlene by the throat, and squeezed so hard that her eyes began to bleed. She fell unconscious and was lucky to survive the attack. The next day, at the end of her tether, she went to the police and Nat was charged with attempted murder. He was held for three days and released on bail. It would be two long years before he was tried, found guilty and jailed (on a reduced charge of assault).

The assault in March 1998 was a watershed in the Fraser marriage. Now it could never be patched up. As Arlene's close friend recalls, he wanted revenge: 'When Nat came out of custody he told Arlene he would never forget what she'd done to him, putting him in jail like that.' Nat moved out of the family home and in with business partner Pedro Taylor.

The disintegration of the relationship gathered pace. Arlene wanted a divorce, custody of the children and a financial settlement; Nat heard that she was looking for £250,000, a sum that would have ruined him, especially when his business was not as lucrative as it once was. For his part he demanded the return of her car – a Ford Granada with the personalised number plates, A19 NAT – on the basis that it was owned by his business. When Arlene refused, the car was torched in her drive and Fraser's company collected the insurance. Such bitterness is common to many failing relationships, but the effect on a man like Nat Fraser must have been devastating. He considered himself God's gift to women and here was the woman he had worked so hard to provide for rejecting him.

Nat began to think the unthinkable. If his wife simply disappeared he could keep his business, his home, his two children and, perhaps, his self-esteem. There was also the small matter of a £125,000 insurance policy Nat had taken out on Arlene's life; a sum like that would go a long way to easing his financial worries. By April 1998, Hector Dick said that Fraser's conversations with him began to take on a sinister air. Fraser speculated about the thousands of people who disappear every year and are never found. He asked Dick, a farmer, how he disposed of animal carcasses and hinted that he knew of people who could be hired for 'hits'. He said that Fraser told him he had been to a library and found out that there had only been two successful murder prosecutions in Scotland in which the body of the victim had not been discovered.

Then, one day in April 1998, Fraser asked Hector Dick to buy an old car for him. Dick – loyal to a friend who had been best man at his wedding – did as he was asked and bought a Ford Fiesta for £400 from a mechanic, Kevin Ritchie. Ritchie remembered that Dick urgently wanted a car with a boot and was surprised to be given a £50 bung by Dick to keep quiet about the transaction. The car was left at Dick's farm for Fraser, or an associate, to collect.

The next day – Tuesday, 28 April 1998 – Arlene Fraser waved her children off to school and was never seen again. All the signs were that she must have left the house in a hurry. The front door had not been locked. She left behind the medicine for a serious condition known as Crohn's disease. She had taken no personal possessions, not even her glasses or contact lenses; nor had she lifted her handbag or taken any money. She failed to cancel two appointments: one with a solicitor to discuss a divorce, and the other with best friend Michelle Scott for lunch. And, most uncharacteristically for a devoted mother, she had made no arrangements for her children to be looked after.

The evidence also suggested that Arlene had not been forcibly removed. There were no signs of a struggle, nor was there a shred of forensic evidence in the house – not even a fingerprint. And the position of the property – on a main road and close to other houses – would have made it very difficult for an abduction to have been carried out without it being witnessed. Police reached the conclusion that she had been lured from the house and speculated on the reasons for her leaving everything behind: she may have gone with someone she knew; she may have been duped by an 'emergency'. This was no ordinary missing person's enquiry; the police quickly suspected foul play, even murder.

A major investigation ensued, and the police were helped by hundreds of local people carrying out painstaking searches of the area. The response from the media was extensive and included a press conference at which Nat Fraser, close to tears, made an emotional plea for his wife to come home. He also announced – albeit under pressure from his wife's family – that he was putting up half of a £20,000 reward for information about Arlene's whereabouts. But it was all to no avail. Despite several sightings of Arlene – which all turned out to be false – the trail quickly went cold.

But what of Nat Fraser? Spouses are invariably the first people to come under the police spotlight in such cases, and Nat had much to gain by his wife's disappearance. He was also due to stand trial for assaulting Arlene, and blamed her for getting him into trouble. But he did have a convincing alibi: on the morning of her disappearance he was out delivering fruit and veg; his van boy confirmed that he had not been out of his sight for more than a couple of minutes. Phone records also revealed that he made a call to a woman friend for forty-five minutes that morning, at exactly the same time Arlene disappeared. His attitude in the early stages of the investigation appeared to confirm his innocence: he was very helpful and accommodating to detective superintendent Jim Stephen and his team; so keen to ingratiate himself with police he insisted on calling detectives by their first names.

But there was something that did not ring true about Nat Fraser's attitude, and it was first noticed by Arlene's relatives. In the immediate aftermath of her disappearance he appeared before her family – who were sick with worry – wearing a false moustache and joked that Arlene had gone without her disguise. He also flippantly remarked that Arlene – something of a shopaholic – would turn up in the Next store in Aberdeen. According to Arlene's mother – Isabelle Thompson – his whole response was all wrong. Her clear impression was that her son-in-law 'was not really all that bothered' about his wife being missing. The good people of Elgin felt the same way; they were shocked that Fraser had not joined them in the search for evidence.

The police of course already suspected Nat Fraser. And then something happened that convinced them Arlene had not just run away. But that he had murdered her. It happened nine days after Arlene went missing: her engagement, wedding and eternity rings turned up in the bathroom of the Smith Street house. The significance was that the rings had not appeared on a video made by the police just after the disappearance; nor were they spotted by members of Arlene's family when they scoured the bungalow for clues to her whereabouts. The police reasoned that Fraser – spooked by their investigation – returned the rings to make it look as if Arlene had run away to start a new life. Another theory was that he had put them back because they were valuable and he wanted to sell them.

From that moment police monitored Fraser's every move. But Nat acted as if he didn't have a care in the world. He took a succession of lovers, and didn't seem to care if they were married or not. One of his most passionate flings was with Pamela Fiske, a 33-year-old senior housing officer with Moray Council. The attractive blonde was a fitness fanatic and despite Fraser's notoriety she fell for him. It is rumoured her marriage to her fisherman husband ended when he caught her in bed with Fraser at a party.

Other aspects of his behaviour were equally bizarre. As his fortieth birthday approached in 1999 he cruised around Elgin in a delivery van bedecked in balloons, with a makeshift banner that read, 'Nat's Big Four-O'. He seemed to enjoy his notoriety and even changed the name of his group to the Nat Fraser Band. This was hardly the behaviour of a husband trying to come to terms with the loss of his beloved wife.

In the meantime police did not let up in their efforts to find Arlene's killer. Hector Dick came under the microscope; he was questioned on several occasions and his farm was searched for clues. When – out of loyalty to his friend – he refused to give detectives information about the purchase of the Fiesta he was charged with attempting to defeat the ends of justice and jailed for a year.

Despite the intense activity, police were no closer to cracking the case. They badly needed a break. And they got one from a most unexpected source. In March 2000 Fraser was convicted on a charge of assaulting Arlene to the danger of her life five weeks before she disappeared and was imprisoned for eighteen months. While in Porterfield prison in Inverness, Fraser was visited by his old pal and former business associate Glenn Lucas. Police knew Lucas and Fraser were close and surmised they would be discussing the case. Unfortunately they could not hear what the two men were saying, even though they could be seen talking on a closed-circuit television tape.

So they turned to Jessica Rees, a forensic lip-reader. She had been deaf from the age of four and had taught herself to communicate by reading people's lip movements. She spent a total of 150 hours transcribing the prison tapes and was able to discern that Fraser spoke of things like, 'Arms off', 'Pulling teeth out' and 'It's all down the plug hole so the police don't know shit so fuck the lot of them.' Fraser also seemed to make several references to 'Heccy' – Hector Dick's nickname – and apparently told Lucas to remind Dick of the importance of keeping his mouth shut.

Although the tapes were not admissible in court they confirmed police suspicions about Fraser and had the effect of galvanising the investigation. The pressure on Fraser was intensified when he was jailed again in April 2001, this time for a year for falsifying an application for legal aid in relation to the assault charge. It was now only a matter of time before the most serious charge of all was proffered: for the murder of Arlene Fraser. In July 2001 police again searched Dick's farm and Fraser's house before charging them and Glenn Lucas with murder.

It was the culmination of a huge effort by Grampian police, an effort that was estimated to have cost £2 million, not surprising when one considers that, at times, more than one hundred officers were working on the enquiry. The man in charge – detective superintendent Jim Stephen – spent so much time on it that he referred to Arlene Fraser as 'the other woman in his life'. Stephen even drafted a specialist fraud investigator into the team: detective constable Gordon Ritchie. His job was to look for any signs that Arlene Fraser was still alive by checking services she may have accessed, such as doctors' practices, pharmacies and banks. Ritchie spent a whole year on this task but found no trace of her, despite the fact that she needed to take medication for Crohn's disease every day.

The trial – at the High Court in Edinburgh – did not start until 6 January 2003, nearly eighteen months after the trio had been charged. Despite the dogged, meticulous investigation by police (an effort that was rightly praised by informed observers) the case was wholly circumstantial; there was no body, no witnesses to the act, no forensic evidence. And Fraser had what some observers considered a solid alibi. Even for prosecuting advocate Alan Turnbull QC – who had won several high-profile cases in which the odds were stacked against him – the going would be tough. And so it proved. The case was on a knife edge and it seemed that the defence – led by rising legal star Paul McBride – would get a not proven, or even a not guilty, verdict. The prosecution's only hope was to get one of the accused to testify against his friends.

Under pressure the prosecution cut a deal with the man they thought was the most vulnerable – Hector Dick, who had already tried to commit suicide while in prison. In return for having the charges against him dropped, he would become a witness for the prosecution (the charges against Lucas, who police always thought was peripheral to the case, were dropped at the same time). And when Dick took the stand he gave the prosecution just what they were looking for. Dick claimed that Fraser told him that he had hired a hitman to strangle Arlene then, after the body was hidden for two weeks, Fraser burned it, removed the teeth and ground down the bones. He then scattered what was left of the corpse to the four winds. Dick also claimed that when he asked what had happened to Arlene, Fraser made a gesture indicating that she had been strangled.

When he took the stand in his own defence Nat Fraser – often close to tears – vehemently denied either killing his wife or hiring anyone to carry out the act. He also rejected the suggestion that he had returned his wife's rings to the bathroom. But he did have to acknowledge, under cross-examination, that he was the only person who stood to gain from his wife's death.

The issue for the jury was whether they could believe Hector Dick's testimony; after all, as the prosecution vigorously pointed out, he was a self-confessed liar and had also been convicted of attempting to defeat the ends of justice. And even if they could, would that – on top of the circumstantial evidence and the fact that Nat Fraser had a motive for killing his wife – be enough to persuade them to bring back a guilty verdict? After deliberating for two hours and forty-five minutes they decided it was. But it was a close-run thing and it is thought the majority in favour of guilty was only 8–6 (bizarrely, the fifteenth member of the jury was dismissed for falling asleep for several hours and missing crucial parts of the evidence).

Nat Fraser was sentenced to life imprisonment on 29 January 2003 by Lord Mackay, and the judge also ordered that he should serve a minimum of twenty-five years. As the sentence was passed Fraser collapsed and had to be propped up by two policemen. Arlene's family was surprised at the length of the sentence, but delighted nonetheless. Her mother said: 'I could not believe twenty-five years. I don't think he will ever come out of jail. He does not deserve to.'

We may never know how this unfortunate young woman met her end. Only one person – her husband – knows the full story. And with an appeal pending against his conviction at the time of writing (July 2005) he is not saying. Many theories have been advanced; some even suggest that Arlene is still alive. And a book by murder accused Glenn Lucas takes the view that Hector Dick lied on oath to protect himself. There may still be twists to come in the Arlene Fraser case.

21. Kim Galbraith

Lying through her teeth

At 1.30 a.m. on the morning of 14 January 1999 police in Argyll received a frantic phone call. 'Please come. My husband has been shot', begged the terrified woman who, her voice breaking, claimed that she had been beaten and raped by two masked intruders. She added that her attackers had set the house on fire, but she was too scared to leave in case they were still hanging around the cottage. When police arrived in the hamlet of Furnace on the banks of Loch Fyne they found Kim Galbraith (33) standing in the road outside her home, barefoot in a bloodstained nightie, clutching her eighteen-month-old daughter Lauren in her arms.

Inside the cottage they discovered that the murder victim, lying dead in his pyjamas on a double bed, had been killed by a single shot to the head. There was no doubting his identity. Local policeman, Ian Galbraith, Kim's 37-year-old husband. Ian had been a popular figure in the towns of Inverary and Lochgilphead where he had his beat. Locals nicknamed him 'Wookie' because at six-feet-six and sixteen stones he seemed the spitting image of the *Star Wars* character, Chewbacca. To others he was simply the 'Big Fella'. Pub landlord Gordon Pirie told detectives: 'People liked him. He kept himself to himself and was just a normal bobby.' Originally a traffic officer with the Metropolitan Police, Ian Galbraith transferred to the Strathclyde force and moved to Argyll because he wanted to live the *Hamish McBeth* lifestyle. Family holidays spent fishing and walking in the Highlands, the home of his grandfather, had opened his eyes to the beauty of the Scottish countryside. He was also a keen hunter.

Detectives soon discovered that Ian had been married before he met Kim Scarsbrook. She was later to claim that after Ian pulled her over for speeding in south London in spring 1989 he asked for her phone number then followed her around before asking her out for a drink. She added: 'I didn't want to go, but I thought that if I didn't he would book me and I would get into trouble. We went out and it was lovely and we carried on seeing each other.' By the following year Ian had divorced his wife of five years, Julie Ogston, and married Kim Scarsbrook.

Kim seemed happy with her life as a newlywed in the flat she shared with Ian in the Camberley district of London. A friend commented, 'Kim was always artistic. She kept her house immaculate. She had a wide circle of friends and an active social life.' But in June 1996, having spent sixteen years in the Met, Ian received a long-wished-for transfer to Strathclyde police and the couple moved to Inverary. In August 1998 they took over a rented cottage, Sandhole, in the tiny village of Furnace overlooking

Loch Fyne. To Ian it was a dream come true, especially after daughter Lauren was born. But Kim was far from ecstatic.

To friends she complained that she did not like the lifestyle in Argyll and wanted to return to London. Kim's stepfather Sid Scarsbrook, who moved to Scotland with his wife Wendy to be near his daughter, said, 'I was helping Kim with some DIY and she would always want her mother and me to stay over. She wanted us to stay more and more.' She told friends Ian and Rachel Cowell of Camberley, Surrey that Argyll was beautiful, but she was lonely and complained that Ian refused to return to London even for a holiday. The wish to return to her former life seemed to become an obsession. Rachel Cowell described a bizarre incident in the run-up to Ian's death. 'Just a couple of weeks before Ian died we got a knock on the door from a guy delivering a dishwasher in the name of Galbraith. I thought it was really strange at the time and phoned Ian. He left a message on my answering machine a week later. I never heard from him again.'

It was never proved, however, that Kim was behind this strange event, but there's no doubt that her mind was drifting down some weird pathways. For several hours on the morning and early afternoon of 13 January 1999 Ian Galbraith was absent from his Furnace home on police duty. Having made sure the coast was clear, Kim Galbraith had quickly implemented a well-prepared plan. She pulled on a pair of surgical gloves then undid the latch on the bathroom window. She next went into the garden, and making sure she left footprints in the ground, climbed in through the bathroom window to make it seem that an intruder had broken into the house.

The next, fatal step required Ian's presence and he had, quite unknowingly, helped Kim to prepare the ground. Guns were unknown territory to Kim Galbraith, so she asked her husband, a keen sportsman, to take her out with him when he went hunting for game. Ian was delighted when Kim showed willing to accompany him. He had often asked her to walk in the hills with him, but previously she had always seemed reluctant. Now he enthusiastically showed her how to load his .27 Ruger hunting rifle with its telescopic sight, little realising that he was signing his own death warrant. Ian appeared to have no suspicions that Kim might have murder on her mind. In November 1998 he had confided to chimney sweep Neil Anderson that someone had used a Stanley knife to cut the brake pipe on his Suzuki four-wheel drive, which he had then had repaired at a local garage. It never occurred to him that his wife might be the culprit.

On the evening of 13 January, Ian went to bed first and quickly fell asleep. In the living room, meanwhile, Kim destroyed cheque books and credit cards and hid two rings under the floorboards, to convince police that they had been robbed. She then climbed into bed beside her sleeping husband, pointed the gun at his head, and, firing at point-blank range, killed him instantly with a single shot.

Kim was prepared to go to any lengths to make sure she was creating a realistic 'set', even banging her head and arm against the corner of the dining-room table to produce bruises she could claim were the result of the assault. Then, to turn herself into a convincing rape victim, Kim cut open her knickers with a kitchen knife and rubbed a condom across the top of her legs to make it appear that that there had been forced entry.

But, from the start, police who arrived on the scene were puzzled by Kim's story of the 'two masked intruders with Geordie accents' who had attacked her and murdered her husband. Why had no one else in this tight-knit community of less than three hundred people seen or heard them? As one close neighbour said, 'I'm their nearest neighbour, but I heard nothing at all. The first I knew anything had happened was when the police came to the door.'

Kim and Lauren were taken to the Vale of Leven hospital in Alexandria near Glasgow where it was quickly established that their injuries were only superficial. Kim was then transferred to Dumbarton police station for questioning and stuck to her story through sixteen hours of interrogation by detectives. But the gaping holes in her account of events that night led her inquisitors to believe that she was lying through her teeth. Eventually she confessed to murdering Ian, adding: 'I'd convinced myself that the men who broke in were for real, and I was really frightened they would come back. I don't know why because I knew they weren't for real.' Kim also admitted the earlier attempt on Ian's life when she cut the brake pipes on his car. 'I didn't want to kill him', she claimed, 'I just wanted to frighten him so he would leave or throw me out. I wanted him to release me.' Kim told police officers that she had finally snapped following years of physical and sexual abuse. She claimed that Ian had terrified her into joining with prostitutes in three-way sex sessions, forced her to have sex inside a dog kennel and watched while, on his orders, she masturbated with a rifle.

Kim claimed that soon after they met, Ian showed a brutal side. She said: 'He sexually started becoming violent. He never hit me but he always hurt me and I just let him do it. I was so frightened.' She added, 'He used to put a knife to my throat during sex. Then he brought home a gun. He would threaten me with it and say it might make me better in bed. I tried to leave several times, but he always said he would kill me and would find me no matter where I went.'

At her trial in Glasgow's High Court the jury dismissed Galbraith's ludicrous version of events, taking only three hours to find her guilty. Judge Lord Osborne sentenced her to life imprisonment. But this was not the end of the story, which had already seen a bizarre twist when her defending counsel, Donald Findlay QC, a fervent Rangers supporter received unwelcome publicity when he was videoed singing sectarian songs. Findlay resigned from his position as vice-chairman of Rangers but carried on as Kim Galbraith's counsel.

But though the effect on the jury was hard to guess, it was not on these grounds that support for Kim grew. There were women's groups who believed her defence that she had finally snapped following years of abuse. A 'Free Kim Galbraith' campaign was started. After hesitating, Kim eventually allowed an appeal against her conviction to go forward. Not, however, on the basis of Ian's alleged abuse, but on her mental state at the time of the murder. In June 2001 five appeal judges heard evidence from experts that she was suffering from diminished responsibility when she blasted Ian. Her mental problems had begun in childhood and persisted into her marriage. She had been treated for depression. Her plea of guilty to the reduced charge of culpable homicide on the grounds of diminished responsibility was accepted and her sentence reduced to ten years, later to just eight. At her Essex home Ian Galbraith's mother, Patricia, responded bitterly, 'The ruling is a farce. I don't think there's any justice.'

In February 2003 Kim Galbraith was released on parole from Cornton Vale women's prison in Stirling, still protesting that she had killed because of the abuse she had suffered. She claimed, 'I am not an evil cop killer. I'm just a woman who suffered years of abuse from my husband and who couldn't take any more.'

But Ian's first wife Julie remembers a much different character, as she told the High Court: 'He was a lovely man and we had a good time when we were together.' It was the picture she drew of Ian Galbraith that the jury, hearing all the evidence, chose to believe.

22. Sheila Garvie and Brian Tevendale
Fatal attractions

Max Garvie was a wealthy young man. He owned a farm, West Cairnbeg, in Fordoun, Kincardineshire, traditional farming country in an area known as Howe of the Mearns and immortalised in Lewis Grassic Gibbon's novel *Sunset Song*. In 1954, at the age of twenty, he met Sheila Watson, a vivacious 17-year-old, at a summer dance in Stonehaven town hall. She came from the other end of the social spectrum and had once lived on the Balmoral estate where her father was a stonemason in the service of the Queen. Max fell deeply in love with the slim, attractive blonde and a year later they married. They were blessed with three healthy children and to the casual observer seemed to have it all: a young family, a luxury home, three cars (including a Jaguar), servants and even a private plane. Sheila, in particular, loved life at West Cairnbeg and quickly grew accustomed to the luxuries her husband could provide.

But there was a dark side to Max Garvie. A very dark side. He became obsessed with nudism, and by the 1960s was travelling to camps in Britain and abroad to indulge his passion. He forced his wife and children to go with him and to take part in naturism, often against their will. Garvie also bought land in Alford, Aberdeenshire, planted trees on it and set up his own nudist colony. His exotic tastes in the bedroom soon became evident. There were orgies with his naturist friends in a house on the colony that became known as 'Kinky Cottage' and Sheila, reluctant at first, soon became an enthusiastic participant. Max Garvie also developed a taste for deviant sex: he regularly sodomised his wife and took photographs of her in the nude, which he would proudly show to his cronies. After a time Sheila became depressed by his behaviour and started to take tranquillisers in disturbingly large quantities.

But Max Garvie had no intention of curbing his appetites. If anything they became even more depraved. He met a young barman, Brian Tevendale, through their membership of the Scottish National Party and they quickly became close friends. Tevendale often stayed at Garvie's home and it became apparent that his genial host wanted Tevendale to have sex with his wife. Although there was certainly an attraction between Tevendale and Sheila Garvie, nothing happened for some time and Max Garvie eventually dragged her naked into Tevendale's bedroom one night in September 1967 when she had consumed a lot of alcohol. They had intercourse, an outcome that gave Max Garvie a considerable vicarious thrill. But Garvie, who had strong homosexual tendencies, also wanted to have sex with the handsome Tevendale, who was then aged 21. He made several passes at him, including on one occasion walking into his bedroom wearing only a nightgown, which was open at the front.

Around this time Tevendale introduced Max Garvie to his sister, Trudi Birse, who was married to a policeman. Birse was instantly attracted to the handsome farmer and later said, 'You could feel the electricity in the air.' She and Garvie began a torrid affair and this eventually led to four-in-a-bed romps, with Sheila Garvie and Brian Tevendale – Birse's own brother – making up the foursome. To ensure that the harmony of these arrangements was maintained, Garvie even procured a girl for Trudi's husband, Alfred Birse. There was no doubting the strength of his attachment to his mistress: Garvie later cruelly told his wife that he got more pleasure from Trudi 'in a fortnight' than he had from Sheila in all their years of marriage. If Birse was unavailable, Max Garvie and Brian Tevendale would often toss a coin to determine who would sleep with Sheila that night.

But despite Max Garvie's liberated approach to life and love he was simply not prepared for what happened next; Sheila and Brian Tevendale fell for each other. When Garvie realised the strength of their attachment he immediately terminated his relationship with Trudi Birse and demanded that Sheila do the same with Tevendale. She refused and was subjected to violence and intimidation from her husband. At around the same time – and in a clear attempt to warn him off – Tevendale was slashed on the face by a man working for Max Garvie. Although Sheila left the marital home on a couple of occasions to live with her lover she returned, apparently taking seriously her husband's threats that he would shoot Tevendale and her children.

Then, suddenly, on 15 May 1968 Max Garvie went missing. In the absence of evidence to the contrary, the police treated his disappearance as a missing-person enquiry and even published details of his disappearance in the *Police Gazette*: the notice read: 'Spends freely, is a heavy drinker and often consumes tranquillisers when drinking. Is fond of female company . . . deals in pornographic material and is an active member of nudist camps . . . may have gone abroad.' But the truth was that Max Garvie was dead, a fact that Sheila Garvie acknowledged to her mother, Mrs Edith Watson, immediately after his disappearance. Sheila Garvie also told her mother that she had 'a strong man at her back', a clear reference to Tevendale. But it took Edith Watson three months to contact the police and it seems she only did so when her daughter said she was going to live with Tevendale and would be taking the three children with her. Mrs Watson disliked Tevendale intensely and she had also made a promise to Max Garvie, her son-in-law, to keep the children away from him.

Armed with Mrs Watson's information the police arrested Sheila Garvie, Brian Tevendale and an alleged accomplice, Alan Peters, and charged them with murder. Tevendale was able to lead police to the body, although he claimed that he had only helped to hide it and that Garvie had been killed by a rifle shot after a struggle with Sheila. And so the scene was set for one of the most high-profile trials of the twentieth century.

Even though this was the end of the 'swinging sixties', the case had stunned this traditional area in north-east Scotland. When the trial started at the High Court in Aberdeen on 19 November 1968 there were long queues for places on the public benches. People across Scotland also found the trial titillating and eagerly anticipated details of the sexual shenanigans to come. Such was the attention focused on the case that the solicitor general for Scotland, Ewan Stewart QC, took charge of the prosecution. In court the three accused all entered pleas of not guilty, blaming their co-accused for the murder.

In court Sheila Garvie maintained she knew nothing about the murder of her husband. She testified that on the night of his death they had made love and fallen asleep together. Wakened by a tug on her arm, she saw Brian Tevendale – who was carrying a rifle – and a fair-haired young man in her bedroom. She claimed that she was bewildered by their presence and had no idea what the gun was for; it 'never entered her head' that he might shoot Max. Tevendale then took her into the bathroom and told her to stay there. She heard thumping noises but did not think they were gunshots and only discovered the awful truth later. She had not gone to the police to report the murder because she felt morally responsible for Tevendale – who had fallen deeply in love with her – and wanted to protect him.

But this account of events, delivered in nine gruelling hours in the witness box, lacked credibility. There was a mass of evidence to the contrary. Sheila Garvie stood to gain financially from her husband's death. There were two life insurance policies worth £55,000 (a very substantial sum in 1968), the house at West Cairnbeg, the three cars, personal possessions and income from the farm. She would be a wealthy woman in her own right as well as being free of an unfeeling and often brutal husband. There was also the fact that she continued to have sex with Tevendale in the three months between Max Garvie's death and her arrest. Why would a wife keep up a relationship with a man who had slain her husband? It was also noted that Brian Tevendale had been best man at the wedding of Alan Peters soon after Max Garvie was murdered and that Sheila Garvie was matron of honour . . . a further sign of the bond between the two.

But the evidence that did more than anything to undermine Sheila Garvie's story was provided by the other man in the house that night: Alan Peters. A rather timid 20-year-old, Peters was a close friend of Brian Tevendale and appears to have been both mesmerised and intimidated by him. In his evidence he told how he and Tevendale went to the farmhouse – which they entered through a side door – and were met by Sheila Garvie. They had a drink together and Sheila Garvie then said, 'I'll show you where to go.' The two men went upstairs and waited in a room. Forty-five minutes later Mrs Garvie returned and told them, 'He's asleep now.' Peters said that he and Tevendale (who was carrying a rifle) then went to a bedroom where a man was lying face down, asleep. Tevendale then smashed the man's head twice with the butt of the rifle, put a pillow over his face and shot him through the pillow. They put the body in the boot of Peters's car and went back into the house, where Sheila Garvie made them coffee. Peters said he saw Tevendale and Garvie kiss passionately on the lips. He and Tevendale then took the body to Lauriston Castle in St Cyrus, Kincardineshire where they buried it in a culvert and covered it with a pile of stones.

It was this version of events that the jury believed. Sheila Garvie and Brian Tevendale were found guilty of murder on 2 December 1968, while the charges against Alan Peters were found to be not proven. Interestingly the jury brought in a unanimous verdict for Tevendale but only found Garvie guilty by a majority. In any event, they were both given life sentences. Before being taken to prison they were allowed a few minutes together and no one who saw them could doubt their love for each other; they kissed passionately, vowed to marry and, in tears, were parted.

Both Sheila Garvie and Brian Tevendale were released from prison in the late 1970s. By that time she had made clear that she did not wish to see Tevendale again. Tevendale subsequently married and, in 2002, was reported to be running a pub in Perthshire. Garvie, who wrote a book about her experiences in 1980, married on two more occasions but both marriages ended in divorce. She is said to be living alone with her dog in a quiet cul-de-sac in Stonehaven, ten miles from Kinky Cottage.

23. Philip Givens

'Phil was such a kindly man'

To friends and relatives Phil Givens appeared a harmless if lonely figure. His sister Margaret had fond memories of him, claiming 'Phil was such a kindly man. He used to bring home injured birds and stray cats and dogs. Almost every spare penny he had went on them. He never smoked or drank. That's one of the reasons we never thought there was the slightest bit of harm in him.' Phil Givens, a 35-year-old, was the sort of person you'd willingly lend your car to as family friends the Scotts did when they went to Canada for a holiday. They couldn't possibly have imagined the use Givens had planned for their kind gesture.

In the silence of his own room Phil Givens was experiencing strange thoughts. He believed the devil was telling him to abduct and tie up young men. There was a strong sexual aspect to his impulse, which the solitary and repressed Givens – living alone with his sister – seemed unable to control. For years he had, unknown to his family, abused himself with knotted ropes. But it had reached a stage where this strange fetish no longer satisfied him and he felt driven to seek new ways to fulfil his bizarre fantasies.

In July 1962, 16-year-old Philip Martin of Salisbury Place, Dalmuir – an apprentice slater who had been sent on an errand – was walking along Clydebank's Glasgow Road when a small black car drew up alongside. The driver, wearing a navy-blue donkey-jacket with a checked cap, and who had a distinct twitch affecting one eye, offered Philip ten shillings to help to move a fireplace. Philip got into the car and was driven to a derelict shop at 69 Stobcross Street in the Anderston district of Glasgow. Philip Martin described what happened:

> A grate was lying in the back shop, pulled out from the wall. It was very dark and the man lit a candle. Suddenly he poked a gun in my ribs and told me to stand by the wall. I laughed at first hoping it was a joke, but it wasn't. The man made me strip, threw me on a chair and tied me up. I thought I was going to die. He gagged me with adhesive tape. Then he snuffed out the candle and left. I managed to bump my way into the front shop and I was getting the gag off when the man came in. He dragged me back, gagged me again then went away. Some children heard my struggle to get free. And a neighbour smashed in the door to save me.

In the darkness the young man could not have guessed that the gun his attacker had threatened him with was a cheap replica he had bought in a shop in town. But it was, nonetheless, frightening evidence that the event had been well prepared and planned. A warning that Glasgow had a serial killer in the making as it was only luck that Philip Martin had survived the attack.

On 3 October 1962 a sanitary inspector, Malcolm Beaton, was called to a disused surgery at 64 West Bridgend in Dumbarton, following a neighbour's complaint about a foul odour originating from the premises. He brought with him, to force open the locked door, 32-year-old joiner Bruce McColl. Inside, the shocked pair discovered the near-naked body of a young man strapped to a chair with a gag still in place across the mouth. His hands and legs had been bound with bootlaces and insulating tape. His ankles had been tied to the iron supports of a sink. The body had been partly burned. The corpse was soon identified as that of 16-year-old Frederick Dowden. From the decomposed state of the torso it seemed clear that Frederick had lain there for some time and had probably been killed soon after he had gone missing on 7 August. However, forensic examination revealed no obvious signs of injuries, which led detectives to speculate that Frederick of 10 Heathcote Place, Drumchapel had been left to starve to death. By explaining his death in this way they could have been trying to save the family from a more awful truth. And the press of that time were far more restrained than today in their reporting. A more likely alternative was that Frederick had slowly suffocated during a prolonged sexual assault by the attacker during which ropes were pulled ever more tightly round his chest. The fact that he had been stripped of clothing, bound and left in empty premises reminded detectives of the case of Philip Martin a few months earlier. An incident that was still under investigation.

Police concern heightened when they learned that a similar incident, not officially reported to the authorities, had taken place at a disused furniture shop at 12 Plantation Street in the Glasgow docklands. Inside the premises, dotted with covered chairs and tables, police discovered items of clothing and a vest. Detective inspector Peter Anderson, head of Dunbartonshire CID, appealed for the youth to come forward, but, to police frustration, he never did.

The police were aware that these were no spur-of-the-moment crimes, but carefully thought through by the man responsible. The killer having first spent time identifying empty shops then contacted the factors in order to view them to make sure they fitted his requirements. For the empty surgery where Fred Dowden met his death the killer had paid James Buchanan two months' rent in advance and given a false address in Dumbarton. He had then painted over windows with black paint so that it was dark inside and hidden from passers-by. He even went to the extent of buying second-hand chairs of the kind he believed would be more suited to his assault on his teenage victims. Some of this detectives learned from their inquiries. The full picture would only emerge after they identified the killer.

Detectives were now desperate to track down the murderer, particularly as Frederick's death was being linked by the press to the unsolved 'twilight murders' in London in which an Admiralty supply officer and a theatrical dresser had been found dead in similar bizarre circumstances. And as a result, for the first time in the history of Scottish criminal law, a decision was taken to broadcast an identikit picture of the attacker on television. As this was a first, detectives were nervous about the potential impact, particularly if and when the case went to trial. No one who was already a witness was allowed to see the identikit and were gathered together under police supervision. Chief detective superintendent Bob Kerr commented, 'In Scotland police have been trying to get permission to telecast pictures of people who could assist them in inquiries, but until now the Crown Office has refused.' But this case was too serious to stand on ceremony. A long-standing ban simply had to go. Too many young men were at risk from a killer who clearly would not stop till he was caught.

On the evening that the identikit was broadcast, Phil Givens was sitting in his home at 98 Ardenlea Street, Dalmarnock in Glasgow. His sister, Mrs Margaret Dick, later described the scene, 'When the identikit picture of Phil flashed on the television screen, he was sitting with my son and daughter. My daughter said, "There's the man with the twitching eyes the police are after." Phil started twitching his eyes and joked that he was the man they wanted. We never believed it for a second.' Perhaps in his perverted mind Phil Givens believed he was innocent of the crime. Or was he, in reality, the cunning, calculating killer his sister eventually came to believe him to be? Although there is little doubt that strange thoughts were swirling in Givens's mind, he was still able to judge that he was in danger and take action to avoid police attention. When news of the attack on Philip Martin hit the headlines, Givens moved out of Glasgow to Dumbarton until things had quietened down.

But he could not control the thrill it gave him to tie up young men and have victims at his mercy. After he had left Philip Martin bound to a chair, he had decided to go back just to look at him. It may be that the sight of the almost-naked young man strapped to a chair sexually aroused him and satisfied for a while his strange urge. When Givens saw that Martin had broken free, the voice that kept speaking to him urged him to tie him up again and this time to make sure he made a better job of it. A short while later Givens, responding to his bizarre fantasy, returned to the shop, and, discovering that his victim had been rescued, actually stood with the crowd which had now gathered and had watched Philip Martin being taken away to hospital.

By the time Givens assaulted Frederick Dowden, he had learned from his mistakes. He made sure Frederick wouldn't escape by tying the chair on which he had strapped him to a sink. From what he admitted to his sister, he decided to return the next day. 'I felt the urge to go back and see the boy. I might have let him go. But the wee boy was dead and I couldn't rouse him. I just burst out crying and walked out of the shop.' Givens's remorse seemed less than heartfelt and Margaret Dick summed him up when she said, 'Phil knows – and I know – that if he hadn't been caught he would have gone on and on. God knows how many people would have died. It's a good job the police caught up with Phil when they did. For he was going to Canada in April. He went to Canada in 1957, but couldn't get work. He was going back to try again.'

Leading psychologists were asked to construct a character profile of Frederick Dowden's killer. In their view, the murderer would be over thirty, unmarried and living with his mother. A remarkably accurate assessment. In fact, the killer's sister had become a substitute 'mum' who he lived with after his mother's death. But, in reality, it was solid detective work that finally nailed Givens. It was known that the attacker used an old black car, which police thought was a 1950 Ford Anglia. In 1962 car ownership had not reached the mass market of a decade later, but there were still ten thousand cars matching the description of the one used by the killer in Glasgow and the surrounding area. The murderer could have been the ten thousandth on the list for all detectives knew but, as luck would have it, detective constable Cameron Wiseman interviewed the sixteenth owner on his list who explained that he had been in Canada over the period of the murder of Fred Dowden. Wiseman then asked if anyone else might have used the car during this time and the name of Phil Givens came up. Wiseman went to the garage where Givens worked as a mechanic and was struck immediately by the similarity between the description of the attacker provided by Phil Martin and Givens. Fingerprint comparison proved that Phil Givens was the man they were looking for.

At his trial in March 1963, psychiatric evidence was presented which showed that Givens achieved a sexual thrill from self-bondage. After a time this failed to satisfy him and he went on to seek sexual pleasure from putting into practice his fantasy of tying up young men. The court was told that, 'He has no girlfriends at all. He has no interest in women.' The coded language of the time for branding Givens as a homosexual pervert. The court's recommendation was that Givens should be confined in a state mental hospital without limit of time, as there seemed little prospect that he would improve. 'Until it does, he might seek to bind someone again with the same dreadful results', a psychiatrist warned. The trial judge, Lord Mackintosh, told Givens, 'I hold that you being a person of dangerous, violent and criminal propensity require treatment under conditions of special security.' Even the experts were forced to admit that Givens was beyond help.

Faces of evil

Owen Anderson,
who murdered salesman
Gary Linn.

William Beggs,
the gay slasher.

Bible John: photofit of a killer
who was never caught.

Robert Black, the child killer who
must never be released.
(courtesy Mirrorpix)

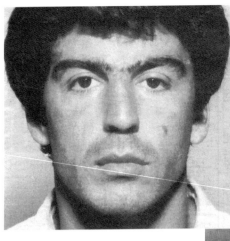

The hit man and the hooker.
Above left: Ricardo Blanco
Above right: Jacqueline Wylie
(courtesy Mirrorpix)

'Every parent's worst
nightmare'
Andrew Cameron (*below left*)
and one of his young female
victims, Kay Wyllie
(*below right*).

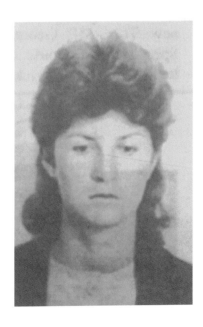

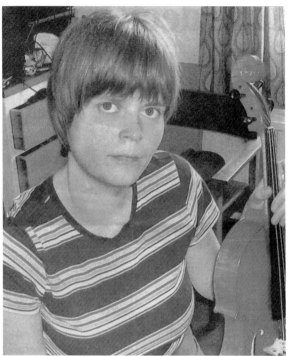

An obsession with necrophilia, rape and consensual asphyxia led Graham Coutts (*above left*) to strangle teacher Jane Longhurst (*above right*) during sex.

The love-crazed teacher. Grant Dunn (*below left*) became obsessed with his pupil, Emanuela Ferro (*below right*). When his feelings were not reciprocated it led to murder.

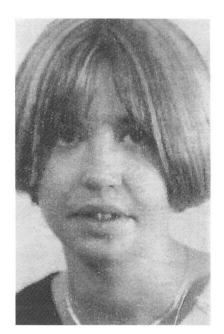

Some people just never learn. Donald Forbes (*above*, at his wedding) escaped the gallows, then committed a second murder and later became a drug baron . . . in his sixties. (courtesy Mirrorpix)

Jack the Lad. Nat Fraser (*below left*) was arrogant enough to believe he could get away with anything . . . even the murder of his wife, Arlene (*below right*)

Deadlier than the male

Kim Galbraith (*above left*) whose ludicrous stories about the shooting of her policeman husband did not save her from a life sentence.

Sheila Garvie (*above right*) whose trial for the murder of her wealthy husband, Max (*also pictured*) scandalised the north-east in the 1960s. Pamela Gourlay (*below left*), who callously cut her neighbour's throat to get money for drugs. Gemma Valenti (*opposite, left*), who, with her mother, murdered a man at a party.

The demon butler: His apparent devotion to wealthy employers was a front for Archibald Hall (*above left*) to commit fraud, robbery and murder. One of his victims, Walter Scott-Elliot, (*above right*), a former MP. (courtesy Mirrorpix)

Thomas Hamilton (*below left*). His massacre of sixteen infants and their teacher at Dunblane primary school in 1996 sent shockwaves round the world.

The 'butcher of Gartnavel'. James Harkins (*below right*) should never have been let out of mental hospital. But he was, and it led to three savage murders. (courtesy Mirrorpix)

Psycho Number One. Christopher Hutcheson (*above left*) wanted to be the 'Godfather' of Glasgow.

The wife, her toyboy and her lesbian lover. The plot instigated by Veronica Little (*above right*) to murder her brutal husband, David (*also pictured*) electrified the sleepy market town of Dumfries in 1982.

Rogue male. Gavin McGuire (*below left*), a grave danger to women everywhere.

The vampire killer. Allan Menzies (*below right*) who murdered his best friend, drank his blood and ate part of his head.

Mad Dog comes home. Glasgow-born Archie McCafferty
(*wearing sunglasses, centre*) arrives in Scotland in 1997 after being
deported from Australia. He brutally murdered four people down
under, after being 'instructed' to kill by his dead son.

(courtesy Mirrorpix)

The case that shocked Scotland. Luke Mitchell (*above left*), the 14-year-old schoolboy who murdered his girlfriend, Jodi Jones (*above right*), who was also fourteen. (courtesy Scotsman Publications Ltd)

He could have been a serial killer! Iain Scoular (*below*) with his two victims: Catherine McChord and Elizabeth Walton.

Catherine McChord

Elizabeth Walton

Break-out from Carstairs! Robert Mone and Thomas McCulloch murdered three people, and seriously injured three others, when they escaped from the state mental hospital in 1976.

(courtesy Mirrorpix)

Daily Record

20p FORWARD WITH SCOTLAND No. 30,367

Alison Murray . . . a glittering future.

Bluebell Woods victim and her callous young killers

Wilson (left) and Murray last night . . . surprised in the woods.   Picture: ANDREW HOSIE

FROM BROTHER TO BEAST

BABY-FACED murderer Iain Murray was behind bars last night...

Branded with his pal Brian Wilson as the Beasts of the Bluebell Woods.

Their victim: Iain's half-sister Alison, the brilliant student who dreamt of a glittering career in cancer research.

The teenagers were found guilty by a jury at the High Court in Glasgow of Alison's savage murder after she surprised them committing an indecent act in the woods near their homes.

But last night the boys' parents vowed to continue the fight to clear their names.

NIGHTMARE NEVER ENDS . . Pages 6 and 7

MAGGIE SOUNDS HER BATTLE CRY

PAGE 2

The Bluebell Woods killers. In a tragic case, Iain Murray murdered his sister, Alison, a young woman with a brilliant academic career in front of her. His best pal, and lover, Brian Wilson, was also convicted of her murder.
(courtesy Mirrorpix)

Killing for company. Dennis Nilsen in 1983, on his way to
begin a twenty-five-year sentence. He murdered six men
and was often loath to dispose of the corpses.
(courtesy Mirrorpix)

Web of the Black Widow:
Happy days. Newlyweds
Stuart and Nawal Nicol
celebrate their wedding
(*left*)

Right: The ample
charms that enabled
Nawal – nicknamed
the Black Widow by
the press – to attract
dozens of lovers.
She was cleared of any
involvement in the
death of her husband.

Left: The men who murdered
Stuart Nicol. Both were said
to be Nawal's lovers:
Muir Middler (*left*) and
Jason Simpson (*right*).

Above left: The scientist, Brenda Page – whose killer has never been caught – at her wedding to Christopher Harrison. *Above right*, Army payroll killer, Andrew Walker. *Middle right*, Douglas Wood, one of the feared brothers known as 'Scotland's Krays'. (courtesy Mirrorpix)

Below left: Robert Smith, the ex-SAS soldier who was convicted of armed robbery and murder. *Below right*: Angus Sinclair, arguably Scotland's most evil man. (courtesy Mirrorpix)

Main picture: Betty Torrance, whose string of extra-marital affairs ended with the 'golf course Casanova', David Watt (*inset*), murdering her dairy-farmer husband.

Death in the suburbs. Iain Wheldon is led away after being found guilty of the culpable homicide of Mark Ayton in the leafy Edinburgh district of Balerno.
(courtesy Mirrorpix)

Ex cop Howard Wilson is driven away from court after being convicted of murdering two former colleagues and the attempted murder of a third. (courtesy Mirrorpix)

24. Pamela Gourlay

'What if you have done the worst thing in the world?'

The trial judge said it all in his summing-up: 'To don rubber gloves, arm yourself with a knife and then burst in on a neighbour and slit her throat in the course of a sustained attack, as it turned out all for the sake of some £20 or £30, a miscellany of personal items and some gift vouchers is a crime of almost unimaginable depravity.' It is perhaps even more shocking that the murderer was a girl aged only twenty and that the victim, a neighbour, was herself aged only twenty-two. This tragic crime took place in Aberdeen in October 1999 and stunned the good citizens of that city with its senselessness and cruelty.

The victim, Melanie Sturton, lived in a bedsit in Great Western Road. She hailed from Ballater on Deeside and was a student at Aberdeen College. She also worked part time as a care assistant at Nazareth House, an old people's home in the city run by nuns. Melanie came from a loving family and was clearly devoted to the elderly people she looked after. She was small with a gentle disposition and was gradually overcoming the shyness and lack of confidence that a slight facial-paralysis had brought in its wake. All in all Melanie Sturton was a daughter any parent could be proud of.

The contrast with her killer could not be more marked. Originally from Inverbervie, a small town close to Aberdeen, Pamela Gourlay was a cold, selfish young woman with a drug habit that had left her deeply in debt. This was despite a job as a chef, an income from dealing cannabis that netted her more than £300 a week and occasional stints as a beggar. Gourlay lived in a bedsit to which her boyfriend Kris Taylor (24), a regular heroin user, was a frequent visitor. The bedsit was on the floor above a similar room occupied by Melanie Sturton.

Like most of her other problems Gourlay's involvement in murder started with drug taking. On the evening of 8 October she and Taylor had been at a friend's house where they had both smoked cannabis and taken Temazepam. They left in the early hours of the morning and on the way home made unsuccessful attempts to get money from two cash machines. Taylor later said that he watched videos until five o'clock in the morning before falling asleep. But Gourlay, anxious for ready cash and probably still high from the drugs she had taken, was wide-awake. Donning two pairs of plastic gloves and a sun hat she sneaked downstairs and knocked on Melanie Sturton's door. Although still in her night-clothes, Melanie was awake as she was getting ready for work. But, when she answered the door, she knew immediately that something was wrong and tried to keep Gourlay out. But her efforts were to no avail. Gourlay forced her way in and, in the course of a desperate struggle, slashed Melanie's throat four times with a razor-sharp kitchen knife. Melanie's screams were so loud that a neighbour on the floor below clearly heard them.

The fact that she had just murdered an entirely innocent human being in such a callous fashion did not faze Pamela Gourlay. Without bothering to check if Melanie was dead or alive she covered her heavily bloodstained body with a duvet and a rug and then, coolly and methodically, gathered up everything in the flat that she thought might be of value: a compact-disc player, two bank cards, some gift vouchers, a purse and jewellery. Gourlay calmly returned to her bedsit with these ill-gotten gains, where she took off her blood-covered clothes, and later that morning she and Kris Taylor headed for Aberdeen's main shopping area in Union Street as if nothing had happened. She even tried to beg money from passers-by for the bus fare. According to Taylor, Gourlay was her 'usual cheery self'. Gourlay used Melanie's bank card and PIN number to steal £10 from a cash machine and she spent the Marks and Spencer gift vouchers stolen from the flat to buy her aunt a vase. She met her parents for lunch – which she paid for with the money stolen from Melanie Sturton – and, according to her mother, was 'fine and cheery'.

But all that was soon to change. Melanie's body was discovered on 11 October and a murder hunt was launched. As part of their routine enquiries Grampian police interviewed Gourlay as a potential witness on 12 October and, two days later in an attempt to eliminate her from enquiries, interviewed her again and took a routine DNA sample. According to police, she was happy to co-operate and to go voluntarily to police headquarters; one officer described her as 'pleasant, plausible and controlled'.

But there was a dramatic change in her mood when police obtained warrants to search her bedsit and the homes of her mother and sister. According to detectives, she became quieter and more withdrawn and said that she wanted to go home. Her sense of foreboding was fully justified as police found much to incriminate her in the bedsit – in particular a Sabatier boning knife with Melanie Sturton's bloodstains on the blade and handle. The police also found a bloodstained jacket and latex gloves as well as a number of Melanie's possessions.

Pamela Gourlay was now on a murder charge. She was strip-searched by two female officers and, through a river of tears, asked them: 'What if you have done the worst thing in the world?' She was then taken for a formal interview, which was video-recorded by police. Gourlay wept throughout the interview process and made a dramatic admission to the detectives who questioned her, 'I murdered Melanie. I slit her throat.'

She said that her unfortunate victim had begged her to stop. She was unable to offer any explanation for her actions: 'I don't know what was going through my head' she told police.

But by the time of the trial at the High Court in Aberdeen in March 2000 she had changed her mind about her guilt. In the dock, charged with murder, she tried to put the blame on her erstwhile boyfriend, Kris Taylor. This of course completely contradicted the confession in the videotaped interview with the police, which was shown to the jury. It also contradicted evidence from her mother who testified that her daughter told her during a telephone conversation from prison that she was the sole killer. Mrs Eileen Gourlay recounted how Pamela Gourlay told her: 'It was me. I am sorry mum. . . . They'll give me fifteen years mum. I am so scared.' Mrs Gourlay put it to her that someone else must have been involved, but she was insistent: 'I am telling the truth' was the tearful reply.

Mrs Gourlay then told the court how, only a few weeks later, her daughter had a completely new version of events: 'She told me it was Kris that done the murder and she took the stuff out of the girl's flat.' The justification for this volte-face was quite simple; she claimed that she was frightened of Taylor and did not want to 'grass' on him. She was also worried about what might happen to her family if she told the truth.

For his part Taylor vehemently denied any involvement in either robbery or murder. There was one piece of evidence linking him to the crime but it was rather tenuous; a DNA test of a bloodstain on Melanie Sturton's front door revealed that it almost certainly belonged to him. But Taylor insisted that he had never been in the bedsit and could offer no explanation as to how it had got there. It would now be up to the jury to decide if Gourlay's version of events was credible. After two-and-a-half hours the members of the jury returned to the courtroom where the foreman announced they had found her guilty by virtue of a majority verdict. Gourlay showed no emotion but Melanie Sturton's relatives uttered a single word, a word that spoke volumes for their state of mind: that word was 'yes'.

In passing sentence the judge, Lord Marnoch, noted that detention for life was mandatory for a murder conviction. But given the nature and circumstances of the crime he went on to say, 'I have decided to mark the gravity of your offence and the degree of depravity, and also the genuine lack of remorse and the sense of outrage which your crime engendered in any right-thinking person. It is appropriate, despite your youth, that I recommend to Scottish ministers that you serve a minimum period of fourteen years detention before being even considered for release into the community on licence.' To loud applause from the public gallery, and shouts of 'bitch', Gourlay was led away to start her new life behind bars.

There is a postcript. Gourlay made an attempt to get a new trial on the grounds that she had suffered a miscarriage of justice because the trial judge, Lord Marnoch, had interrupted her evidence 186 times. Although this plea was rejected by the Court of Criminal Appeal in Edinburgh she later persuaded it to quash the recommendation that she should serve a minimum of fourteen years behind bars. The effect of this was that she would only have to serve a 'normal' life sentence, which would have meant an earlier release date. This decision horrified Melanie Sturton's mother who complained bitterly that no one was able to speak up for her daughter in court. But there was a final twist. Under European human rights legislation, judges in Scotland must now specify the length of time murderers should spend in jail as a punishment for their misdeeds. In October 2002, Gourlay found herself back in the High Court where Lord Marnoch confirmed his original minimum sentence of fourteen years.

And Gourlay found a way to get into even more trouble. In February 2004 she received a four-year sentence for drug dealing in Cornton Vale women's prison in Stirlingshire. Her plan was to sell £4,000-worth of heroin to fellow prisoners during a church service. But unfortunately for her, prison officers conducted a search and Gourlay was caught red-handed. It seems that some people will never learn.

25. Archibald Hall
The demon butler

Archibald Hall was born in July 1924 in the modest surroundings of 15 Albert Road in Glasgow's Victoria Park. Although life financially was not easy for the family, Hall was far from being destitute, but from an early age he grew to resent his father who, as a soldier and lay preacher, constantly warned his son to beware of straying from the 'straight and narrow'. Advice Archie ignored. But he doted on his mother, even to the extent of excusing her secret affair with an army major, which led to the birth of a half brother, Donald. For whatever reason, Hall turned to stealing and throughout his adolescence continually fell foul of the police. He became through time a talented con man who loved mixing with the wealthy and titled while he thought up plans to rob them. Hall, who preferred the first name Roy, and used the alias Roy Fontaine, was also a bisexual who sought out both male and female lovers. It was his passion for gay sex that was eventually to bring about his downfall

But that lay in the future. For years he lived the high life. A suave communicator, he landed several jobs as a butler to rich families and then fleeced their homes of jewellery, antiques and paintings. Often his employers had no idea they had been robbed. He became a bit of a connoisseur, better able to judge the worth of the valuables he sold than the professionals in the trade. But Hall turned his hand to every kind of stealing, even taking part in more down-to-earth smash-and-grab raids on London jewellers. He was no fool, commuting regularly between London and Glasgow so that he could carry out crimes in both cities then get away from the area. However, he came to prefer life in the south, which he saw as the ideal location for his style of crime.

In his twenties and thirties, Hall was on the way up, making a fortune from his criminal activities. He claimed to have been a guest at gay parties where he mixed with such famous homosexuals as Lord Louis Mountbatten, Prince Charles's favourite uncle. He also boasted of having sexual affairs with the playwright Terence Rattigan, Lord Boothby, a leading Tory of the 1950s, and with Victor Oliver, a son-in-law of Winston Churchill. Whether these encounters were real or all in Hall's vivid imagination, no one could be sure, but that didn't stop Hall boasting of his time with the famous of the land. He was desperate to be accepted by the rich and titled as an equal. He was even a fervent royalist. But Hall could never be a part of high society. It was a pipedream. He was an accomplished thief but, even so, many years of his life were spent in prison. Though he saw himself as a professional criminal he never managed to evade the law. That was the reality behind Hall's 'glamorous' lifestyle.

But he tried hard. Hall would spend hours studying upmarket publications like *The Times* and *Tatler*. He wanted to learn everything about upper-class society so he could home in on wealthy people to rob. In June 1977 he came upon an advertisement in the magazine *Country Life*. Lady Margaret Hudson, widow of a former Tory MP, living alone on her Kirtleton estate in Dumfriesshire, had a butler's position to fill. Hall's forged references helped him to get the job, but his sole purpose in going to Kirtleton was to help himself to Margaret Hudson's collection of valuable antiques.

But his plan hit a snag when a former gay lover, David Wright, turned up. Hall had enjoyed a sexual relationship with Wright at Worcestershire's Long Martin prison in the early 1970s. At Archie's suggestion, on his release, Wright had burgled a stately home, Grimshaw Hall, but had failed to give his 'friend' a share of the loot. Hall bore him a grudge because of this, but when he heard that Wright was on the run following the murder of an Asian man he had enticed into a toilet, Hall invited him to Kirtleton. He was desperate to resume their sex life together. It was Hall's biggest mistake. Wright was a liability and Archie still harboured resentment over events at Grimshaw Hall. It was a bad combination. Now Wright's behaviour would drive Archie over the edge. Wright stayed with Hall at Kirtleton for several weeks, during which time he stole several items of jewellery. Hall, carefully planning a major job, made him put it back. But Wright, enraged that Hall refused to let him burgle the house when he had run up thousands of pounds of debt, got drunk one night and fired a gun at Hall as he lay in bed. Hall thought he was going to be killed and begged for his life. Though Wright eventually calmed down and apologised, it was too late. Hall was bent on revenge.

The next day he took Wright into the woods on the pretence of rabbit shooting. Hall waited till Wright had used up all his bullets then blasted him in the head and chest with a .22 rifle, burying the body on the bank of a nearby stream. Hall next concocted a story that Wright had left to take up a job in Devon. No one suspected. No one cared. Wright was simply forgotten.

But though he'd committed the 'perfect murder', his time at Kirtleton came to an end. A former female lover tipped off Lady Hudson about Hall's criminal past and he was forced to quit. Hall moved to London and, again using forged references, landed a butler's post with Walter Scott-Elliot and his wife Dorothy, in their London flat in the exclusive district of Knightsbridge. Scott-Elliot was a former Labour MP, Eton-educated and wealthy, but by the time Hall arrived a frail 82-year-old shadow of his former self. Hall looked forward to relieving the ageing couple of their collection of antiques.

Hall, meanwhile, had taken up with 33-year-old Mary Coggle who he'd first met while working on prison release at Whittington hospital for the insane. Archie explained that he was looking for a younger criminal to help him with his plan to rob the Scott-Elliots. Coggle introduced him to 29-year-old Michael Kitto and soon all three were close drinking companions. A potentially explosive trio had been created.

On 13 December 1977, after a bout of heavy drinking, Hall offered to show Kitto round his employer's flat so that his friend could see for himself what real wealth was like. It was an act of bravado on Hall's part, which was to go badly wrong. Hall knew that Walter would be heavily sedated, as he always was at bedtime, and that Dorothy was staying overnight in a nursing home. But as the three wandered through the flat, Dorothy, who had changed her plans for the night, suddenly appeared and demanded to know what Kitto was doing in her home. Panicking that they would be rumbled, and the police sent for, Kitto and Hall attacked Dorothy, smothering her with a pillow. Hall then hatched a bizarre plot which he hoped would convince witnesses, even her husband, that she was still alive, and had not been murdered at the Knightsbridge flat. The ageing Walter Scott-Elliot was fed a drugged glass of whisky and persuaded to get into a grey Cortina that Hall had hired. Unknown to Walter, Hall had hidden the body of Dorothy in the boot of the car. It was a macabre touch. He was practically sitting on top of his dead wife. Hall, meanwhile, had persuaded Mary Coggle to impersonate Dorothy and she, dressed in the dead woman's clothes, got into the car, even convincing Walter, in his drugged state, that she was his wife. They then visited a succession of banks, withdrawing large sums of money from the accounts of the Scott-Elliots.

The party headed north, staying overnight at a cottage, Middle Farm, that Hall had rented in advance in Newton Arlosh on the Cumbrian coast about fifteen miles from Carlisle. That evening they visited a local pub, the Joiner's Arms, taking Walter Scott-Elliot with them. Clearly in a confused state, Scott-Elliot appeared quite happy to be there, convinced that Mary Coggle was his wife. In fact, Dorothy's body was still lying in the boot of Archibald Hall's car.

The following morning they drove into Scotland, eventually reaching the village of Comrie in Perthshire. At an isolated spot between Comrie and the village of Braco they buried Dorothy's body. Hall then drove to the village of Tomich near Inverness, about two hundred miles away. Walter Scott-Elliot survived two more days before he was strangled. He was buried in a grave above a waterfall in Glen Affric. The three then returned to the cottage at Newton Arlosh.

Hall and Kitto were now in a dangerous position from which they could only escape by careful planning. The police were still unaware that the Scott-Elliots were missing. They thought that they had gone to Italy for a holiday even though they had found their London flat ransacked and bloodstains on the wall. But Mary Coggle seemed blissfully unaware of how close they all were to being caught and appeared to have learned nothing from her association with Hall and Kitto. It had not dawned on her that she was involved with a pair of psychotic killers who showed no mercy to anyone who might land them back in gaol. Mary boasted openly to friends of her newly found wealth and refused to stop wearing Dorothy's mink coat. Evidence that could sink them all. Hall knew that if she was allowed to carry on their freedom would be jeopardised. He and Kitto decided that there was only one way to silence her. Kitto held her down while Hall battered her head with a poker. They dumped her body in a stream near Annan, Dumfries-shire, on the Middlebie to Waterbeck road.

Hall and Kitto were now out of control and, having tasted blood, found it impossible to stop. It was simply a question of the next victim. Hall focused his anger on his half brother, Donald Hall, a convicted burglar, who had just been released from prison. Hall loathed him and branded him a child molester. He decided to kill him. With Kitto's help he chloroformed Donald and drowned him in a bath. Putting the body in the boot of his maroon Ford Granada, Hall drove to North Berwick, searching for a likely spot to hide the body, stopping at the Blenheim House Hotel for dinner. It was here that Hall's con-man persona uncharacteristically slipped. His nervous babbling manner aroused the suspicion of manager Norman Wright who suspected that Hall's car might have been stolen. He rang the police who, on checking the registration, found it did not match the make of car. Hall, in fact, had put on false number plates. A police search quickly discovered Donald Hall's corpse in the boot. The ground had been frozen hard and it had not been possible to bury the body.

On 27 January 1978, Hall and Kitto were charged with murdering Walter Scott-Elliot by 'pushing him to the ground, compressing his throat with their hands and a scarf, stamping on his throat and strangling him'. Hall then admitted, and was charged with, the murder of David Wright.

For all his years in crime, Hall had never shown a tendency towards violence. So why did this smooth-talking con-man turn into a vicious and cold-blooded killer? Hall was to blame it on the death of the only person he truly loved, David Barnard. Barnard was serving eighteen years for armed robbery when Hall met and fell in love with him, in Hull prison. After their release, Hall hoped they would set up home together. But soon after, in 1974, Barnard was killed in a car crash. Hall sank into depression and his judgement began to go awry. His argument with another lover, David Wright, was the final push that set him on the slope to self-destruction.

On 2 May 1978, at the High Court in Edinburgh, Archibald Hall received two life sentences. He was never released and died, still a prisoner, on 16 September 2002.

26. Thomas Hamilton

Slaughter of the innocents

At quarter past nine on the morning of Wednesday, 13 March 1996 Thomas Hamilton walked through the front door of Dunblane primary school, a building he knew well. He was carrying two semi-automatic pistols, two Smith and Wesson revolvers and 743 rounds of ammunition. He saw two teachers in the corridor and immediately opened fire. Although he hit them both they managed to evade serious injury. But it was not teachers Hamilton had come for; it was the children of Dunblane.

He marched purposefully through the dining area and then passed the school kitchen on the left. Turning right into the assembly hall, he strode on until he reached the school gym, where twenty-nine pupils – mostly 5-year-olds – were playing under the supervision of their teacher, Gwen Mayor. Hamilton burst in and, without further ado, took aim. The most infamous crime imaginable was about to be perpetrated.

Hamilton became a killing machine. He stood over the children and, despite their sobbing, shot them in the head at point-blank range. When others, unable to comprehend what was going on, huddled together he simply shot into the pile of bodies. Others tried to run away; Hamilton chased them round the room before killing them too. He also shot and killed Mrs Mayor, who courageously tried to protect her pupils by covering them with her body. Hamilton then pushed open the emergency doors of the gym and started firing wildly at the windows of classroom huts. Inside three minutes he had fired 104 rounds. Then, having done his worst, he turned the gun on himself and blew his brains out with round 105.

Meanwhile Agnes Awlson, the assistant head teacher, had been taking her primary-seven class to an art room when she heard 'sharp, metallic noises' accompanied by faint screams. She raced to the gym but stopped short when she saw cartridges outside the door: 'I realised something dreadful was happening,' she later recalled. She made for the office of head teacher, Ron Taylor, crouching in terror, afraid that the gunman was behind her. Taylor had also heard bangs but they were indistinct and he assumed they had been made by builders. He was on the phone but broke off his call when he saw that Mrs Awlson was very agitated. She told him, 'There is a man in the school with a gun,' and advised him 'to get down'. The head immediately dialled 999.

At 9.38 a.m. Taylor gave emergency services a chilling message: 'A man with a gun is running amok in Dunblane primary school.' He then rushed to the gym where a scene of 'unimaginable carnage' was revealed. There were sixteen dead children on the floor – most with terrible head injuries – along with another twelve who had suffered gunshot wounds. Three other teachers had also been hit in the course of Hamilton's rampage, but survived. Apart from the blood-spattered walls and floor the room was 'thick with blue smoke and cordite'. The headmaster spotted Hamilton's body with a gun beside it and another in his hand. 'He seemed to be moving. I asked Mr Currie, the janitor, to kick the gun away. A voice behind us shouted, "Leave the gun alone". I became aware that an off-duty policeman had arrived.'

Another teacher who was also quickly on the scene helped to identify the dead and injured children. She was nursery teacher Elaine Isle who knew the children well, as she had taught them the year before. It must have taken incredible courage – not least because her 5-year-old son Jack was a pupil at the school. For an awful moment she feared that he might be among the piles of dead bodies. Thankfully for her he had gone missing amid the confusion and turned up later safe and sound.

Even for paramedics, used to the aftermath of accidents, it was hard to take. John McEwan, who co-ordinated the ambulance teams, said the gym was 'like a medieval torture chamber'. Such was the enormity of what had taken place that ambulance personnel were not ordered to take the bodies out; their senior officers thought it appropriate to ask for volunteers. For the first time in his career McEwan was tempted to act in an unprofessional way: 'I saw him [Hamilton] lying there with his head blown off and a handgun by his side. I had this overwhelming desire to mutilate that corpse – I know that sounds terrible. I had to really force myself not to kick him as I walked by.'

By any standards it was a massacre, and one rendered more poignant by the age of those killed. The world's media converged on Dunblane, a small, affluent, respectable town in Perthshire popular with commuters who work in Glasgow or Edinburgh; the last place one would expect gun crime. Reporters and cameramen mingled with two hundred anxious parents and relatives waiting desperately for news of their children. Thanks to the bravery of Elaine Isle the identification process was completed quickly (although some families were unhappy about the length of time it took police to confirm what had happened to their loved ones). Many parents were then faced with the awful task of being taken to the school to identify their children.

And then, when the initial shock had subsided, and the funerals had taken place, people began to ask questions. Very pertinent questions. Why had 43-year-old Hamilton acted as he did? Could the deaths of sixteen schoolchildren and their teacher have been prevented? What did the authorities know about the killer and his background? What could be done to stop it happening again? In the months after the tragic events of 13 March 1996 some very disturbing answers began to emerge.

Thomas Hamilton, like many criminals, came from a dysfunctional family. His mother, Agnes Watt, had a very unusual upbringing; she was born illegitimate in 1931 and was given away by her mother to her late husband's brother – James Hamilton – and his wife who legally adopted her. At the age of nineteen Agnes met bus driver Thomas Watt and they married in Bridgeton, Glasgow in 1950. But Watt left Agnes for another woman before their son, Thomas, was born in 1952. Agnes was distraught and moved back in with her adoptive parents, who then took the unusual step of adopting her son Thomas. So, as he was growing up, Thomas Hamilton treated his grandparents as his father and mother; he regarded Agnes not as his mother, but as a sister. The family then moved from Glasgow to Stirling, where Agnes found work in local hotels. Eventually Thomas was told the truth about his origins; no one can say for certain what effect this had on an impressionable mind, but it was certainly a highly unorthodox background.

As an adult Thomas Hamilton was outwardly respectable. He was politely spoken, owned his own business (a DIY store in Stirling) and, despite a reputation as a loner, got involved in a range of voluntary activities in the community. A confirmed bachelor, he was a dutiful son to the woman he now knew was his real mother, visiting her twice a week and phoning every night to make sure she was all right. Many who knew him said he appeared plausible and came across as capable and intelligent. But he had two passions in life, passions that would drive him to the edge and beyond: a lust for young boys and an obsessive interest in guns.

In the early 1970s, now in his twenties, he was a member of the Scout Association, taking boys on weekend trips to Aviemore and other locations. But, in 1974, he blotted his copybook by sleeping with eight young Scouts in the back of a van instead of taking them to a hostel for the night. He later tried to cover up his actions by claiming that he had taken them to a hostel; a deliberate lie. Although there were no allegations of a sexual nature the Scout Association felt that it could no longer trust him and he was expelled from the movement. Hamilton bitterly resented the expulsion and spent years trying to have the decision overturned, but to no avail. It was the first in a long line of grievances Hamilton was to harbour against society.

It was around this time that his true sexual tendencies came to the fore, and he was soon attracting the attention of both the police and social workers. He was at his most depraved during the residential summer camps he ran on Inchmurrin, an island on Loch Lomond. The camps took up to seventy boys aged between eight and eleven. It seems that in setting up the camps Hamilton had been inspired by the movie *Lord of the Flies* – based on a novel by William Golding – in which a group of pre-pubescent boys are marooned on a desert island without any adults to supervise them. The only difference was that the Loch Lomond camps had an adult to write the rules: Thomas Hamilton.

At the start of the holiday, which lasted up to three weeks, boys were expected to hand over their clothes and dress in skimpy, black, wet-look swim trunks. The trunks Hamilton supplied were deliberately on the baggy side so that they would fall down. One of his favourite pastimes was to make videos of the scantily clad boys, which he would then watch at his leisure at home in the winter months. If a boy 'stepped out of line' he would take them to a 'punishment' tent where he made them rub baby oil into his private parts. One mother, whose 10-year-old son attended the camps, explained what happened in the punishment tent and elsewhere:

> He'd pick up a couple of boys to do it every night. The kids spoke of him moaning, and wriggling about making funny noises. The boys were dressed in baggy trunks issued by Hamilton. As they ran around the trunks would slip down, and their wee bums would be exposed to him.
>
> Hamilton kept going on about the kids needing proper discipline, and saying this generation was ruined. He went on and on like a maniac. He would pull the boys' pants down and smack them with a hairbrush. He went on about them turning into scum, thugs and vandals unless they were disciplined.
>
> The camp looked like a prison. There were no toilets. The boys would have to go into the woods and I'm sure he spied on them.

It is thought that Hamilton ran around sixty such camps over a period of twenty years, giving him almost limitless opportunities to abuse the boys in his charge. Although he banned visits to the camps by parents, and did not allow boys to phone home, the truth filtered out. There were then, inevitably, complaints from parents about the goings-on at the camps, and three Scottish police forces launched investigations into his conduct in the late 1980s. However, no charges were ever proffered. It was the first in what would become a long line of failures by officialdom in dealings with Thomas Hamilton.

He also ran many boys' clubs in the towns and villages of central Scotland and hundreds of boys attended over the years; one was in Dunblane, and was held in the gymnasium where he would later perpetrate his atrocity. Again there were complaints from parents about his behaviour. One worried father remembered that he made his 7-year-old son do vaulting exercises wearing only swimming trunks; while a concerned mother told how Hamilton would take topless pictures of her little boy.

Following further incidents a number of independent witnesses – most holding down responsible jobs – approached the police. One woman, Shona McKay, a former prison officer, caught Hamilton with an 8-year-old boy in a locked gym in Denny, Stirlingshire after bursting in through the fire exit with other worried mothers. The boy, wearing only skimpy black trunks, was doing press-ups while Hamilton, just three feet away, took photographs of him. Although police wanted to prosecute, and considered McKay a highly credible witness, the Crown Office refused to act.

Hamilton's passion for firearms was every bit as pronounced as his desire for young boys. He had a fearsome arsenal of weapons and ammunition at his flat in Kent Road, Stirling. It included six handguns, four rifles and a Kalashnikov assault rifle. Although he was a member of various gun clubs this went way beyond a hobby; it was an obsession and a very dangerous one. And he liked nothing better than to boast about his collection and even to show it off. He also got a particular thrill from allowing the boys who attended his clubs to fire the guns.

On one occasion his twin obsessions came together in a very sinister way. It happened when he heard that a worried mother – Doreen Hagger of Linlithgow, Midlothian – was going to report him for his perverted activities at the Loch Lomond summer camp. Hamilton turned up at her door and said he had a way of dealing with people who told nasty stories about him. He pulled out a gun, held it to Mrs Hagger's head and threatened to blow her away. Fortunately she did not panic and told him to 'fuck off or I will ram the gun down your throat'. Doreen Hagger reported the incident to the police but once again nothing was done. Police rather lamely informed her that Hamilton had a licence authorising him to keep guns.

However, the most shocking example of official incompetence was the repeated renewal of his firearms certificate by senior police officers. Hamilton had, after all, carried out his killing spree with legally held weapons. This was despite the litany of complaints about the abuse of children and his highly irresponsible behaviour with the guns. One relatively junior officer, detective sergeant Paul Hughes, even wrote to his superiors in 1991 – five years before the massacre – outlining his misgivings about Hamilton's character. In an excellent, perceptive report Hughes outlined how Hamilton had been investigated on many occasions by police and noted that, 'Hamilton is an unsavoury character and unstable personality . . . a scheming, devious and deceitful individual who is not to be trusted.' Hughes recommended that Hamilton should not only be prosecuted for child abuse but also that his firearms licence should be revoked. However, the recommendations were not acted on by Douglas McMurdo, the deputy chief constable of Central Scotland police. Hamilton was then granted another licence, signed by no less a personage than the chief constable, William Wilson.

The question must be asked: why did the authorities not recognise the signals Thomas Hamilton was sending out and act accordingly? An important reason was that Hamilton knew his rights and was not afraid to exercise them. On one occasion he was denied the use of Dunblane primary school as a base for his club by Central Regional Council because of allegations about his conduct towards boys. He made an official complaint to the local-government ombudsman, who ruled in his favour. Another time, when he was being investigated about sex-abuse allegations, he wrote furious letters to the chief constable, his local MP and the Scottish Office; the result was that police were instructed to back off.

More sinister, and as yet unfounded, allegations emerged. One concerned the scale of his homosexual activities. He had been warned by police on at least one occasion about his activities in well-known gay haunts, and neighbours noticed that he entertained many male visitors at his flat in Stirling. One woman recalled: 'Most callers were in their thirties. They were all smartly dressed and drove posh cars. I never saw a woman. The men would often stay for a couple of hours or more. I don't know what they got up to.' Could it have been that some of his visitors were policemen, or people with even more influence, such as politicians? And that they were having gay sex with Hamilton? Perhaps he evaded prosecution simply because of who, and what, he knew.

There was a public enquiry into the Dunblane massacre. It was headed by a senior judge, Lord Cullen, and his report was highly critical of the decisions taken by Central Scotland police consistently to renew Hamilton's firearms licence. Among Cullen's other recommendations were that the ownership of guns should be restricted and that school security should be tightened up. These seemed to be appropriate and proportionate in the wake of a tragedy unlike any other in peacetime Scotland. Indeed, the Labour government elected in 1997 went further than Cullen had proposed; it banned handguns completely in November 1997, even for sporting use. The ban came about largely as a result of the efforts of the Dunblane parents themselves, who had formed the Snowdrop Campaign to lobby politicians for such an outcome.

But many – including some of the bereaved parents of Dunblane – felt that the Cullen report was an exercise in damage limitation. Some speculated that Hamilton (like his grandfather, the man who had raised him) was a mason and that he was being protected by senior figures in freemasonry. Indeed Lord Burton, a former grand master of the Grand Lodge of Scotland, said that Lord Cullen's report was a massive cover-up to protect leading members of the Scottish establishment.

Others raised the issue of Hamilton's sexual abuse of pupils at Queen Victoria school, an establishment located near Dunblane that caters for the children of personnel serving in the armed forces. The Cullen inquiry failed to investigate why Hamilton was allowed to roam round the school whenever he liked, even venturing into the dormitories at night. The school has close links to the Scottish establishment and senior government figures are represented on its board. A former housemaster at the school, Glenn Harrison, believes that Hamilton was a personal friend of a senior policeman. Perhaps that was why Harrison's complaints about Hamilton's behaviour were, like those of so many others, ignored.

There is also the question of the report compiled by detective sergeant Hughes. After being used in the Cullen inquiry it was deemed top secret and ordered to be sealed for 100 years. This caused intense speculation and it was thought by some that the report names a number of top people Hamilton had links with: a senior politician who gave him a reference; a leading lawyer who helped him to get a gun licence; the police officers he was friendly with. In October 2005 political pressure forced part of the report to be made public, although suspicion remains that embarrassing details about Hamilton's connections with people in high places have been withheld. Given the secretive nature of Scottish society we may never know the truth about why Thomas Hamilton was able not only to roam the towns of central Scotland abusing innocent children but also to build up an arsenal of weapons that would not have been out of place in a 'Dirty Harry' movie.

And what of Hamilton's motives? Until that fateful day in March 1996 he had displayed no violent tendencies. He was a non-smoking teetotaller who did not use drugs. He had no criminal convictions despite the litany of complaints about his behaviour towards minors. Nor did he have a mental illness; two leading psychiatrists confirmed this to the Cullen inquiry, concluding only that he had certain personality disorders, in particular a need for control over others and paranoid tendencies.

The fact of the matter is that Hamilton seems to have acted as he did because of deep-seated grievances towards those he believed were portraying him as deviant. They included the Scout Association, the police, local councils and, crucially, teachers at Dunblane primary school. These grievances seemed to gnaw away at him and became the main driving force in an otherwise empty life. This becomes clear in a series of letters he wrote to the then secretary of state for Scotland, Michael Forsyth, from 1992 onwards. In one letter – written on 26 January 1996, only six weeks before the massacre – he complains bitterly: 'At Dunblane primary school, where teachers have contaminated all the older boys with this poison, even former cleaners and dinner ladies have been told by teachers at school that I am a pervert.' Hamilton also wrote to the parents of boys who attended his clubs railing furiously against those who painted him as a pervert.

The Dunblane massacre was carried out by an evil, uncaring man who was intent on revenge towards those he believed had wronged him.

27. James Harkins

The butcher of Gartnavel

Would the sight of your fiancée being murdered drive you out of your mind? In 1969, James Harkins, originally from the Gorbals, became engaged to a girl in Perth, Western Australia where he had emigrated with his parents. But the girl's father had developed an intense dislike of 19-year-old Harkins and wanted her to have nothing to do with him. During one bitter row something snapped, and the man picked up a knife, viciously stabbing his daughter. Harkins was in the room when it happened, but could do nothing to save her. Harkins may have been mentally suspect before the tragic events, but the death of his future bride drove him over the edge. Just days after his fiancée's father was handed a life sentence, Harkins poured paraffin over his clothes and set himself alight. Incredibly, in spite of severe burns which required plastic surgery, he survived his suicide bid and shortly after moved back to Scotland.

On the surface, Harkins appeared to have got back on an even keel. A year after the traumatic events in Australia, he met and married in Glasgow, Marie Craig, and enrolled to train as a psychiatric nurse. But by 1973 Marie had divorced him, on the grounds of adultery after he met up and moved in with Joyce Flynn. In 1975 the couple had a child, christened James, but known to his parents as 'Little Jim'. A year later the couple married. While Harkins moved from psychiatric nursing to working as a mortuary technician at Glasgow Royal Infirmary, Joyce took up a job in the records office at Gartnavel hospital.

In 1979 Harkins, still employed at Glasgow Royal Infirmary, was promoted to senior mortuary technician, but away from work his life was on a downward spiral. His relationship with Joyce was at breaking point. He had assaulted her on a number of occasions. After Harkins told Joyce several times to 'get out', she eventually left on 4 January 1980 taking Little Jim, and moving in with her parents in Balloch, on the shores of Loch Lomond. At the same time Joyce made it clear to Harkins that she was going to divorce him.

On 7 January, three days after his wife's departure, Harkins visited Gartnavel hospital where Joyce still worked in the records office. Little Jim attended the hospital nursery close by. After a violent struggle, Harkins snatched the child and took him back to his house at 22 Cally Avenue, Drumchapel. He then rang Joyce and threatened that if she didn't come back he would kill Little Jim and take his own life. Later that day, Harkins was arrested and, after appearing at Glasgow Sheriff Court on 8 January, charged with attempting to strangle his son. He was sent to

Woodilee hospital in Lenzie so that the state of his mental health could be properly assessed. A disturbing conclusion was reached. The police doctor's report said of Harkins: 'this man is psychotic and is insane and unfit to plead.' Harkins was clearly regarded as unstable and documents recorded that he was a 'special-risk prisoner with suicidal tendencies and an extremely violent nature'. In fact, he did make a half-hearted attempt to kill himself with a razor blade and went on hunger strike, all in a vain attempt to get Joyce and Little Jim back. Though they may have been little more than cries for help, they did indicate that Harkins's mind was in a severely disturbed state. As the Sheriff Court had realised when it refused Harkins bail and ordered him to be detained in Woodilee.

But for reasons never fully explained the hospital authorities did not place Harkins in a secure ward. Instead, he was allowed the freedom to wander unsupervised in the hospital's extensive grounds. It was true that he did not have permission to leave the hospital without prior agreement, but there was no security in place to prevent it. On 5 February, Harkins simply walked out, travelling to Glasgow Royal Infirmary where he picked up his back pay of £125, explaining that he had been granted a pass out for the day. At lunchtime he joined work colleagues in the pub, chatting and enjoying a few drinks. Afterwards, he returned to the infirmary where he managed to steal a knife-length scalpel from a locked cabinet in the mortuary. It was not till several hours later, around nine, that the authorities at Woodilee informed the police that Harkins had disappeared. By then it was too late.

Harkins had hatched a chilling plan. One that would have served as the plot of a horror film. He later confessed that he planned to force his wife, son and brother-in-law to go with him to a secluded spot. The first to die would be his brother-in-law, 18-year-old Peter Flynn, whom he detested. He then planned to kill Little Jim, in front of Joyce. She would be the last to die, slowly tortured to death. Events, however, did not go according to plan.

Around 4 p.m., Harkins hailed a taxi which took him to Gartnavel hospital. Having paid the fare, he sheltered among trees opposite the nursery. He was seen by several witnesses, but no one suspected, or could have suspected, what Harkins had in mind. Harkins had earlier checked to make sure his son was at nursery that day, having phoned pretending to be a social worker asking after Little Jim.

At 5 p.m. Peter Flynn arrived by car to pick up his sister, Joyce, and nephew, Little Jim. At this moment, Harkins came out of the trees and grabbed his son. He brandished the stolen scalpel and dragged the boy back into the nursery where he discovered his wife standing in the nursery office. Without saying a word to Joyce he stabbed her several times. Little

Jim was thrown to the floor and slashed repeatedly by Harkins who then turned on his wife and cut her again. As Peter Flynn burst in he too was stabbed. Forensic examination would later show that Joyce and her son had received more than twenty-five wounds each.

Although he would later claim that he was insane when he carried out the murders, at the time Harkins had the self-control to jump into Peter Flynn's Volvo to escape from the scene. He drove to the house of Ray Murray, a friend, at Lochiel Road in the Arden district of Glasgow. Ray Murray arrived home at 6.30 p.m., surprised to discover Harkins sitting in his living room chatting to his wife Moira. Thirty-year-old Ray later recalled, 'I thought Jim must have been released from Woodilee and was amazed to see him. He was in pain and showed me his hand. There were horrible cuts on his fingers to the bone.' Harkins claimed that he had fallen on broken glass, but Ray Murray did not believe him, convinced that Harkins had been in a fight. Eventually Harkins admitted, 'It's worse than that. I have done in my wife, kid and brother-in-law.' He then pulled open his jacket and revealed the bloodstained scalpel hidden in the lining.

Ray's nightmare continued when Harkins insisted that they go out for a drink. They got into Peter Flynn's stolen Volvo, which was parked outside. Harkins again revealed the murder knife and when Ray asked him to throw it away, refused, saying, 'No way. This is my passport out. If any police come near me, I'll use it on them and then myself.' The bizarre evening continued with a drive to Victoria Infirmary, where Harkins abandoned the Volvo, then took a bus to the Thornlie Arms Hotel. Here, using cash from his pay, Harkins bought a round of drinks and confessed to more of the day's events. He claimed, 'It wasn't meant to happen the way that it did. I wanted to get my wife, son and brother-in-law into the car. I was going to use the string I'd taken from the mortuary to tie her in the back seat with Little Jim. I was going to hold the knife to Peter and force him to drive to the country. Then I was going to kill him in front of Joyce. Kill my son in front of her and then slowly torture her to death.' But that wasn't the end. Afterwards he planned to drive to Balloch to murder Joyce's parents.

But, as Harkins explained to Ray, in the heat of the moment it all went wrong. He grabbed Little Jim, but when Joyce tried to defend him he slashed her across the breasts and then 'hacked the little boy five or six times'. When Peter Flynn burst in, Harkins shouted, 'You are getting it you bastard', and stabbed him to death. Harkins then went round each body plunging the knife into the heart to make sure they were dead. That was how he had injured himself as his hand slipped on the blood-soaked weapon and cut through his fingers. Ray Murray would remember with disgust that 'there wasn't a hint of remorse in his voice. He just kept repeating how he didn't like the look on Joyce's face as she died with her eyes rolling.'

But justice was about to catch up with Harkins. By the time he and Ray returned to Lochiel Road, police had surrounded the house. Ray slipped out to get help on the pretext of contacting a friend, but to his dismay the police would not let him return to the house. Moira and the couple's three young children were on their own facing a self-confessed murderer. It must have been a chilling experience to hear Harkins's explanation of why he had killed his wife and son. Moira recalled, 'He said his wife was going to divorce him and eventually she would meet some-one else who would become a father to Little Jim.' He added, 'I wasn't going to have that. If I'm not going to get him nobody else is.' Moira's ordeal lasted till the early hours of the morning when police burst in and seized Harkins who, in spite of his boasts to Ray, offered little resistance.

At his trial, the Harkins defence was one of insanity. His lawyer claimed that Harkins had, in fact, gone to Gartnavel with the intention of killing himself in front of his wife. However, when he found her his self-control snapped. His defence argued that, 'whatever psychiatrists think of this man's condition, there is no doubt that looking at the extent of the injuries inflicted in what must have been a very short time there were certainly indi-cations of a frenzied loss of control. A minute or so of madness.'

But it was not an argument that convinced the court. Harkins was judged to have a gross personality disorder, but was considered sane and fit to plead. There could be little doubt about the outcome. The facts were beyond dispute. On 8 April 1980, Harkins was gaoled for life for the murder of his wife Joyce (25), son James (4) and brother-in-law Peter Flynn (18). Lord Weir told him: 'It may be that you will never be released to be a danger to the public. A life sentence in your case is liable to mean just that.'

In February 1996 Harkins caused fresh controversy and heartache when he was allowed out of Edinburgh's Saughton prison to marry Sandra Randall, his third wife. In a bizarre twist for the 'Butcher of Gartnavel', as the media had christened him, the wedding ceremony took place in a hospital chapel in Edinburgh Royal Infirmary. Hugh Flynn, father of Harkins's victims Peter and Joyce, commented, 'I find this amazing. He is totally evil and should never be released.'

28. Christopher Hutcheson

Psycho Number One

Christopher Hutcheson was a small-time gangster with delusions of grandeur. Inspired by films like *Goodfellas*, *Scarface* and *Gangster Number One* he wanted to become the 'Godfather' of Glasgow. He was flash, cocky and loved the trappings that his ill-gotten gains could buy: attractive women, designer suits, expensive holidays and big cars. As one former associate explained, 'Hutch liked to surround himself with good-looking young women, preferably blonde, and he could turn on the charm when he wanted to. He lived life the way he thought a gangster should and that meant the glamorous blondes, holidays and cars. But they all dumped him when they realised what a monster he was.' Despite his pretensions the reality is that the 23-year-old was – in criminal terms – a nobody who made a living by pushing £10 bags of heroin to pathetic junkies. But he craved recognition, and told friends, 'I will make the front page. I will do something that will go down in history.' Sadly for his victims he would do just that.

Hutcheson worked hard to keep his customers in line. He had a multi-gym in his flat in Glasgow's Govan district and he pumped iron every day to enhance his massive physique. Recognising that psychology was important in his line of work he practised the chilling stare used by the lead character in *Gangster Number One* and, like his fictional counterpart, would carry a small machete to make his threats more credible. Hutcheson even had his own gang of street punks and dealers who would willingly carry out his orders; men like his closest associate, 19-year-old Andrew Ferguson.

The punishment inflicted on bad payers was instantaneous and ruthless. When his customers crossed him he left them in no doubt about his intentions: 'I'll hang you like a rabbit' he would sometimes tell them, or in the words of his favourite warning, 'I am gonnae murder you'. When threats did not have the desired effect Hutcheson upped the ante. Beatings were routinely administered to defaulters but often he would go much further. One debtor recalled how Hutcheson had pulled out a crossbow from under his coat and fired a bolt into his thigh. In another incident Hutcheson knocked at a neighbour's door and asked for a rope; he had been torturing victim Blair McCallum for hours and decided to finish the job by hanging him. Fortunately the hapless McCallum escaped with his life.

Having gone so far in his campaign of violence and intimidation Hutcheson was ready to take the next step and commit the ultimate crime: murder. His victim was John Mitchell, a small-time drug dealer and heroin user, who depended on the would-be 'Glasgow Godfather' for supplies and ended up in his debt. In July 2001 he was summoned to Hutcheson's flat after failing to repay £350. Angered at Mitchell's lack of funds Hutcheson viciously stabbed him in the leg and gloated that he had pierced an artery. Two months later – and still indebted despite begging for money on the streets of Glasgow – Mitchell was subjected to ten hours of the cruellest torture imaginable. He was handcuffed and locked in a bathroom Hutcheson called his dungeon. Like the famous scene at the end of the movie *Braveheart*, where William Wallace is shown the instruments he is to be tortured with before being put to death, Hutcheson had neatly laid out an array of tools: it included a rope, hammer, gun, knife and metal dumb-bells. We can only imagine the terror Mitchell must have experienced at the thought of what lay ahead.

Wearing his rubber 'torture gloves' Hutcheson subjected the man he called 'John the beggar' to ten hours of extreme pain and suffering. The poor man was punched, choked by a rope, had his fingers pulverised by the metal dumb-bell and, in a sickening finale, had a kettle of boiling water thrown on his raw and bloodied hands. As one detective said later this had no logic to it; it was simply violence for the sake of violence. Having come so far Hutcheson decided to finish the job. Two days' later he bundled his victim into a car, drove him to a bridge over Halls Burn near Strathaven and pushed him into the water fifty feet below. He later told an acquaintance of his disappointment that Mitchell had not shouted 'aargh' as he fell to his death.

Given John Mitchell's drug habit and chaotic lifestyle, police put his death down to a tragic accident. Christopher Hutcheson was elated and boasted to friends that he had 'got away with it'. Drug dealing, extortion, abduction, assault and now murder. He had perpetrated them all, and with impunity, helped by the fear he inspired in those around him. Perhaps he was, like the fictional Godfather, above the law. And it may have been this confidence that drove him to commit a crime that was to shock the nation.

Daniel Hutcheson (19), a former soldier who had served in Northern Ireland and Bosnia, was Christopher Hutcheson's cousin. Although his loving family had high hopes for him he had drifted into petty crime and drugs after being discharged from the army for smoking cannabis. He was, like John Mitchell, one of Christopher Hutcheson's team of dealers and like Mitchell had become indebted to him. When he was unable to pay he was summoned to Hutcheson's flat where he was told by his cousin that 'he had bitten the hand that fed him'. Daniel was told by his tormentor: 'I'll give you a choice. I'll either cut your hand off or I'm going to murder you.' When Daniel burst into tears Hutcheson snapped and told him, 'Fuck it. In fact I'm going to murder you.'

Watched by his henchman, Andrew Ferguson, he forced Daniel to kneel down, put a rope around his neck and began to garrotte him. Ferguson noticed that Daniel was clawing at the ligature, that his tongue was hanging out and that blood was streaming from his eyes and nose. Hutcheson loosened the rope and Daniel took a deep breath, but the process was repeated. Accounts about what happened next vary. Ferguson claimed that Daniel died from the garrotting. However a witness at their subsequent trial, Amanda Bain, testified that it was Ferguson, not Hutcheson, who wanted to go further and to kill him: 'Daniel was still alive and Andrew drowned him' she later said. Whatever the truth, Hutcheson and Ferguson, apparently without a care in the world, went out clubbing that night with pals.

But the duo still had a problem: how to get rid of a body. Hutcheson may well have remembered the scene from *Scarface* – starring Al Pacino, in which a corpse was dismembered with a chainsaw – because he ordered Ferguson to cut up Daniel's body with a hacksaw. As Ferguson later testified, 'It just seemed to take forever. Chris showed me where to cut his arms and legs then told me just to cut his head off.' But Hutcheson was having the time of his life. He later boasted that he had played football with Daniel's head and gouged one of the eyes out with a spoon. He had even invited friends to come and gawp at Daniel's body in the bath; one described how he heard banging and a ripping noise and then saw Daniel's body minus its legs, arms and head.

Over the next few days Hutcheson and Ferguson set about the task of disposing of the body parts. They wrapped up the torso and threw it in the river Clyde. And showing once again his contempt for human life, and a complete indifference to the forces of law and order, Hutcheson spent the next five days coolly drinking beer, listening to music and burning Daniel's limbs in an oil drum in his back garden before throwing the remains into a skip. As one lawyer said at his trial, it 'must have been Scotland's most terrible barbecue for years.' It was also said by another witness that Hutcheson had told her he cut out Daniel's tattoos with a craft knife to make identification more difficult. He bragged openly about his misdeeds, threatening to do a 'Daniel' on anyone who got in his way.

But the decision to throw body parts into the river was their downfall. Two men out hunting rabbits spotted a parcel on the shoreline; it contained Daniel's torso. A police investigation linked this murder and the death of John Mitchell and, when Andrew Ferguson confessed while being interrogated, the writing was on the wall. A jury of eight men and seven women at Glasgow's High Court in April 2003 found both Christopher Hutcheson and Andrew Ferguson guilty of murder and of a string of other offences. Both were given life sentences, the former to serve at least twenty-five years and the latter a minimum of seventeen years.

Hutcheson, callous to the last, stood with his hands in his pockets and then raised his hands above his head and clapped. The families of both victims cheered as the two murderers were led away to start their sentences. Lorraine Hutcheson, the mother of Daniel, was particularly emotional and she thrust a photograph of her son into their faces: 'I took Daniel's photo so it would be the last thing those monsters saw before starting their sentences' she explained.

29. Veronica Little

The wife, her toyboy and her teenage lesbian lover

Dumfries – a sleepy, prosperous town in the rural south-west of Scotland – has very few murders. Let alone murders that involve the contract killing of a violent, rapist husband by the wife's toyboy lover, and a teenage girl who was the lover of both husband and wife. So it is hardly surprising that, in March 1982, this cold-blooded killing shocked not only Dumfries but also the whole nation.

Veronica Little, an attractive brunette, quickly came to rue the day she married smooth-talking car dealer David Little in 1976. His pleasant demeanour and easy charm hid a violent and unpredictable streak that could erupt at any time. Little had been married before – to Sylvia McEwan, the girl next door – and the couple had a son. But only three years into the marriage, in 1970, he was in serious trouble. He stalked a young woman who was walking to her home on the outskirts of the small Dumfries-shire town of Annan, and leapt on her from behind a bush. Little forced his victim to undress and brutally raped her. It was discovered at his trial that he had a long history of psychiatric problems and he was ordered to be detained without limit of time in the state mental hospital at Carstairs. Many who came into contact with him thought that he should never have been released.

But, in 1974, he was allowed out under supervision and by 1977 – when he had met and married Veronica – the supervision order was lifted. The couple set up home in Cairn Circle, a quiet street in a Dumfries council estate. But life was far from peaceful for Veronica Little: her husband beat her up regularly, breaking her nose and jaw and leaving her a partial cripple; he raped her when she came home from hospital after a miscarriage; and he threatened to kill their daughter, Samantha, a threat that drove his wife to take an overdose of sleeping tablets.

But it was the presence of pretty 17-year-old Elaine Haggarty in the marriage, and the bizarre sex triangle that ensued, which was the catalyst for murder. Haggarty was a near neighbour of the Littles and, to earn a bit of pocket money, she would babysit 4-year-old Samantha. She grew close to the couple and went out drinking with them both to local pubs. But then her relationship with 34-year-old David Little deepened and, leaving Veronica at home, they regularly visited bars where Haggarty drank brandy and played fruit machines endlessly. Soon they were having a torrid affair and Haggarty fell pregnant, but later lost the baby.

David Little's cruelty was not confined to mistreatment of his wife. In a childish code in her secret diary, Haggarty recorded not only their torrid sex sessions but also how her older lover abused her: in his own bed; after she had been at church; on the bathroom floor. He had also threatened to kill her on several occasions. Despite the abuse she continued to see him; she had become, in effect, his sex slave. But Little underestimated the extent to which his cruelty was turning the women in his life against him. And he could not possibly have foreseen two developments that spelled the beginning of the end for him: his wife and Elaine Haggarty had become lovers; and Veronica was also having an affair with an impressionable teenage boy, William McKenzie.

McKenzie – a quiet 18-year-old, said to be a bit of a dreamer – had been brought up on a farm and had only recently moved to Dumfries where he was a close neighbour of the Little family. While he was living in the countryside he had learned how to use a gun to shoot rabbits and his expertise with weapons had been developed by service in the Territorial Army. He was the owner of a .22 rifle and he fancied himself as a crack shot. There is no doubt that he was flattered by the attentions of an attractive older woman and would have been keen to ensure that their sex sessions continued. So, when Veronica Little and Elaine Haggarty offered him £120 to kill David Little, he no doubt saw it as an ideal opportunity to earn money to impress his older lover.

In a statement to police, McKenzie described how he had waited for two-and-a-half hours in Elaine Haggarty's garden with his rifle before David Little arrived. He said that he shot him once as he walked across the garden and, when Little got up, he pumped two more bullets into him. Then, when his victim went down for a second time, McKenzie said, 'I walked up to him and shot him again in the head.' He then told police that, with the help of Veronica Little and Haggarty, he bundled the body into a wheelbarrow, put it in David Little's car and drove to a lay-by near Irongray church a few miles from Dumfries where they hid the body.

Veronica Little, Elaine Haggarty and McKenzie were charged with the murder of David Little. When the case came before the High Court in Dumfries, McKenzie changed his story and said that Veronica Little had shot her husband after she borrowed his gun. Little and Haggarty denied murder and also denied paying McKenzie £120 to murder David Little. But, in addition to McKenzie's damning statement to police, the evidence against Little and Haggarty was compelling: it was discovered they had withdrawn money from their building-society accounts on the day of the murder, money that McKenzie had later paid into his account; letters were produced in court in which Little said she prayed for her husband's death; and of course both Little and Haggarty had clear motives for murdering David Little, a man who had brutalised them both.

After a week of hearing the evidence, the jury of nine women and six men took only one hour and thirty-eight minutes to find Little, Haggarty and McKenzie guilty of murder. In front of a packed courtroom, the judge, Lord Allanbridge, ordered all three to be detained for life. It was too much for Veronica Little who shouted and screamed hysterically and had to be carried bodily from the court. Elaine Haggarty, who had been composed throughout the proceedings, wept uncontrollably as she learned her fate. William McKenzie showed no emotion, and seemed calmly to accept his punishment.

30. Peter Manuel

No expression of remorse

Killers are born liars who usually try to play down their own guilt and blame the victim in some way, particularly where a sexual crime is involved. Peter Manuel was true to type. An arrogant individual with no compassion, who saw murder as his way of grabbing the limelight and who seemed ready to confess to almost anything. A man who toyed with his victims and played cruel games with their families.

On Friday, 30 December 1955 sisters Anne and Alice Kneilands attended a dance at East Kilbride town hall. There 17-year-old Anne met a man who she agreed to a date with on the following Monday, the second of January. Around 5 p.m. Anne, wearing a blue-and-red coat, black shoes and stockings and carrying a tan-leather shoulder-bag waved goodbye to her sister and mother as she left her home at the Stables, Calderwood estate, East Kilbride. She had arranged to meet 26-year-old Andrew Murnin, on home leave from the army, at the nearby bus terminus. Mr Murnin did not appear. He had decided to 'stop off' at a friend's house where a party was being held. A fateful decision. A disappointed Anne caught the 6.40 p.m. bus into East Kilbride town centre. The conductress on the bus remembered her as did a number of other witnesses, but then the trail ran cold. Anne did not arrive home that night. Her parents guessed she had stayed over at a friend's. But when she had not returned by Wednesday morning, her father, John Kneilands (46) an engine fitter, notified the police.

It was already too late. On that morning, Wednesday, 4 January 1956, George Gribbon, walking on East Kilbride golf course came across a girl's body, the head split open, lying near the fifth tee. He called the police. First on the scene was inspector William Woods. He noted that the body lay in a hollow in the ground and was only visible from a few yards away. The skull had been badly battered and brain tissue and blood were spattered all around. The detective reported: 'The left stocking, both shoes and part of her underclothing were missing. The clothing was ruffled up as though the body had been pulled along the ground.' This confirmed his suspicion that a deliberate attempt had been made to hide the body. It was soon established that these were the remains of Anne Kneilands, whose route from the bus stop would have taken her close to the golf course. Several items belonging to Anne were missing including a watch, earrings, a belt and a handbag. It was clear that Anne had run in terror from her killer, scrambling over barbed wire in her panic, as muddy footprints and shreds of clothing caught in the fence revealed.

As the hunt for the killer intensified, an unrelated investigation was taking place that would eventually assume a significance that could not have been appreciated at the time. Constable James Jardine from East Kilbride was looking into an alleged theft from a gas-board hut and amongst the workmen he interviewed was 29-year-old Peter Manuel. Jardine noticed that Manuel had scratches on both sides of his face and had not shaved for several days. It was as if he was trying to hide something. Manuel had aroused Jardine's suspicions, but there was nothing that appeared to connect him to the Kneilands murder so, for the moment, Jardine let the matter pass. As did Manuel's workmates who had also remarked on the abrasions on his face after his return to work following the New Year break. 'I asked him', Richard Corrins, the foreman, would later recall, 'where he had got the cuts and he said he had been in a fight.' Another employee voiced the opinion that they were scratches made by fingernails. But like Jardine they made no connection to Anne Kneilands's disappearance and murder. Manuel behaved like a model employee. They had no reason to suspect him. But in due course these facts would help to convict a killer.

Peter Manuel was American by birth, having been born in the New York borough of Manhattan in 1927. His parents, however, were Scottish, having emigrated to the USA in search of a better life. Like many immigrants of the time, they were hit by the advent of the Depression and were forced to return home, bringing 5-year-old Peter with them. Manuel was a talented individual with a high IQ. Teachers spoke in glowing terms of his intelligence. He showed real ability as both an artist and musician. He excelled at games and was highly rated as a promising professional boxer. Employers praised his commitment and work rate. But in spite of all this potential, Manuel had a dark side. He liked easy money and spent his spare time developing his talents as a thief and burglar. He was also a sexual predator who carried out his first recorded assault on a woman when aged only fifteen. Manuel had also served an eight-year sentence for rape. He could become sexually aroused and orgasm simply by terrorising women with threats of violence as yet another rape case in which Manuel had been implicated showed. He was an obvious threat to women though not yet, as Anne Kneilands's body was being removed to the mortuary, a proven killer.

There is no evidence that Manuel had heard of William Watt, a master baker who had developed a chain of baker's shops in the Glasgow area. Manuel had, however, burgled houses close to the street where Watt and his family lived and was known by his associates to be on the lookout for other properties to rob. During the week beginning Monday, 10 September 1956, Mr Watt had left his bungalow at 5 Fennsbank Avenue, High Burnside for a fishing holiday. Occupying the house were his wife Marion (45), and 16-year-old daughter Vivienne. Also present on the night of Sunday, 16 September was Marion's sister, Margaret Brown, who was staying over to keep Marion company during William's absence.

Around 8.45 a.m. on the morning of Monday, 17 September, Helen Collinson, the family's daily help, arrived at the bungalow. Marion Watt was a semi-invalid who spent a lot of time in bed. Helen had worked with the family for several years because of Mrs Watt's health. She knew the family's habits well and was surprised to discover that the curtains had not been opened and that the back door was still locked. She later told a jury at Glasgow High Court:

> This was unusual because Vivienne usually unlocked it before she left the house for college. I thought Vivienne had not gone out that morning and I rapped on the door. When I got no answer I rapped on Vivienne's bedroom window and still got no answer. I didn't want to disturb Mrs Watt and I thought I would try and ease up Vivienne's window. I managed to get it up about three inches. I could see the bed and what I thought was a figure at the foot and half roads up. At the top of the bed all the clothes were turned down.

Just as she was setting off to get help, local postman Peter Collier arrived and managed to open the front door by reaching through a broken glass panel. Exactly as, the police later guessed, the intruder had done. Helen Collinson went inside, just long enough to take in the scene of devastation. She was later to tell the court:

> I went into the house and into Mrs Watt's bedroom. I could see that Mrs Watt and Mrs Brown were both dead. They both seemed to be in the same position. Both faces were turned slightly to the window. One was bleeding from the nose and the other from the mouth. I went into the rear bedroom to look for Vivienne. I saw she was covered up by bedclothes and I saw the pillow was covered in blood.

Forensic expert professor Andrew Allison was later to tell the court, 'The first bedroom where Mrs Watt and Mrs Brown had been shot showed no signs of disturbance. Both women lay side by side, their heads turned towards the window.' They had probably been shot as they slept. But the picture in 16-year-old Vivienne's room was different. Here, professor Allison claimed, 'the killer tried to "arrange" the room to disguise the fact that there had been a struggle'. Vivienne's black pyjama bottoms and yellow-and-black pyjama jacket had been torn off as buttons lying on the floor showed. Bruises to her face and body, which looked like the result of repeated punching, suggested that Vivienne had fought her attacker before being overpowered and shot. In police eyes husband and father William Watt became the chief suspect and he spent several uncomfortable weeks locked in Barlinnie gaol while they investigated the murders.

William Watt, however, was eventually cleared, as he had an alibi supported by witnesses, but the case was no closer to being solved when the killer struck again. On the evening of 28 December 1957, Isabelle Cooke (17) went out to meet her boyfriend who lived in Uddingston, taking her usual shortcut along a footpath connecting Mount Vernon Avenue and Kenmuir Avenue. Somewhere along the route she was attacked. Isabelle was forced into a field and her clothes ripped off. Her attacker then wrapped her bra around her neck and, stuffing her headscarf into her mouth, strangled her. He then robbed her of several items including shoes, a brush, cosmetics and a handbag. The killer, however, did not carry out a sexual assault. When Isabelle's naked body was eventually unearthed from a shallow grave on a Lanarkshire farm, forensic examination confirmed that she was still a virgin. The only marks on her body were bruises on the left side of her cheek and forehead. It looked as if her attacker had punched her on the face before murdering her.

The pace of death now quickened. On New Year's Day, 1958 Manuel broke into a house at 38 Sheepburn Road, Uddingston. There he shot and killed Peter and Doris Smart and their 10-year-old son, Michael Smart. In a confession Manuel later gave he told detectives:

> I left my home about 5.30 a.m. and went down the path to the foot of the brae crossing the road and into Sheepburn Road and broke into the bungalow. I went through the house and took a quantity of banknotes from a wallet I found in a jacket in the front bedroom. I then shot the man in the bed and next the woman. I then went into the next room and shot the boy.

The bodies of the Smart family were not found for another six days. And then purely by chance. A car had been discovered abandoned in the Gorbals district of Glasgow. A check revealed that it was registered to Peter Smart of 38 Sheepburn Road. On 6 January 1958 police sergeant Frank Hogg (40) went to the house on what seemed a purely routine inquiry. He recalled, 'The windows and doors were shut and both doors were locked. The curtains of the two front rooms were drawn back, but those of the two bedrooms, the kitchenette and bathroom were closed.' He then broke into the house. 'In a bedroom I found a man and woman lying in a sleeping position. I went into the smaller bedroom and found a boy in bed there. He was obviously dead. There were no signs of disorder in the room or bedclothes.' It was discovered later that Manuel had returned several times to the house to make something to eat and had even fed the Smarts' pet cat. It revealed the grisly side of the man that lay hidden behind a charming exterior.

On 2 January 1958, the day following the murders, but before the bodies were discovered, constable Robert Smith thumbed down the driver of a grey Austin A30, only yards from the Smart bungalow, and asked for a lift to Glasgow. The driver, a small, neat man with distinctive deep-set brown eyes and swept-back hair, obligingly agreed and chatted affably to the policeman throughout the journey. A fortnight later constable Robert Smith positively identified the man who had given him the lift as Peter Manuel. The car was of the same description as that stolen from the Smarts and later found abandoned in Glasgow.

The net was closing in on Manuel who almost seemed to be goading the police into arresting him. In the aftermath of the murders at 5 Fennsbank Avenue, when William Watt had been arrested, Manuel, incredibly, approached Watt's lawyer, Laurence Dowdall, claiming to know who the real killer was. Dowdall took statements from Manuel and reported their contents to the police. Manuel gave information that only the killer could have known. The police were not at first convinced that Manuel had been involved, but began to take a closer look at him and whether he had any connection to the previous unsolved murders. The identification provided by Robert Smith linked him to the scene of the Smart killings, but the clinching factor was the discovery that money spent by Manuel at a hotel bar had been stolen from the Sheepburn Road bungalow. On 13 January 1958, Manuel was arrested on theft charges, but ever searching for the limelight he soon confessed to his involvement in eight murders.

It was only now that detectives learned how Anne Kneilands had met her fate. Manuel gave his account to police in a manner which sounded as if he was describing an afternoon stroll. He claimed:

On January 1st 1956 I was in East Kilbride about 7 p.m. About 7.30 I was walking towards the Cross when I met a girl. She spoke to me and addressed me as Tommy. I told her my name was not Tommy, but she said she thought she knew me. We got talking and she told me she had to meet someone, but she did not think they were turning up. After a while I asked her if she would like some tea or coffee. We went into a cafe. When we came out she said she was going home and I offered to take her home. She said she lived miles away and I would probably get lost if I saw her home. But I insisted so she said 'All right'. We walked up to Maxwelltown Road. There we went along a curving road. About halfway along this road I pulled her into a field, but she struggled and ran away. I chased her across the field and over a ditch. When I caught up with her I dragged her into a wood. She started screaming. I hit her over the head with a piece of iron I picked up. After I killed her I ran down a country road which brought me out at the General's bridge on the East Kilbride Road. I don't know where I flung the piece of iron. I ran down to High Blantyre and along a road. I went along the road and over a railway, up to where I lived. I got home about 10.15 p.m.

Manuel was charged not only with murder, but also with housebreaking including offences involving properties in Fennsbank Avenue where Marion and Vivienne Watt had been murdered. This was to show that Manuel was skilled at breaking into houses, and used a method of smashing glass panels on a door to gain entry, as had happened at the Watt house. Manuel's trial was held in Glasgow High Court during May 1958. He refused to plead insanity, which might have saved him from the rope, preferring to blame the murders on others, including the unfortunate William Watt. He claimed that his confession was a fabrication, the result of police bullying, and that he had an alibi for every murder.

In the event, Manuel was found guilty of the Watt murders, the Smart murders and the death of Isabelle Cooke. He was cleared of the Anne Kneilands murder, on the instructions of the judge, Lord Cameron, on the grounds that no link had been proved between Manuel and her death. It made no difference to his fate. He was sentenced to death. Manuel had caused a sensation during the trial by becoming the first person in Scottish legal history, facing a murder charge, to sack his lawyer and conduct his own defence. An action born of arrogance or foolishness, or both. It did him no good though it no doubt satisfied his ego. The evidence against him was overwhelming.

Manuel's execution was set for 11 July 1958 at Barlinnie prison. For most of the time he was, as an official report describes it, 'pleasant and bright'. On 20 June his behaviour changed. It was suspected by the authorities that he was feigning madness in order to escape the noose. He started foaming at the mouth, twitching, pouting his lips, jerking his head from side to side and crouching on his bed with his legs crossed. He ignored his mother when she visited him. But psychiatrists were not convinced. They reported, 'there is no good reason to think Manuel is insane and no evidence that he was insane at the time of the murders'.

On the evening before his execution Manuel had returned to his typically cheerful persona, playing cards and chatting affably with the warders. The final note he sent to his family read: 'I feel OK today. I was told it was 9 July. I can remember back to June. I got cracked by an officer called Sutherland he is not here now.' It is hardly the message of a normal person facing imminent death. He was due to hang at 8 a.m. and after having breakfast, and hearing mass, he asked the governor to thank the staff for their kindness. A minute after eight, Manuel was dead. His body was buried in the grounds of Barlinnie prison. He died with no expression of remorse, even for the sleeping 10-year-old child who proved to be his final victim.

31. Stephen Martin

The cowboy builder

Driving from job to job in his Transit van, Stephen Martin was a well-known figure in the small Renfrewshire town of Neilston. The self-employed builder was a hard worker with a reputation in the trade for doing a quality job. His personal life could best be described as happy and contented: the 42-year-old lived with girlfriend Linda Fairnington and her two children. And he had his extended family all around him: his mother, Mary, his four brothers and three sisters all lived minutes away from the house he and Linda shared in Neilston's Manse Road.

But there was something eating at Stephen Martin. It started as a minor business problem. Probably the type of problem that builders face all the time; a client was dissatisfied with his work and had refused to pay him. The client in question was wealthy businessman and landowner, Archie Pollock (43), who lived in a six-bedroom farmhouse four miles from Neilston. Pollock had spent a small fortune renovating the farmhouse. Indeed, such was the extensive nature of the works that he had employed close friend Gordon Wallet, an architect, as his technical adviser and site manager.

Part of the refurbishment involved the construction of a second floor on the house. And when, in late 1999, it was time to do the plaster work and roughcasting, Wallet put the job out to tender. Stephen Martin's original estimate of £4,500 was much cheaper than other firms and, after checking his references, Wallet awarded him the contract. But it soon became clear to both architect and client that Martin was simply not up to the job. Archie Pollock had doubts from day one, as he later explained: 'As soon as he came on the job I knew he was a cowboy.' Their instincts were right; the work was so badly botched that the plaster manufacturer refused to issue the standard twenty-five-year guarantee.

Archie Pollock went through the normal commercial channels: letters were sent to Martin – some by solicitors threatening legal proceedings – demanding that the defective work be put right. Nothing was done and there was no reply to any of the letters. And in the meantime Gordon Wallet advised his friend not to pay the builder's bill, which had now gone up to £6,000. Months passed, but nothing changed; the defective work was not rectified and Stephen Martin was still waiting for a cheque.

By March 2001 it was almost a year since Martin submitted his invoice to Archie Pollock. It must have been preying on his mind. He had spent two months on the work, much of which had been done in the cold Scottish winter. The £6,000 represented a fair chunk of his annual income.

And, after all, he had a family to support. Why would Archie Pollock not pay his bill? The sense of injustice he harboured may well have been overwhelming.

The dam finally burst on 19 March 2001. Martin drove to Archie Pollock's Mossneuk farm at six o'clock in the morning, armed with a meat cleaver and a handgun he had rented from a Glasgow gangster. Jumping from his van he used the cleaver to hack the tyres on the farmer's Land Rover to shreds. When the alarm was raised by his 13-year-old son, Pollock raced from the house to confront Martin. He asked the builder what he was playing at and was told: 'Pay your fucking bills.'

After smashing fifteen windows Martin jumped into his car and drove away very slowly. Pollock, a former policeman, ran after him, with the intention of seeing him off the property. But this was exactly the reaction Martin wanted, as Archie Pollock later explained:

> He was driving really slowly as if he wanted to lure me away from the house. Then he stopped, jumped out of the car and pointed the gun at my head. He fired it at point-blank range. The noise was deafening. I ducked and he fired again, but the bullet jammed.
>
> Then he pulled out a meat cleaver from the car and chased me for about thirty yards. You can imagine I was quite fast on my feet. Then he went back to his car and drove off.

Despite this failed attempt at cold-blooded murder Martin was not finished yet. Not by a long chalk. He raced towards the hamlet of Uplawmoor, no doubt realising that police would have been alerted. In fact such was his speed that he skidded off the narrow farm road and ended up in a ditch. The noise of the crash alerted a van driver refuelling in a nearby petrol station and – completely unaware of what Martin had just done – the Good Samaritan drove up to see if he needed help.

Martin asked for a lift to Neilston Road, Uplawmoor. It was where Gordon Wallet lived. The man who had advised Archie Pollock not to pay his bill. In all innocence the van driver took Martin to Uplawmoor, where he dropped him off. Without further ado, the builder marched up the drive and rang the bell of the Wallet family home. When the door opened, Martin pumped two shots at point-blank range into Mr Wallet's head. The 45-year-old father of two died instantly. Tragically, his wife Margaret saw the whole thing.

By this time a full-scale police operation was in full swing. Roads were closed-off, searches carried out and hundreds of police roamed the quiet villages and surrounding countryside. A team of armed officers swooped on Martin's council house in Neilston, but he was nowhere to be found.

It was a fair bet that with so many relatives in Neilston, Martin would be hiding out in a safe house in the town. And so it proved. After a search lasting fourteen hours police found him in his niece's council flat in Craig Road, which was unoccupied because it was being redecorated. But Stephen Martin had spared them the trouble of making an arrest: he had turned the gun used to kill Gordon Wallet on himself. By the time he was found he had been dead for several hours. In a further gruesome twist the flat was next door to where Martin's brother, Dennis, lived with his wife and family.

Who can say why Stephen Martin acted as he did? He was well liked, so much so that some four hundred people attended his funeral in Neilston cemetery. A neighbour said of him: 'Steve was a nice guy. Never any bother, always do you a turn. The last guy on earth you'd think would kill anybody.' Some put it down to the stress caused by financial problems. One acquaintance said his 'back was up against the wall' as suppliers hounded him for payment. Newspapers compared him to the Michael Douglas character in the movie *Falling Down*, in which a mild-mannered, middle-aged man goes on a shooting spree in Los Angeles as his life comes apart at the seams. In fact, drugs may have been a factor; police found cocaine in Martin's wallet and it was known that he had been hooked for more than a year. He was also a recovering alcoholic, which must have made his inner torment worse.

We shall never know the whole truth. All that we do know is that a respected, hard-working member of the community was brutally murdered, simply for doing his job. As one of his neighbours said, 'Gordon was an absolutely lovely man who brought great joy to us and was a loving father.' And Mr Wallet's advice to his client not to pay for the building work was correct; Archie Pollock had to pay another builder £12,000 to rectify the mess Stephen Martin left behind. But at least he was still around to sign the cheque.

32. Archie McCafferty

They called him 'Mad Dog'

The seventeenth of March 1973 marked a turning point in the life of 23-year-old Archie McCafferty. It was the day that his wife Janice accidentally suffocated their 6-week-old son, Craig. Archie, however, refused to accept that Craig's death had been an unfortunate accident. The event threw him over the edge. An edge that Scots-born McCafferty had lived on for most of his life.

In 1960, when Archie was ten, his family emigrated from Glasgow to Australia. McCafferty later admitted, 'One of the reasons we went overseas was because I had got into trouble and caused my parents a problem.' But the change of scenery did nothing for him. In fact, moving to a new country cemented his bizarre behaviour. By the age of twelve he had already clocked up a long record of offences and served his first spell in a correction home for adolescents. The pattern continued into adulthood. By the time of Craig's death in 1973 McCafferty had served several sentences for burglary and theft. But though he blamed his behaviour on beatings he claimed to have received from his father as a child, McCafferty did not have a reputation as a violent criminal. That was about to undergo a dramatic change. Little Craig's death set him on a downward spiral that would rapidly earn him worldwide notoriety as Australia's 'Mad Dog'. A nickname that became as instantly recognisable as any company trademark.

In his teens McCafferty developed a fascination for the occult and became highly superstitious. As he explained: 'The number seven was totally important to me. It ruled my life. If I combed my hair, I would count seven times. If I struck a match I would count to seven. If I scratched my leg, I would count to seven.' With the death of his son his occult obsession rapidly gained control of his mind. Visiting Craig's tomb at Sydney's Leppington cemetery, McCafferty saw a light shining above the grave and a figure, dark and shadowy, appeared out of the light and spoke to him, asking, 'Dad is that you?' McCafferty was immediately convinced that the voice was that of his dead son, who then promised McCafferty that if he killed seven people he would return from the dead. McCafferty was sure his son had spoken from beyond the grave and that if he followed Craig's instructions and murdered seven, Craig would somehow be reincarnated.

On 24 August as the inquest into his son's death opened, McCafferty drove around the streets of Sydney with his gang looking for a victim. They spotted an easy target in 50-year-old George Anson. A veteran of the second world war, Anson sold newspapers outside the Canterbury Hotel where he was also a regular customer at the bar. Late on that evening as

Anson staggered home McCafferty dragged him into a side street. Drunk and only five-feet tall, Anson was no match for Mad Dog and his gang. Anson's shout of anger to McCafferty, 'Fuck off! You young cunt!' only provoked Mad Dog who completely lost control, kicking Anson repeatedly on his body. As Anson collapsed to the floor Archie heard a voice calling, 'Kill seven. Kill seven'. McCafferty pulled out a flick knife and stabbed his victim seven times in the body and neck.

Leaving Anson dying in the gutter, the gang drove off and stopped on the way at a fast-food outlet. When McCafferty visited the toilet he heard his son talking to him through a mirror above the washbasin, calling to him to go with him. Back at the flat, where the gang, Carol Howes (26), Julie Todd (16), Mick Meredith (17), Dick Whittington (17) and Rick Webster (17), were hiding out McCafferty admitted to his associates, 'I couldn't help myself. I couldn't stop. I can't understand why I did it. Craig's voice told me to kill, kill, kill.'

Three days after the murder of George Anson, McCafferty again visited the grave of his son. As he brooded, Julie Todd and Mick Meredith arrived at the cemetery in the car of 42-year-old Ronald Cox, who they were holding at gunpoint. Cox, a miner who was returning home after his shift, had made the mistake of pulling over to give the two hitchhikers a lift. Cox was forced to lie beside Craig's grave while a gun was pushed against his head. The shadowy figure again emerged from the tomb and urged McCafferty to kill. Cox begged for his life saying that he had seven children. This was the trigger for the superstitious McCafferty to shoot him in the head. As McCafferty drove off the light shone more intensely over Craig's grave with the figure, still visible, laughing out loud.

McCafferty, however, had still not satisfied his son's request 'that seven must die' and so Craig continued to demand more deaths. The morning following the murder of Cox, Julie Todd and Dick Whittington took Evangelos Kollias, a 24-year-old driving instructor, back to the gang's flat at gunpoint. He too had made the mistake of picking up two apparently innocent hitchhikers. Kollias, according to the gang's testimony, fell asleep in the back of the car so Whittington shot him twice in the head then dumped his body. Three of the seven killings had now been carried out, but McCafferty had more victims in his sights. He was convinced that, far from being an accident, his wife, Janice, had murdered little Craig. McCafferty wanted revenge and his plan was to drive to his wife's house and kill everyone he found there. That would bring the tally to six. The seventh was going to be gang member Rick Webster who seemed unsettled by McCafferty's violent behaviour. According to McCafferty, 'I was going to Blacktown to kill three people. I was going to go into the house and just start blasting away until they were all dead. They were very lucky people that the car didn't have enough petrol that night.' The car ran out of fuel on the way.

McCafferty still planned to kill Janice, but decided to murder Rick Webster first. Webster, however, learned that Mad Dog had him next on the list and when he saw Whittington and Meredith in a van outside his workplace he called the police, describing McCafferty's murder spree. Armed officers surrounded the area and arrested McCafferty, who had been hiding inside the van. He put up no resistance and willingly admitted to the murders, even warning police that he would go on killing.

McCafferty went on trial in February 1974. Four days into the trial he coldly informed one of the lawyers defending other members of the gang 'I'd like to cut your head off'. It confirmed McCafferty's reputation as a cold-blooded killer. It was understandable that the authorities prescribed Mad Dog powerful sedatives to keep him calm. During the trial the press labelled him 'Australia's Charles Manson'. Like Manson, psychiatrists called in to give a verdict on McCafferty's mental state could not agree on whether or not he was insane at the time he committed the murders. McCafferty himself had no doubt, claiming from the dock 'at the time of these crimes I was completely insane. I did this for revenge of my son's death. That is what made me do it . . . if given the chance I will kill again, for the simple reason that I have to kill seven people, and I have only killed three.'

Whatever drove Mad Dog to a killing spree the jury was not convinced either of his insanity or of his innocence. McCafferty was found guilty and given three life sentences. Even as he was led from the court, McCafferty swore that he would kill four more to avenge his son. The prison authorities were left with the problem of keeping under control a man overwhelmed by bizarre thoughts and full of rage. It proved an impossible task. In September 1981 McCafferty was charged with the murder of Edward Lloyd, who was stabbed in his cell. He was sentenced to fourteen years for manslaughter. Mad Dog furiously protested his innocence. He claimed he knew who had carried out the murder and told the authorities who was responsible. It was a serious mistake because now hardened criminals turned against him and his life was at risk from his fellow convicts. Somehow he managed to survive though much time was spent isolated from the other prisoners.

Although it might have been expected that a killer with McCafferty's personality and background would never be released, on 1 May 1997 he was put on a plane and sent back to Scotland. McCafferty had never taken out Australian citizenship and his adopted country was only too relieved to dump the problem of Mad Dog on the land of his birth.

McCafferty claimed to be a changed man, but years in prison, an unstable personality and returning to a country he had left almost forty years' before did not help his situation. Soon after his return he moved in to the Merlin guest house in the Morningside district of Edinburgh with his former wife Mandy Queen, who he intended to remarry. The couple were asked to leave when the owner saw Mad Dog's picture on television. The intense publicity brought death threats to McCafferty. It was feared that he might be allocated a council house in Glasgow's Sighthill where he still had relatives. So Mad Dog was forced to move from hotel to hotel in a bid to hide from the media. An angry McCafferty told reporters, 'I just want to be left alone. I don't think I deserve any hassle. I've completed my sentence and just want to start a new life.'

But McCafferty could not escape his violent past. For one thing he was too easily identifiable.

McCafferty had an obsession with tattoos and had over two hundred separate figures on his body. These included sexually explicit designs and one that read 'kill and hate cops'. In October 1998 McCafferty was put on two years' probation for threatening Edinburgh police officers following a car chase. An attempt to move to New Zealand in 2000 failed when his identity was discovered and he was deported. But even when lying low McCafferty could not escape attention. In July 2002 his Edinburgh flat was surrounded by police after a man was stabbed to death nearby. It made headlines even though the police admitted: 'We are not linking him with what happened.'

Then, in early April 2004, McCafferty's past caught up with a vengeance when he was charged with attempted murder and abduction following a two-hour siege at a flat in Hawick in the Scottish Borders. It was alleged that he had tried to kill his wife, Mandy, and then had to be persuaded to release his 5-year-old son to police custody. The charges were dropped but, in September 2004, McCafferty was handed a six-month sentence for threatening to stab police officers. In the interim, Mad Dog's wife and child had fled Scotland and returned to Australia, well out of his reach. A senior detective told reporters, 'The guy is a psycho, but fortunately gave himself up before any lives were lost.' Meanwhile, in Australia, the law was changed so that, in future, mass killers like McCafferty will never be released. Too late for Scotland where by accident of birth the bizarre life of Archie 'Mad Dog' McCafferty will continue to be played out and still, it seems, has a way to run.

33. Gavin McGuire

The death of innocence

The dogs in the street knew that Gavin McGuire would murder one day. From petty offences, his crimes had grown more serious until they culminated in the most heinous of all; the murder of an innocent 16-year-old schoolgirl. He had also displayed a capacity for unfeeling cruelty from an early age that marked him out as someone capable of perpetrating the most unspeakable acts. The tragedy is that he could have been stopped at a much earlier stage were it not for the astonishing laxity shown by the judicial system in Scotland to those who are truly evil. It is a case that sums up the feelings of many that the system is designed for the offender and not the victim.

Gavin McGuire was born in the working-class town of Stevenston in Ayrshire in 1958, the first child of Jimmy and Nettie McGuire. The family were always short of money despite the fact that Jimmy had a steady job as a labourer in the steel industry. They lived in a council house with few luxuries and Jimmy's only real pleasure was looking after the pigeons he kept in a loft in the garden.

By the time he reached the final year of primary education McGuire – the class loner – had already embarked on a criminal career. He started with shoplifting and graduated in his teens to stealing cars and housebreaking; habits that spells in List D schools and young offenders' institutions could not break. But there was one act that those who knew him thought beyond the pale; an act that first revealed his limitless capacity for cruelty. It happened when he was fourteen: he poured petrol over the pigeon hut in his back garden and set it alight. Then he just laughed as his pets were burned to death. As one classmate later said: 'I remember him torching those poor animals. He showed no remorse for what he had done. He is really evil.'

Worse was to follow. At the age of just seventeen he raped a 15-year-old girl, sexually assaulted another and attacked a woman. Then, incredibly, he was let out on bail by the authorities, a decision so controversial that it was debated in the House of Commons. But the thought of trial, and imprisonment, did not seem to deter him; while he was on bail he brutally raped another woman. McGuire was jailed for ten years at the High Court in Ayr in 1977, a sentence that many felt was far too lenient. Then, to add insult to injury, he was released in 1983, having served only six years. He was now free to carry out an attack so depraved that it should have put him away for ever.

It happened on a warm summer night in 1986. Doris Thomson, aged thirty-three, was on holiday with her husband and five children; the youngest was just nine months. After a family night out in the pub there had been a spat and she decided to make her own way back to their holiday caravan in the seaside resort of Saltcoats in Ayrshire. Stopping off to use a public toilet, Doris was seized by the throat by McGuire. He dragged her to a summer seat and subjected her to a terrifying ordeal:

> He made me lie on my back. Then he pressed his hand hard against my throat. I could feel myself blacking out and heard the click of him squeezing my throat. He told me to take off my pants and tights. He grabbed the tights and told me to open my mouth. I thought he was going to gag me but he put them round my throat and held them like a dog's choker chain.

At that point a taxi drove past and McGuire marched Doris onto the beach, ranting and swearing all the while. He even taunted her by saying over and over again: 'You are a big girl but you haven't learned to take care of yourself properly.' Then he laughed mockingly; a laugh that his victim says she will never forget.

Although at one point she managed to break free from his clutches he caught her when she was only feet from a caravan and safety. McGuire then made her pay for her attempt to escape by punching her hard in the mouth and in the stomach. He then dragged her to the pier and squeezed her into a gap in the sea wall. Forcing her on to the sand McGuire made her strip and then raped her, becoming enraged when she would not give him oral sex.

But it was not enough for McGuire simply to assault and rape Doris Thomson. He also had to indulge in psychological intimidation. Discovering that she had five children, including a baby of nine months, he said: 'I hope you said cheerio to him tonight. Because you'll never get the chance to say cheerio again. I hope you have left plenty of pictures for him because he will never know his mother.'

When McGuire had sated his desires he decided to deliver the coup de grace by killing Mrs Thomson. She recalled the agony of what happened next:

> At the water's edge he gave me the most hellish punch in the stomach and then punched me on the face again. He got a hold of me by the throat, this time with both his hands, and started squeezing. I saw the frenzied look on his face and felt my neck click. I thought of my children and how I wanted to see my baby. As he squeezed I slipped down to my knees, praying to God I had convinced him I was dead.

McGuire was convinced but still kicked her between the legs, shouting obscenities as he did so. Doris Thomson had never felt such pain but somehow managed not to cry out. He then grabbed her by the hair and threw her into the water. When she struggled back to shore she thought she was safe but McGuire came back to find her; anxious to ensure she was dead. At one point he was only a few feet away, and she held her breath and ducked under the water.

Eventually the victim, battered and bruised, managed to get away and raise the alarm. For the two nights after the rape she toured Saltcoats in disguise with the police until they spotted McGuire in a chip shop. He was followed to Bobby's Bar (owned, incidentally, by former Celtic FC great, Bobby Lennox) and after Doris's husband punched him in the face McGuire was arrested.

McGuire was charged with attempted murder and rape. It ought to have been the opportunity to send him away for life (a life sentence can be imposed for rape under Scots law). But McGuire plea-bargained and was found guilty of only an attempted rape. His unfortunate victim did not even get the chance to tell her story in court; perhaps if she had been able to give details of her horrific ordeal the judge may have handed down a realistic sentence. But McGuire got only ten years, the same as he had copped for the rapes and assaults in 1977. He would soon be free to strike again.

Gavin McGuire was again released early and by 1993 he was, inevitably, in serious trouble. He was charged with the attempted murder of a prostitute, but the jury at the High Court in Glasgow brought back a not-proven verdict. He had been in custody again – for three months – in the winter of 1995 but was set free on 27 November 1995 without the case going to court, some say because of blunders by the Crown Office. If it was an official error it was a disastrous one. Just nineteen days after being turned loose McGuire was to perpetrate his most depraved act yet.

McGuire had gone back to live with his mother in Stevenston. At first he tried to keep a low profile and left the house only to take the dog for a walk. But he had to get out and on Saturday, 16 December 1995 he told his mother he was going to Kilmarnock to buy Christmas presents. After wandering round Kilmarnock town centre and having a few drinks the 37-year-old decided to go home and made his way to the town's bus station at about twenty past nine. But then someone caught his eye; an attractive 23-year-old mother-of-two called Shona Ronald who was walking on her own through the Burns shopping mall.

When he spotted Shona Ronald, McGuire immediately changed direction and started to follow her. She left the mall and walked up to her friend's flat in the town's London Road. As she approached the flat her pal, Lorraine Dorrans, leaned out of the window and threw the keys to Ms Ronald, who let herself into the house. It was a move that almost certainly saved her life. If McGuire had cornered her in a quiet spot she may not have lived to tell the tale.

This meant that McGuire – full of drink – had had his passion aroused and been frustrated; a very dangerous state of affairs as others had found out to their cost. He now found himself in the vicinity of the Palace Theatre, where a Christmas panto – *Sleeping Beauty* – was about to end. Within minutes hundreds of people would pour out of the theatre into the dark winter night, many of them young women.

Among the panto audience was Mhairi Julyan, a fun-loving 16-year-old with long, curly red hair. Caring and popular, she wanted to become a nurse. When she was not at school or working in a local fish-and-chip shop she spent most of her free time with either her best pal, Julie Holland, or her boyfriend, Jim Caldwell. It was the life of a normal teenage girl. A life that was about to be cut short in the cruellest possible way.

Like the rest of the audience she had enjoyed the panto and had laughed at lead actor Johnny Beattie's corny jokes. So she was in high spirits when she came out of the theatre and waved goodbye to her friends outside. She started to make her way to her home in Samson Avenue, where she lived with her parents and big sister Claire. She felt safe; it was a short walk in an area she knew like the back of her hand.

But Mhairi Julyan was never to reach home. Gavin McGuire saw to that. He pounced on the schoolgirl and subjected her to an unspeakable attack. She was sexually assaulted, gagged with her bra and strangled with her blouse. McGuire inflicted no less than forty-seven injuries on the helpless young woman before killing her. He then dragged her across rough ground and stuffed her body into a disused coal bunker.

Police immediately put McGuire in the frame. He was interviewed three times but claimed he had been drinking until 10.45 p.m. and had not gone near the murder scene when he left the pub. But police came up with a security video that showed McGuire stalking Shona Ronald in the Burns shopping mall at 9.23 p.m. – eighty minutes before he said he left the pub. Forensic evidence made the case against him almost watertight: fibres from his shirt matched those found on Mhairi's jacket; and DNA tests revealed that blood on the sleeve of Mhairi's jacket matched his blood.

The jury at the High Court in Glasgow had no doubt about McGuire's guilt. The nine women and six men took only thirty minutes to find him guilty on charges of sexual assault and murder. The judge, Lord Clyde, said he 'was guilty of an atrocity without mercy' and, on 30 May 1996, handed down a life sentence with a recommendation that he should spend at least thirty years behind bars. A sentence that was long overdue.

But it seems that the Scottish legal system is incapable of punishing Gavin McGuire properly. In September 2002 he had his sentence cut by eight years because of human rights legislation. He will now be eligible to apply for parole after twenty-two years, in 2018. He will then be fifty-nine, still young enough to kill again. As victim Doris Thomson said when she heard the news: 'He'll just repeat this if he is ever let out. If he's released, no matter how old he is, some other wee girl will get it again.'

34. The Renee MacRae case

No trace was ever found

'If I go first then please make sure I am cremated not buried because I would hate to be buried alive.' Those haunting words, spoken by Renee MacRae to a close friend, are a poignant reminder of her still-unexplained disappearance. Around 10 p.m. on 12 November 1976 a passing motorist spotted a vehicle on fire in a lay-by on the A9 near Tomatin, several miles south of Inverness. By the time the emergency services arrived the car was a blazing shell, but having checked that there was no one inside it seemed that all that was left to be done was to have the fire brigade extinguish the flames. On checking the registration number – JAS 219P – the police identified the metallic blue BMW 1602 series as belonging to 37-year-old Mrs Catherine MacRae, an attractive petite blonde, known to her friends as Renee. Estranged from her husband, she lived with her two young sons Gordon (9) and Andrew (3) at 4 Cradlehall Park, Inverness. The fact that Mrs MacRae was neither in the vicinity of her car when it was found, nor at her home, did not cause undue concern. Following initial inquiries, the police believed that Renee had gone away for a 'lover's weekend' and, having parked her car at a secret meeting place, had been unlucky enough to have it vandalised.

That Renee's death might be suspicious only emerged following a chance interview with a friend. It was discovered that she had been involved in a long-term affair with her husband's business colleague, Bill MacDowell. The affair was so intense that she had fallen pregnant by MacDowell who, the police learned, was the father of 3-year-old Andrew, the toddler who had been in the car with Renee at the time of her disappearance. Further digging revealed that in the weeks before she vanished, Renee had been led to believe that she and MacDowell were going to start a new life together in Shetland. MacDowell had even convinced Renee that he had got a job there and bought a house. He had been lying, but on the basis of his story Renee MacRae had packed her belongings in readiness for the move which she believed would take place at the end of November. A complicating factor in this tangled situation was that Bill MacDowell worked as an accountant for the building company owned by Renee's husband, Gordon MacRae. The two men appeared to get on in spite of MacDowell's affair with Renee. And though they had been apart for a number of years, Renee and Gordon also kept in touch. In fact, the last confirmed sighting of Renee was at the offices of Gordon's building firm, H. MacRae & Co.

While all this information slowly emerged, the initial belief of the police that they were dealing with a routine case of vandalism had allowed the killer crucial time to cover his tracks. Clues to the fate of Renee MacRae and Andrew had disappeared in the flames which consumed her BMW and in the clean-up of the site that followed. All that the police could be sure of, following an examination of the car, was that neither Renee nor Andrew had been in the burnt-out BMW. So where could they have gone?

If Renee and Bill MacDowell had planned to meet up, on the weekend Renee had disappeared, then MacDowell was clearly the key to the inquiry. But MacDowell at first denied that he had arranged to meet his lover. His wife Rosemary commented: 'My husband has told me that such a suggestion is untrue and I believe him.' However, as the evidence built up, his claim was undermined. He eventually admitted that on the weekend in question they had intended spending time together and had discussed moving to Shetland. However, according to MacDowell, at the last moment he changed his mind and decided that he did not want to go through with it. He had not kept the date with Renee so could throw no light on what had happened to her.

Establishing Renee's movements on the last afternoon of her life was clearly going to be crucial. Renee had been seen leaving her bungalow at around four in the afternoon, smartly dressed in a three-quarter-length, dark-tan sheepskin coat, maroon slacks, chunky navy-blue cardigan and brown knee-length boots. She had then driven to her husband's office where there was a last confirmed sighting of her, made by a female employee of the firm, at around quarter to five. So just five hours before her blazing car was discovered on the A9, Renee MacRae was still very much alive.

So where had Renee and young Andrew been in the intervening time and where were they now? Renee had put it about that she was going away for the weekend to stay with her sister in Kilmarnock, but there was no truth in it and her sister was not expecting a visit. And no confirmed sightings of Renee after 5 p.m. on 12 November had emerged in spite of nationwide publicity, all of which suggested that she was not staying in a hotel or similar accommodation. So had she gone into hiding for a reason known only to her? Or could Renee and Andrew be lost, wandering through unfamiliar countryside? The police dismissed these possibilities and as the days passed with no word from Renee gave up hope of finding them alive.

One witness had described seeing Renee pushing Andrew in a blue silver-cross pushchair through Inverness. The distinctive pushchair was not in the car nor was it at her home. It appeared to have disappeared with Renee and Andrew. This had a clearly sinister implication. But if the two were now dead, discovering their bodies would be the key to identifying the murderer and bringing him to trial. Divers were called in to search local lochs while police and volunteers scoured woods, hills and any potential hiding place. Nothing was now left to chance. Planes from the Royal Air Force photographed miles of remote countryside and used heat-seeking equipment in the hope of locating the missing mother and son.

But in spite of one of the most extensive missing-person hunts ever undertaken no trace of either Renee MacRae or Andrew was ever found. The case remains unsolved though by no means forgotten. In 2004, a retired policeman, sergeant John Cathcart, who had been involved in the original search, claimed that the bodies had been dumped in Dalmagarry quarry, close to the A9. In fact, a witness had also claimed to have seen a man pulling a heavy object through undergrowth in the area of the quarry on the night that Renee Macrae disappeared. Could this be the same man seen earlier that evening – at around eight – standing beside a car close to the lay-by where Renee's BMW was found? This individual was never identified.

During the search for Renee, Dalmagarry quarry, though identified as a potential hiding place, had not been thoroughly investigated as it had been in the process of being filled in. Strangely, in 1977, a psychic claimed that Renee MacRae's body would be found buried beneath rubble. But policeman John Cathcart was more direct in his assessment of the evidence. He reported: 'We took off the top soil when I got this terrible smell. And on the second run down the slope the digger driver got the smell inside his cab. I was convinced that the smell was that of the dead bodies.' The excavation was stopped for the simple reason that the equipment for the dig had only been hired for a week and there were many other more likely spots to look at. So could the disappearance of Renee and Andrew have been solved all those years ago if fate and police budgets had not intervened?

A huge volume of publicity was generated by John Cathcart's claims. Northern Constabulary came under massive pressure to reopen their search of Dalmagarry quarry and in August 2004 mechanical diggers and police investigators once more began to work their way through the site. From his London home Bill MacDowell broke a twenty-eight year silence on the case to claim, 'I didn't kill her'. But the investigation came to nothing. After several weeks of sifting though vast quantities of earth and debris the quarry had revealed no hint of a body and the search was brought to an end.

Even as the hunt at the quarry was winding down, however, two workmen came forward to claim that Renee and Andrew could have been buried under a section of the A9, which was being relaid at the time of their disappearance. The truth is there is no shortage of potential sites where two bodies could have been hidden. And unless the remains of

Renee and Andrew are discovered the killer can be sure that he will never have to face a charge of murder. On the other hand those who believe themselves wrongly suspected of the crime will never be free of suspicion till the fate of Renee and Andrew is finally resolved.

35. The Willie McRae case
Did they get him first?

In the early 1980s Glasgow lawyer Willie McRae enjoyed a short period of fame when he masterminded a campaign to halt the disposal of nuclear waste in Ayrshire's Mullwarchar hills. And though he rapidly fell from public view the impact he had was long lasting. Not only was Scotland's nuclear industry forced to abandon its plans, but also it was left with the serious problem of locating an alternative site for burying waste. And McRae made it clear that he was determined to stop them, wherever they went. But would opposition to the nuclear industry really be enough for a man to lose his life?

In 1985 McRae was sixty-two and had been a lifelong supporter of Scottish independence. But somewhere along the line he had become convinced that achieving independence through the ballot box was too slow a process. Unknown to his friends, he had linked himself to 'tartan terrorists'. Individuals who believed that only direct action with the bomb and the bullet would set Scotland free from English rule. Could it have been this hidden part of McRae's life that brought about his still unexplained death?

Of course, officially, Willie McRae was not murdered. On Good Friday, 5 April 1985, McRae left his top-floor flat at 6 Balvicar Drive, Glasgow for the four-hour drive to Dornie near the Kyle of Lochalsh where he had a holiday home, Camusty. Neighbours caught a last glimpse of him as he set off down the street around 6.30 p.m. At ten the following morning, Saturday, 6 April, Alan Crowe and his wife, on holiday from Australia, driving along the A87 road from Invergarry, spotted a car lying about a hundred yards down a steep slope leading to Loch Loyne. At the scene they discovered a maroon Volvo, lying in a burn. The rear window was shattered and the window on the driver's side wound down. The driver's door was wedged shut against the burn's bank. Inside the car the driver lay slumped in his seat, his head resting on his shoulder, a stream of blood ran from his hair to his forehead. Crowe ran back to the road and flagged down the first car that passed. By an odd coincidence it contained leading Scottish Nationalist politician David Coutts, a prominent Dundee councillor. When Coutts reached the Volvo he immediately recognised its occupant. It was Willie McRae, still alive, but unconscious. He was well beyond medical help and though taken by ambulance to hospital in Inverness, then Aberdeen, he died on Sunday, 7 April.

At first glance, the cause of death might have seemed obvious. Driving along too fast for the road he had misjudged a bend and crashed down the embankment. But this was no road accident. McRae had died of a gunshot wound. A bullet lay embedded in his brain having entered through his right temple. Amazingly, the cause of death was not established till the Sunday and it was only then that the police returned to the 'accident' scene to investigate. In the meantime, as far as a forensic investigation was concerned, the death site had been effectively destroyed, having been thoroughly walked over with no attempt to preserve clues or keep it free from contamination. Articles found in the vicinity that appeared to belong to McRae had been removed, most of them by David Coutts who had been asked by a police constable to gather them up. And McRae's Volvo had been taken away to a garage with no formal examination of its interior.

To explain the circumstances in which McRae had been found the police put forward a new theory. McRae, they suggested, had committed suicide. He had used the Smith & Wesson .45 revolver found at the scene – his own – to shoot himself in the head. He had been only partially successful. The bullet had not extinguished his life immediately and it was judged that McRae had been alive though critically injured for several hours before he was found. This explanation had one serious flaw. The gun that McRae had supposedly used was lying several yards from the Volvo. This could only mean that after shooting himself in the head McRae had somehow thrown the gun a considerable distance. This would have been nothing short of a miracle. The injury McRae had sustained to his brain would have made movement impossible. It was clear that, however it had happened, McRae died where he had been shot, in the front seat of his car. So who had moved the gun?

According to those who knew him, McRae was in good spirits in the time leading up to his death. He was, apparently, writing a book on the nuclear industry and was preparing for a fresh battle with the authorities having put his name forward as an objector to a proposal to build a nuclear-waste-processing-plant at Dounreay. He had an established law practice and money did not seem to be a problem. Furthermore, at around 9.30 p.m., only a short time before he was to die, McRae had stopped to change a punctured tyre. An odd act for a man who then drives two miles up the road to commit suicide. And where was the suicide note? Wouldn't a man with the intense political conviction of Willie McRae have left some kind of personal statement? Normally, the absence of a last message would set alarm bells ringing for detectives, but not in this case.

In spite of the fact that a figure well known within political circles had died in bizarre circumstances – which on the face of it merited further investigation – the authorities claimed that McRae's death was not suspicious. Even though it was discovered that the book he was compiling on the nuclear industry, and his briefcase containing key documents, had disappeared from his car. They have never surfaced. Pressure mounted for an official investigation, but in July 1985 the Crown Office announced that there would be no further action. Scotland's solicitor general, Peter Fraser (now Lord Fraser of Carmyllie), later said: 'I personally took the decision that there should be no fatal accident inquiry. This is not unusual where the circumstances, so far as ascertained, reveal no criminality on the part of another person known or unknown.' Unfortunately, little effort was made to establish whether or not another party had been involved. Even the Scottish National Party, of which McRae had been a devoted member, was reluctant to turn McRae's suspicious death into a major incident. So who did get away with the murder of Willie McRae?

There's little doubt that the security services had worked to encourage nationalist extremists in the hope of discrediting Scotland's independence movement. So had McRae somehow learnt more of their secret activities than was safe for him to know? But if British Intelligence had killed McRae, which some have speculated, it might have been expected that his death would have been more professionally set-up to look like suicide. Which leaves open the possibility that the site was deliberately arranged in the way it was found, with the gun some distance from McRae as a warning to others. Unlikely? The day intended for his death, 6 April, was the anniversary of a key event in nationalist history – the signing in 1320 of the Declaration of Arbroath, a document that asserted Scotland's independence from England. Was this a coincidence too far? On the last day of his life McRae was excitedly claiming, without explaining exactly what he meant, 'I've got them! I've got them!' But did they get him first?

36. Allan Menzies
Blood of the vampire

'I drank his blood and ate a bit of his head.' That was the chilling statement given to police by Allan Menzies as they investigated the disappearance of his close friend, Thomas McKendrick. It was January 2003 and the quiet, unassuming 21-year-old had not been seen, or heard from, since 11 December 2002. What had started as a missing-person enquiry in the small town of Fauldhouse, West Lothian turned into something altogether more sinister. So sinister that it led to the most disturbing confession in Scottish criminal history.

The evidence detectives gathered during a search of Menzies's bedroom convinced them that he knew much more about Thomas McKendrick's disappearance than he had previously revealed. It was clear that the 22-year-old, an unemployed security guard, was obsessed by vampirism, human sacrifice and murder. They found the novel *Blood and Gold* by Anne Rice, which is about vampires. Inside the book Menzies had written several notes: one read, 'I have chosen my fate to become a vampire. Blood is much too precious to be wasted on humans.' There was a video, *Queen of the Damned*, which tells the story of a seventeenth-century vampire, Lestat, who returns from the dead to the twentieth century and also includes a memorable female vampire, Akasha. Another video, *Leon*, portrays the life of a contract killer. Menzies had previously told police that he had changed his name to Leon. But, of far greater importance, there was also physical evidence of foul play in the house. Despite attempts to clean it up forensic scientists found evidence of massive bloodstaining on the walls and floorboards.

All that police were missing was a body but, only eight days' later, constable Kenneth Gray, a member of the search team, noticed a hand and a forearm sticking out of a drainage ditch in woods near Fauldhouse. They belonged to Thomas McKendrick. Shortly after the body was found Menzies made the infamous statement to police about drinking Thomas's blood and eating part of his head, adding: 'I am going to get twenty or twenty-five years, but I have got his soul.' A friend would tell later how Menzies had admired a young Welsh murderer who had killed an old lady, cut out her heart and drunk her blood.

With the evidence now stacking up against him Menzies knew he would be found guilty of killing his friend and tried every trick in the book to avoid going to prison. He offered to plead guilty if 'he could get Carstairs' (the state mental-institution). When this was rejected he and his legal team devised a new strategy: he confessed to killing

McKendrick but entered a plea of culpable homicide on the grounds of diminished responsibility. This was rejected by the prosecution who wanted him convicted of murder, given a life sentence and sent to a mainstream jail. Desperate to keep up the pretence of being mentally unstable, Menzies wrote sinister letters home while on remand and signed them 'Vamp' in blood. He addressed the letters to Akasha and wrote in one: 'Dear Akasha, everything is going as planned. I will kill for you again soon. These humans are nothing but animals, fodder for us.'

But it was the evidence given by Menzies at his trial in Edinburgh's High Court in the autumn of 2003 that shocked everyone who heard it. He claimed that he was completely under the influence of Akasha after watching the film *Queen of the Damned* more than one hundred times. In fact all he was doing was following her orders; orders that she gave him while sitting on his bed. To be guaranteed eternal life, she told him, all that he had to do was kill, and then drink his victim's blood. Anyone would do. Even his best friend.

On that fateful December day Menzies and Thomas McKendrick were in his kitchen, along with, he said, Akasha. Menzies claimed his friend called Akasha a 'black bitch' and he told him to shut up. When Thomas asked why, Menzies told him it was because Akasha was in the kitchen with them. His friend's response was, 'What do you mean? Don't be stupid.' Menzies claimed that Akasha was offended: 'She wasn't pleased. Then she turned her back to me.' Asked why Akasha was angry, Menzies replied: 'Because Thomas had just insulted her and I had let him away with it.' So Thomas McKendrick's young life was about to be snuffed out because his best friend did not want to 'let down' a fictional character.

In a rage Menzies picked up his heavy hunting-knife and stabbed his friend in the neck, back, face and shoulders. When Thomas fled screaming at the top of his voice into another room, and banged on a window in a vain attempt to summon help, Menzies followed him and battered him to death with a hammer. Menzies then put Thomas's body on its side, cut his throat and let the blood flow into a whisky cup. 'I drank two cups of his blood. A fragment of his skull was on the carpet so I ate that', he told an incredulous courtroom. He then put the body in a wheelie bin before taking it to Fauldhouse moor and burying it in a shallow grave. Far from feeling either remorse or fear Menzies was coolness personified and returned home, where he watched television and a video before feeding the family's pet ferrets.

The jury did not accept his plea of diminished responsibility. They were no doubt influenced by the three psychiatrists who told the court that he was not mentally ill. On his vampire fantasies, one noted: 'It does occur to me as one possibility that they are manufactured to avoid conviction for the crime of murder.' Judge Roderick MacDonald was in no doubt about the criminal predilections of the man before him: he told him 'You are an evil, violent and highly dangerous man who is not fit to be at liberty.' Menzies showed no emotion as the judge passed a life sentence on 8 October 2003, with a recommendation that he should serve at least eighteen years in prison.

After the trial several theories were advanced for his descent into barbarism. Some blamed the influence of violent films, which even as a teenager he would watch alone in his room for hours on end. Others, including his cousin, Jim Menzies, laid the blame at the door of the young killer's father, Tam. According to him, Tam Menzies had brought up his son on tales of his exploits as an assassin for the feared paramilitary group, the Ulster Volunteer Force. But the stories were a figment of his father's imagination; he was, in reality, a humble joiner. As Jim Menzies said, Tam Menzies 'filled the boy's head with shite for years'. Discovery of this deception proved to be a devastating blow to his son and his self-esteem was further eroded when his parents began divorce proceedings. Could one or more of these factors have caused him to kill? Or was he simply a violent thug who had difficulty in containing his volcanic temper? Family members and friends had observed that he was moody and prone to violent rages and there is evidence that he had attacked several relatives, including his grandmother. And, significantly, he had a history of extreme violence involving the use of knives: when he was fourteen he was sent to a secure unit for stabbing a classmate who had beaten him up. We will never know the truth; Allan Menzies hanged himself in Shotts prison in November 2004 after only twelve months inside.

37. Luke Mitchell

Tomorrow never came

The killing of an innocent schoolgirl is bound to attract a great deal of attention. And so it proved with Jodi Jones who, at just fourteen, lost her life in the most appalling circumstances imaginable. Her age and the way she was killed would have been enough, on their own, to provoke a media frenzy. But there were other factors to consider; factors that pushed the murder to the top of the news agenda and have kept it there ever since. Scotland has produced many high-profile murderers: Thomas Hamilton, Nat Fraser and Bible John among them. But none have provoked the degree of fascination Scotland has with the teenage boy who killed his girlfriend.

Born in 1989, Jodi Catherine Jones was from the former mining village of Easthouses, a tightly knit working-class community in the county of Midlothian. She lived with her mother, her mother's partner, her brother and sister in a modest end-terrace house in Parkhead Place, and attended St David's High School, a Roman Catholic secondary in Dalkeith. She had known tragedy in her short life: in 1998 her father, James Jones (39), a postman, hung himself from a tree in the back garden of his mother-in-law's house in Dalkeith and was found by his wife and son. Jodi, then only nine, had bravely overcome this devastating loss and even made her own tribute to him: a stone carved with the words 'J—— J—— luv Jodi. XX', which she had carefully placed next to his headstone in Gorebridge cemetery.

Jodi Jones – nicknamed 'Toad' by her family – was bright, outgoing and popular. Her teachers considered that she would do well in the public exams that she was expecting to sit in the years ahead. Despite the death of her father she brightened up her home and was described by her mother, Judy, as a 'ray of sunshine to family and friends'. Like all teenagers Jodi began to experiment and – more free-spirited than most – even mildly to rebel. One day it was by wearing a ring through her lip; the next by putting corn rows in her hair. Her musical tastes became more sophisticated and she had a particular passion for what is known as grunge music, a passion shared by several of her contemporaries at school.

It was perhaps her musical tastes and individuality that attracted one of those contemporaries: Luke Mitchell, a class mate at St David's. They met in early 2003 and quickly became an item, enjoying films and music together. A particular favourite for both Luke and Jodi was the American grunge band Nirvana, whose lead singer Kurt Cobain had committed suicide. Cobain's best-known lyric (which was written on Jodi's bedroom wall) had proved to be prophetic: 'The finest day I ever had was when tomorrow never came.' Another pastime enjoyed by Jodi and Luke was less innocent, but nevertheless common among their peer group; they smoked cannabis together. It was clear only weeks into their relationship that Jodi had already fallen for Luke. Before much longer the couple, both aged fourteen, became lovers. Jodi penned a touching entry in her diary, explaining the depth of her feelings for him: 'I think I am actually in love with Luke. Not in a stupid way. I mean real love. God, I think I would die if he finished with me.'

But when Judy Jones – a caring and protective parent – found out about the drug-taking she was shocked; so shocked that she grounded Jodi. This meant that her daughter was not allowed to leave the house before six in the evening and had to be back no later than nine. It had little effect and Jodi continued to smoke cannabis, although without her mother's knowledge. On Monday, 30 June 2003 Judy Jones relented; when Jodi got home from school she released her from the grounding and the youngster was free to come and go as she pleased provided she was always back home by ten at night. The first thing Jodi did was to text Luke Mitchell and arrange a date. She was ready to leave the house at about ten to five and gave her mother a kiss, saying, 'That's me off now mum.' As she slipped out Jodi noticed that her mother was cooking lasagne, a family favourite, and said, 'Mind and keep me some.'

When she left Parkhead Place Jodi headed for a path known locally as Roan's Dyke. She and Luke often met at the top of the path, on Easthouses Road, a short walk from where Jodi lived and about the same distance from Luke's home in the village of Newbattle. But something had gone wrong. Luke phoned the Jones house about 5.40 p.m., asking for Jodi. It was almost an hour after she had left home on a journey that should have taken only two minutes. Allen Ovens, the partner of Judy Jones, took the call but did not realise the obvious time discrepancy and simply told Luke that Jodi had already left.

Later that evening Luke Mitchell called some male friends and they met up in the woods near Newbattle Abbey to smoke a few joints. When one of his pals asked where Jodi was, Mitchell replied: 'She isn't coming out.' By ten Judy Jones was concerned that her daughter had breached the curfew. At twenty to eleven she sent a text to Jodi, via Luke's phone. It read: 'Right that's you grounded for another two weeks.' Then, about two minutes after the text, Luke phoned Judy Jones and said he hadn't seen Jodi all night.

Frantic with worry Judy Jones began to call friends and family, asking if they had seen her daughter. When it became clear that no-one knew where Jodi was she alerted the police. In the meantime a mini search party – made up of Jodi's sister Janine, her fiancé and Jodi's grandmother – walked up the Roan's Dyke path. At the top they met Luke Mitchell, accompanied by his Alsatian, Mia. He told them he had seen nothing and the search went on. Then, when walking past a V-shaped break in the wall that runs parallel with the path, Mitchell climbed over and started searching on the other side of the wall. Almost immediately he shouted to the others that he had seen something. Alice Walker, Jodi's gran, joined him on the other side of the wall and was confronted with a mutilated body. It was her grand-daughter, Jodi Jones.

When police arrived on the scene they discovered that Jodi had been subjected to a savage attack. One senior detective said it was the worst sight he had seen in thirty years of service. She had been punched in the face and throttled, and then forced to her knees before her assailant cut her throat, an action that almost severed her head. The killer stripped her and tied her hands behind her back before mutilating her body in a very methodical manner: he slit her eyelids and cut her left cheek from ear to mouth and then cut her left breast. Her stomach was ripped open in three places and the killer had also opened her mouth and pierced her tonsils with the knife. There were more than three hundred injuries to her cheeks, throat, ears, eyes, breasts and torso. Strangely – in what seemed to be an attempt to preserve her dignity – her right leg had been lifted and placed over the left leg, thus concealing her private parts. There were no signs of sexual assault.

Led by detective superintendent Craig Dobbie and detective inspector Tom Martin of Lothian and Borders Police, a police team that numbered fifty officers swung into action. In the first few days hundreds of people were questioned, roadblocks were set up to stop and question drivers and appeals for information were broadcast on radio and television. A reconstruction of Jodi's last walk was enacted, with a woman constable taking the part of the murdered girl. But despite the resources deployed there would not be an early breakthrough, leaving detectives not only frustrated but also worried that the killer might strike again.

The scale of the police operation was matched by interest from the media; the story was front-page news from the start and would remain so for months. And this intense scrutiny led inevitably to speculation about the killer's identity: one theory was that Jodi had caught a man performing a sex act and, out of embarrassment, had killed her. Others put in the frame included a group of vagrants who often slept rough in the woods in the summer months. There was also talk of a man in his early twenties with a rucksack who had been seen stalking Jodi on the afternoon she died. Then there were the experts; psychologists contacted by newspapers eager to steal a march on their competitors and paid to write articles on the type of disturbed personality that would commit such a horrific crime. Incredibly one paper even ran a big story about a blind psychic who offered to use her 'sixth sense' to find the murderer.

For their part the police were convinced of two things: the killer was a man (the level of violence meant it could only be a man); and he was a local (only a local could have so easily navigated the network of paths and woods around Roan's Dyke). They were becoming increasingly interested in one local in particular – Luke Mitchell – and carried out two detailed searches of his house. Spouses, partners and lovers are always near the top of the suspects list in murder cases, but when details of Mitchell's character and lifestyle began to emerge it became clear to detectives that he was someone worthy of further investigation.

Luke Mitchell lived with his mother Corinne in a semi-detached villa on the outskirts of Dalkeith. Corinne Mitchell, popular and outgoing, owned her own business, a caravan dealership. She had divorced Luke's father in 1999 and worked hard to support her two sons, Shane and Luke. But while she may have been a relatively successful businesswoman this would not have been apparent at first sight; Corinne Mitchell dressed unconventionally and often revealingly – in what one neighbour described as 'gypsy-style' clothes – and sported a number of tattoos. She was adopted and was said to be insecure about her roots and upbringing. Described as 'laid back' when it came to Luke's upbringing, Corinne Mitchell was said to have allowed him a virtual free rein to behave as he liked. It is clear there was a particularly close relationship between Luke and his mother, despite the fact that Shane was the older of the two boys.

Without a father's guiding hand, and with relaxed discipline at home, Luke Mitchell was hardly the model schoolboy. He was a heavy user of cannabis and regularly sold it to friends; in his bedroom he had scales and the other paraphernalia associated with dealing. Bizarrely, he also kept large bottles filled with his own urine in the bedroom. Local youngsters flocked to his house because, as one said, 'his mum let him get away with anything'. When the parents of his friends found out what was going on they were concerned; one mother said she was horrified when she arrived home one day to discover Mitchell and Jodi in bed together smoking dope.

His artistic tastes matched his drug use; he was a devotee of the notorious Goth rock star Marilyn Manson, whose song lyrics on the themes of murder and the supernatural were of concern to many people. Manson had an obsession with the so-called Black Dahlia case of 1947 – in which the Hollywood actress Elizabeth Short was murdered and her body cut in half – and had produced a number of paintings that graphically depicted Miss Short's wounds. When police downloaded these paintings from the Internet they discovered a remarkable similarity between the injuries suffered by the actress and those inflicted on Jodi Jones. More disturbing still was Luke Mitchell's interest in Satanism and the occult. His school jotters were covered with disturbing references; in one he had written, 'I offer my flesh, blood and soul to the dark lord of hell,' while another noted, 'Life is merely an inconvenience between being born and going to hell.' Indeed one of his teachers was so disturbed by two of his school essays that she referred him to specialist guidance teachers because she thought he needed help.

But the most chilling part of his character was his deep interest in knives. He had an impressive collection and enjoyed showing them off to friends, boasting that he knew how to slit someone's throat. He even said to one pal that he imagined it would be a good laugh to get stoned and kill someone. This was not just talk and there were several incidents that showed Mitchell was willing and able to use a knife. When he was twelve he threatened his then girlfriend with a blade when she refused to have sex with him. Two years later, at a party, he repeatedly poked Jodi Jones hard in the leg with a knife before other partygoers intervened. And, just weeks before Jodi was murdered, Mitchell terrorised another girl-friend, Cara Van Nuil, with a knife. She remembered how Mitchell had grabbed her from behind and pressed a knife to her throat with some force. Although he let her go when she punched and kicked him, and dismissed the incident as a joke, Van Nuil was petrified because she thought he was serious.

As the dossier on Luke Mitchell grew thicker police became convinced that he was the killer. As one officer said, 'Once we started digging into his background, we found plenty to interest us.' Formal interviews with him did little to dissuade them from this view. Craig Dobbie remembered how cocky and smart-mouthed he was in those encounters: 'He was always a very resilient, defiant and lippy lad, not at all what you would expect of a 14- or 15-year-old. . . . He was challenging and he liked to taunt. He seemed to have this vision that Dalkeith police were numpties. It was almost as if he was saying, "You will never solve this".'

The problem for the police was that the case against Luke Mitchell was wholly circumstantial. There were no witnesses to the killing, nor had they been able to find the murder weapon. To make matters worse there was not even any forensic evidence linking Mitchell to the crime scene; it was particularly noteworthy that none of Jodi's blood was found on Mitchell, or on his clothes, despite the fact that it was an extremely gory murder. Nevertheless, as other leads melted away, the list of suspects shrunk to one name, that of Luke Mitchell. This was confirmed by the *Scottish Daily Mail* in an exclusive front-page story on 5 September 2003, ten weeks after the murder of Jodi Jones. The paper reported that detectives had sent a report to the procurator fiscal in Edinburgh naming Mitchell as the only suspect.

The Jones family had no doubt about his guilt. They had banned Luke from attending Jodi's funeral, a moving ceremony held on 3 September in Gorebridge cemetery at which hundreds of locals paid their last respects. Fittingly, Jodi was buried next to her father. Luke and his mother turned up later that day – along with their pet Alsatian – at Jodi's newly dug grave and laid a bouquet of roses; thirteen red and one white, representing Jodi's fourteen years. A card read 'Jodi, luv you always Luke. XXX.' When Judy Jones found out she removed the flowers and drove to the Mitchell home where she dumped them on the doorstep. It was not the first floral tribute from Luke: shortly after Jodi's body was found he left a bouquet on the Roan's Dyke path. Accompanying it was a card with the words 'I Love You' printed on it, and a handwritten section with the Nirvana lyric: 'The finest day I ever had was when tomorrow never came.'

It could hardly have been a coincidence that Luke Mitchell chose the day of the funeral to break his silence on Jodi's murder. He agreed to talk to a reporter from *Sky News* in his living room and it was, by any standards, one of the strangest events in the whole case. He had placed fourteen lit candles in the corner of the room and they illuminated a message that read 'Goodbye Jodi'. This little tableau had clearly been designed as a 'shrine' to his former girlfriend: it was not visible to viewers but was witnessed by the reporter who gave viewers details later. During the interview itself Mitchell was calm and measured and he flinched only when he was asked if he had killed Jodi. He replied: 'No, I never. I wouldn't even think of it.' Throughout the interview his mother tenderly stroked his neck, as if to comfort him. If this touching denial was meant to fool the police it had precisely the opposite effect; when a psychologist, expert in the field, viewed the tape he came to the conclusion that Mitchell was lying.

Although police were sure of Luke's guilt as early as September 2003 it would be another seven months before he was charged, on 14 April 2004. During this time many stories circulated to the effect that the Crown Office had informed the police that not enough evidence had been gathered to secure a conviction. The caution of the prosecuting authorities is perhaps understandable given the circumstantial nature of the case. Nevertheless the die was now cast and the trial that would transfix a nation began in the High Court in Edinburgh in early December 2004.

Because it would be so difficult to convince a jury of Mitchell's guilt, Scotland's top prosecutor, Alan Turnbull QC, was assigned to the case. Turnbull – a dogged, quietly effective advocate – had secured many high-profile convictions where the evidence was less than conclusive, including those of 'Limbs-in-the-Loch' killer William Beggs, the Lockerbie bomber, Abdelbasset Al Megrahi and Nat Fraser, who murdered his wife Arlene. But he would be up against a formidable opponent in the shape of Donald Findlay QC, (the often controversial former chairman of Rangers Football Club) who had a track record second to none in engineering acquittals against the odds. His achievements included notorious gangster Paul Ferris walking free from a charge of murdering Arthur 'Fat Boy' Thompson. Findlay advised Mitchell to enter a plea of not guilty, based on a defence of alibi and incrimination.

The prosecution – without material witnesses, a murder weapon or forensics – was nevertheless able to lead a good deal of circumstantial evidence. Some witnesses recalled seeing Mitchell, or someone looking like him, near to Roan's Dyke at the relevant time and one even said that he looked as if he was 'up to no good'. Then, in an attempt to illuminate Mitchell's character, other witnesses testified to his drug use, his interest in weird music and of course his passion for knives. A neighbour told how he noticed an unusual burning smell coming from the Jones garden on the day Jodi was killed. Then Corinne Mitchell was quizzed as to why she bought Luke a new parka just after Jodi's murder when several witnesses had testified that he owned a parka before Jodi died.

His ownership of knives was raised. A police constable told the court that Corinne had bought Luke an £8.95 hunting knife in December 2002. But when police searched his bedroom there was no trace of the knife. They did however find a knife pouch with the initials 'JJ', the numerals '666' (the Satanic code for the 'number of the beast') and the dates 1989–2003 (the year that Jodi Jones was born and the year of her death) inscribed on it. Inside the pouch the following words had been written: 'The finest day I ever had was when tomorrow never came.'

The witness who caused the greatest commotion at the trial was 15-year-old Kimberley Thomson. A dead-ringer for Jodi Jones, she told the court she thought that *she* was Luke's girlfriend, and not Jodi. She said that Luke had been two-timing her with Jodi and that she had been hurt to discover his cheating. Nevertheless he and Ms Thomson were regularly in touch after Jodi was killed.

But the most damning evidence against Mitchell stemmed from the night Jodi's body was found. It was given by her sister, Janine, and her grandmother, Alice Walker. They made clear that when Mitchell climbed over the V-shaped opening in the wall at the Roan's Dyke path he knew exactly where to look. In other words he knew what only the killer would know; where to find Jodi's body. This must have made an impact on the jury who had not only visited Roan's Dyke at the start of the trial but also were assisted by a replica of the wall that had been specially built for use in the courtroom. Janine Jones also testified that Mitchell seemed neither up nor down about the gruesome discovery – a complete contrast with the other members of the search party – as the following exchange illustrates:

QC: 'How was Mitchell reacting?'
Janine: 'He was fine.'

QC: 'Did he seem to have changed in any way?'
Janine: 'No.'
QC: 'Was he crying?'
Janine: 'No.'
QC: 'Was he shaking like your grandmother was and did he show any of the emotion on his face that your grandmother did?'
Janine: 'No.'

Then, on 21 January 2005, after a trial that had lasted nine weeks, it was over to the jury. Despite the eloquence of Donald Findlay most of them did not buy Mitchell's defence of alibi (he claimed to have been at home at the time Jodi was killed, a claim supported by his mother) and incrimination (that persons unknown had murdered Jodi). After deliberating for six hours they brought back a majority verdict of guilty on the murder charge. As he listened to the jury foreman Luke Mitchell showed no emotion and looked straight ahead, as he had done for the entire trial. Although the judge, Lord Nimmo Smith, had warned the court that he would not tolerate any outbursts, it was too much for Judy Jones. She shouted: 'Mrs Mitchell, go to hell.' Nimmo Smith – his voice shaking with emotion – handed down a life sentence and later decided that Mitchell would have to spend a minimum of twenty years in prison before being considered for release.

But why did Mitchell – one of the youngest murderers in recent Scottish history – do it? Why did he kill an innocent young girl, a girl who was in love with him? He was clearly unstable and came from a dysfunctional family in which there were few constraints on his behaviour. Then there was the music he favoured, with its violent and misogynistic lyrics. Some psychologists have argued that he must have been under the influence of drugs to have perpetrated such a frenzied attack. But there may be a simpler explanation and it is one that has been advanced by the policeman in charge of the investigation, superintendent Craig Dobbie. He argues that Jodi may have found about a holiday Luke was about to take with her love rival, Kimberley Thomson, and the two of them got into an argument (and it is likely that Jodi did know about Kimberley; her class mates remember seeing her looking upset on the afternoon of 30 June, just a few hours before she was murdered). Dobbie believes that Mitchell was a fantasist with a strong desire to kill and that a row about the other girl could have sparked off the frenzy of violence.

There is one more disturbing, but perhaps predictable, aspect to the case. Luke Mitchell has become something of a cult hero to hundreds of young girls, many of whom are adherents of the so-called Goth lifestyle. He has received adoring letters from these girls, who see him as a role model and sex symbol. This is no doubt fuelled by the continuing blanket coverage of the case: his life in prison is a source of fascination for the press and stories about him putting on weight, arguing with his mother during visits and a romance with his new girlfriend have all featured on the front pages of national newspapers. Like Myra Hindley, the Yorkshire Ripper and other notorious killers, Luke Mitchell will always be newsworthy.

And the final chapter in the story may not have been written yet. On 3 August 2005 it was announced that Luke Mitchell is to lodge an appeal against his conviction.

38. Robert Mone and Thomas McCulloch
Breakout from Carstairs!

At Carstairs hospital in Lanarkshire – since 1948 Scotland's state institution for the criminal insane – Robert Mone (28) and Thomas McCulloch (26) were regarded as model prisoners. Mone, in fact, was hoping for an early release. His father was arranging a legal petition to the courts. But behind the facade of tranquillity, the pair who had become strangely attached to each other were planning a bizarre escape. A road to freedom that would leave three people dead and cause a national outcry.

Mone had already gained public notoriety. On 1 November 1967, Mone – then a 19-year-old private home on leave from the Gordon Highlanders – held eleven schoolgirls and their teacher at gunpoint in St John's secondary school in Harefield Road, Dundee. For no reason he turned his shotgun on their teacher, 26-year-old Nanette Hanson. Nanette, a bride of just seven months, died with her unborn child, from her wounds.

Mone was a former pupil of the school, but what he hoped to achieve by going there is unclear. He later claimed that a few months before the shooting, while with the army in Germany, he had joined a Nazi devil cult and had vowed to spill blood before he reached the age of twenty-one. It was probably, however, nothing more than a fantasy of his deluded mind. In any event at 2.30 p.m. that day he burst into a needlework class with his shotgun and barricaded the door. Police were called and the school surrounded. In a shouted conversation with the police, Mone said that the only person he would negotiate with was Marion Young, a girl he had known at the school. Miss Young, who was studying to become a nurse, was contacted and volunteered to go into the classroom to speak to Mone. The siege had now lasted an hour. Ten minutes later, at 3.40 p.m., Marion Young persuaded Mone to let the pupils go. Nanette Hanson, Miss Young noted, was very collected and doing her utmost to keep Mone calm. But by 4 p.m. Mone was becoming increasingly agitated and started firing his shotgun. As the bullets flew, Nanette Hanson was hit in the body and collapsed. Marion Young would also have been a target if Mone's gun hadn't jammed. She then persuaded Mone to let Nanette be taken out. At half-past four, police burst in and Mone was overpowered and arrested. A few minutes later the news came that Nanette Hanson was dead. Following psychiatric examination, Mone was found unfit to plead and, after a brief court appearance, sent to Carstairs. As he heard the sentence, Mone beamed at the judge, shouting 'Well done'!

Five years later, in 1973, Thomas McCulloch joined Mone in Carstairs. McCulloch believed he had been insulted by staff at the Erskine Bridge

Hotel. He was furious when they ignored his protest that there was not enough butter on his sandwich. His reaction said everything that needed to be said about his state of mind. Grabbing a shotgun and strapping a bullet belt around his chest, McCulloch returned to the hotel. First to feel his rage was chef John Thomson who McCulloch blasted with his gun. By sheer luck Thomson was only hit on the cheek. McCulloch then dashed upstairs firing through the door of a staff bedroom, striking hotel manageress Mrs Lilias Rodger in the shoulder. Next he burst into the function room where fifty members of the Milngavie and Bearsden Round Table were holding a social evening. For several minutes he held the group hostage, but abruptly had a change of heart and apologised. He tamely allowed himself to be arrested by police. Detectives soon realised that they were dealing with a disturbed mind. In McCulloch's house they found an arsenal of weapons. During an interview he expressed the wish to 'go to Vietnam' where the US was still fighting the Vietcong, 'to shoot the North Vietnamese'. McCulloch was found not fit to plead and sent to Carstairs.

Mone and McCulloch quickly struck up a weird friendship. They held hands in chapel. Decorated their rooms in the same style. And wore identical silk dressing-gowns with a dragon motif.

By November 1976 both men knew each other so well that they planned to break out of Carstairs together. There was no hint of what was to come. A former patient was later to recall that both 'were quiet types'. Both had their security category reduced by two grades. Mone, who was doing a university correspondence course, was trusted. Unlike most inmates they were allowed, during the day, to move freely round many parts of the hospital. It was the calm before the storm. The storm broke after dinner on 30 November 1976.

Mone and McCulloch were members of a drama group which was run by 46-year-old nurse, Neil McLellan, who also acted as recreation officer. Widely liked by both patients and staff, McLellan, who had worked at Carstairs since 1961, enjoyed his job so much that on the evening of 30 November he was holding the drama group in his own time. Members of staff and inmates were jointly involved in producing a play. But McLellan was soon to become the first victim of the evening's horrific events. Around seven o'clock, Mone and McCulloch were collected from their wards and taken to the recreation room for their drama class. McCulloch was carrying two boxes. Mone had a parcel. But neither was challenged. In fact, both men had spent time in the hospital workshop preparing for their escape. They had stolen a knife from a tool kit and replaced it with an imitation they had made so that no one would notice the genuine tool was missing. McCulloch somehow got hold of an axe kept by McLellan in his office safe for use in case of fire.

The only witnesses to what happened next were the two prisoners.

McLellan must have realised what Mone and McCulloch were up to and tried to stop them. McCulloch, according to Mone, 'went berserk' and hacked at McLellan with the heavy-duty axe. Ian Simpson, a trusted prisoner, whose hobby was collecting butterflies, was also a member of the drama group. Forty-year-old Simpson was a double murderer who having hitched a lift from a man called George Green then shot him and stole his car. A few weeks later he picked up Swiss student Hans Gimmi (24) then murdered him in a forest at Eskdalemuir in Dumfriesshire. But Simpson, who had been at Carstairs since the events of 1962, now came to the aid of McLellan. He, in turn, was viciously assaulted by McCulloch with a knife and garden fork, slashing off his ears during the attack. Leaving the two men dying from their injuries, Mone and McCulloch headed to the security fence surrounding the prison to put the next stage of their plan into action.

In the weeks leading up to the breakout the pair had gathered money, a map with a route marked on it, clothes, false papers and a weighted rope-ladder. It was this last item they used to get over the fifteen-foot-high barbed-wire security-fence.

On the road outside, Robert McCallum was driving by when he saw a man lying in the road. A second man, wearing a peaked cap, waved him down with a torch. Robert McCallum had no idea that he was dealing with two escaped patients from the hospital. Mone started to explain that there had been an accident, but at that moment a police car arrived with constables John Gillies and George Taylor. A torch was shone in Mone's face. He reacted immediately, attacking the two officers. McCulloch then joined in, striking constable Taylor, a 28-year-old married man with four children, with his axe. He was then stabbed and left dying. Covered in blood, Mone and McCulloch stole the police car, driving past the hospital gates with lights flashing. Meanwhile a bus arrived and George Taylor, who had survived the assault, staggered towards it. He was taken to a local doctor's surgery and then transferred to Law hospital where he later died from serious head wounds.

Around twenty-past-seven, William Lennon and Ian McAlroy were heading in their van along the A702 Peebles–Edinburgh road near Biggar when they saw a police car lying halfway down an embankment. A man dressed in a uniform waved them down and asked for help with an escaped prisoner. As Lennon and McAlroy got out they were axed and stabbed. Lennon was repeatedly knifed in the back with such force that his lung was punctured and a rib broken. McAlroy was battered on the head with an axe. Amazingly both men survived this murderous attack. Mone and McCulloch drove off in the van but, within fifteen minutes, had crashed the vehicle on the outskirts of Roberton village.

Abandoning the van, the two convicts walked over to Townfoot farm and confronted Rennie Craig on his doorstep, threatening to axe him. They were handed the key to his car and immediately drove off. Meanwhile, Mr Craig's daughter, Catherine, hearing the commotion, had called the police and gave a description of the vehicle and its registration number RVO 858M. The gold-coloured Austin Maxi was spotted near Beattock summit on the A74 and chased over the border into Cumbria on the M6. A police car forced the Maxi into a slip road at Rosehill roundabout, a few miles outside Carlisle, and, at 9.20 p.m., it crashed into a lamp-post. Uninjured, Mone and McCulloch attempted to grab another car from a nearby pub, but were overpowered by police. The pair were driven in handcuffs to be held overnight in cells at Carlisle police station.

In an escape lasting a little over two hours, three men had been killed and three seriously injured. It sparked a massive public outcry and the tightening of security at Carstairs. It had been the first escape in the hospital's twenty-eight-year history to result in a death, but in the three years leading to the breakout £500,000 had been spent on security. Security that had been breached with tragic consequences. With 341 patients and fifty murderers housed inside its grounds lessons had to be learned.

On 28 February 1977 Mone and McCulloch were sentenced to life imprisonment with the recommendation that 'they should be detained in prison for the rest of their natural lives'. They were sent to separate gaols. McCulloch admitted all three murders. Mone was found guilty of one, that of police constable George Taylor. Twenty-six years passed before they both found themselves in the same institution when, in May 2003, Mone was sent to Peterhead prison, where McCulloch was already held, to take part in a sex-offenders rehabilitation-programme. Both continue to be viewed as highly dangerous individuals and, in spite of European human rights legislation, it remains an open question whether either will ever be released.

39. Iain Murray

'He is still my son'

Alison Murray had overcome many obstacles in her life. The girl from Drumchapel, a deprived housing scheme in Glasgow, had clawed her way up and was on the verge of a brilliant career. At school she had been thought of as backward and could barely read or write at the age of ten. Then one day her mother, Elizabeth, found a barely legible note on her pillow. It read simply: 'Mummy, I'm so lonely'. Suddenly it dawned on Elizabeth Murray that her daughter was not backward at all; she was dyslexic.

From that day on her mother set out to persuade Alison's teachers that she was in fact highly intelligent; a girl with the potential to go on to university. But that was typical of Elizabeth Murray. She was a mother who was determined that all seven of her children would make a mark in life despite their modest background and she had a staunch supporter in her common-law husband, Iain. The couple met in the late 1970s after the breakdown of Elizabeth's first marriage. She already had three children by then: two boys, Derek and Keith, and Alison, who was then just a toddler. The couple went on to have four children of their own: Iain, the first born, and then Alistair, Eilish and Jamie.

Elizabeth Murray and her close-knit family spent years teaching and encouraging Alison and gradually their efforts paid dividends. She began to excel at Waverley, her local secondary school, and even became dux. From school she went to Strathclyde University to read for a degree in microbiology and genetic engineering. In May 1986 she was about to sit her final exams and, such was her record of academic excellence, that she had already been made an offer by the prestigious Imperial College of London to study for the degree of doctor of philosophy; her field was to be cancer research.

Alison was not the only one in the Murray family who seemed destined for greater things. Alistair and Jamie were doing well at school and had ambitions to go on to university, while Eilish hoped to study art. Another brother, Keith, had a good job with an insurance company in Glasgow, while the oldest sibling, Derek, spent his days looking after his 4-year-old son, Christopher. And for advice and encouragement the younger Murrays had unwavering support from Iain and Elizabeth Murray who worked tirelessly to give their children a head start in life.

If there was an odd man out in this happy and boisterous household it was Iain Murray junior. He was a quiet boy who failed to shine at school and had left without any idea about a career. He started a training scheme in motor engineering but decided to leave after a year, a decision that he tried to conceal from his parents. When they found out he ran away. In fact, he would be away for a year – during which time he lived with another family – before returning home. This did not surprise Derek Murray, who felt it was characteristic of his younger brother: 'Iain was always the coward. He would always run away from things rather than face up to them.'

His only real interest seemed to be music and he spent hours walking the streets with a ghetto-blaster. As often as not he was accompanied by his best friend and former class mate, Brian Wilson, who shared his taste in music. Worried about his aimless lifestyle his father and mother often lectured Iain about getting a job, but to little avail. Perhaps surprisingly he was invariably defended by sister Alison, the brightest and most ambitious of the Murray clan. As Elizabeth Murray said: 'It was always Alison who championed his cause. She was always protective towards him. We used to push Iain to get a job and Alison would always say, "Oh mum leave him alone".' Alison encouraged Iain, helped with his home-work and threw a protective arm around him when he was down. For his part he adored his sister; it seemed to their mother that there was a special bond between them.

But Alison Murray had pressures of her own. In May 1986 she was about to sit her final exams at Strathclyde and, as ever, had studied extremely hard. When she needed a break she would walk through the Bluebell woods close to her home. It helped to clear her head before getting back to the slog of revision. So it was no surprise when she decided to go for a walk on Thursday, 22 May, especially as it was such a fine sum-mer evening. But as she strolled through the woods deep in thought she stumbled upon a scene so shocking that it caused her to cry out in panic.

She saw two teenagers with their trousers around their ankles engaged in mutual masturbation. That alone must have caused her great distress. It was made even worse when she realised who the boys were: one was her 17-year-old half brother, Iain; the other was his best pal, Brian Wilson, who was a year older. Hearing her cry the two youngsters turned and chased after her. When she was finally caught they launched a frenzied attack. Alison was pushed to the ground and had her clothes ripped off. For the next half an hour she screamed for help as the two friends took it in turns to assault her. Then, in a final, desperate act, her assailants tied her bra around her neck and choked the life from her. Her partly clothed body was found eighteen hours later by schoolboys playing in the woods.

For the first three weeks of the investigation police were baffled. The trail was going cold and they badly needed a break. Then they heard rumours that Iain Murray and Brian Wilson were lovers; rumours that the two boys were undoubtedly keen to suppress. But when detectives confronted Murray with a youth who claimed to have had sex with him, his composure broke down and he told his interrogators exactly what had happened on the night that Alison died.

Murray said that when his sister saw them having sex they panicked, afraid that she would tell their parents about the relationship. He described what happened next: 'I put my hands around her throat to strangle her. She was screaming and struggling and after a time she went quiet. I picked up her bra and strangled her.' In another police station, Wilson gave a remarkably similar account of the attack and also told how he tried to have sex with Alison. They then dragged her body by the heels through thick brambles and did their best to hide it in undergrowth. Both young men seemed remarkably unaffected by what they had just done; they calmly went back to Wilson's house for a cup of tea before Murray set off for home as if nothing had happened.

By contrast, the jury at their trial in the High Court in Glasgow were deeply affected by the level of violence perpetrated on Alison. They were shocked by a videotape showing her naked body lying spread-eagled in the undergrowth. And they were stunned to hear that she had been strangled so tightly that the bra had to be cut from her neck by a pathologist during the post-mortem. One juror was relieved midway through the trial such was the horrific nature of the evidence.

As often happens, both Murray and Wilson recanted their confessions. Charged with attempting to rape, strangling and murdering Alison, they pleaded not guilty and lodged a special defence of alibi. Murray claimed that the police constantly shouted at him during interviews and called him a 'poof, pervert and a homo'. In the end he said that he signed a confession because, 'I just wanted to get them off my back.' And it is true that the evidence was rather scanty; even the prosecution acknowledged the case relied heavily on the boys' confessions, while the judge, Lord Robertson, noted in his summing-up that the evidence was 'sparse'.

The jury clearly found it difficult to reach a decision; it took nine hours – and an overnight stay in a hotel – for a guilty verdict to be returned on all three charges. Even then the verdict was on a majority basis. On 10 October 1986 Lord Robertson sent 18-year-old Wilson to a young offenders' institution for life; Murray, aged seventeen, was detained without limit of time in a place to be determined by the secretary of state for Scotland. An appeal was lodged against the convictions and came to court in April 1987; it was, however, thrown out. The crucial piece of evidence, in the opinion of the judges, was the almost-identical accounts given by the two accused of what happened on that fateful night, despite the fact that they were questioned in separate police stations.

The outcome of the trial was devastating for the Wilson family; his mother, Jessie, collapsed on the steps of the court building and had to be taken to hospital. The effect on Iain and Elizabeth Murray was even more pronounced; after all, their son had just been convicted of brutally murdering their brilliant daughter; a daughter that both parents had invested so much time, effort and love in. As Mrs Murray said, 'This is a dreadful day. We have lost a daughter and we have lost a son as well today.' She described how in the months leading up to the trial she almost lost the will to live, and only pulled through with the help of her family . . . and the memory of a special daughter: 'I knew life had to go on. Alison wouldn't have wanted me to give up.'

In the immediate aftermath of the trial both parents were convinced of their son's innocence. They felt that many leads had not been properly investigated by police; leads that would prove their son was innocent. As she left the court a tearful Elizabeth Murray said: 'Alison's killer is still on the loose. Iain is just a silly little boy. I sat through the court hearing, and even the video showing Alison's body, and I know that Iain didn't do it.' They had been persuaded of his innocence at an emotional meeting when Iain was on remand and awaiting trial. Elizabeth Murray recalled the exchange with her son: 'I asked him to look me straight in the face and he told me, "Mum. I never did it." I believed him.' Despite all that had happened, the love of a mother could not be extinguished. As she said: 'He is still my son.'

40. Brian Neill

Killers were allowed to run amok

There are certain crimes that capture the attention of the public. The murder of Devlin McIndoe was one of those crimes, and there were good reasons for the high profile. The backgrounds of the killers and their victim could not have been more marked: Mr McIndoe came from the affluent suburbs of south Ayr, while the gang who murdered him lived in council houses on dreary estates. The killing was not the result of a 'square go' between working-class protagonists determined to fight. There were severe criticisms of the police for the failure to apprehend the killers well before the fatalities occurred. And, finally, it was one of the most depraved murders ever committed in Scotland.

The events that were to lead to Devlin McIndoe's murder began in the quiet seaside town of Troon on the evening of 27 March 1992. Four youths were prowling the streets looking for trouble. They were Brian Neill (20), Kevin Kirkland (20) and Terence McIntosh (19) all of Dundonald, and Lorne Thomson (20) from Irvine. Neill and McIntosh were both out on bail after having been charged with other offences. The quartet caused mayhem in Troon. They punched and kicked a number of local youths and caused a breach of the peace by shouting, fighting, threatening people and brandishing knives at them. Not satisfied with this they travelled to Ayr where they stole a car from the car park at Ayr Hospital and then headed for the area around Ayr harbour. It later transpired that police had been told on three separate occasions about a group of knife-wielding youths but failed to apprehend them.

During the time that Brian Neill and his cronies had been causing trouble in Troon, another group of young men had been enjoying a night out in Ayr. Devlin McIndoe (22), Clive McIndoe (18) Curtis Briggs (19), Maxwell Dawson (24), Steven Taylor and John Morris (18) had all been to a nightclub in the town and, like many young people, made their way to the harbour area at the end of the night. The attraction was probably the late-night coffee and hamburger outlets that operated on both sides of the river Ayr. To an observer the young men would have appeared carefree and in high spirits. They were also very well dressed, reflecting their affluent backgrounds. Devlin McIndoe lived in Broomfield Road, which has some of the most expensive houses in Ayrshire, and he had attended Drumley House, a private school near Ayr.

The trouble started when a passenger in a silver Vauxhall Cavalier leant out of the back window and shouted something about the jacket being worn by John Morris. It was an expensive Chevignon designer jacket with leather sleeves. Morris thought the man was asking where he had got the jacket and he told him it had been a present. But this was no innocent enquiry; the man in the car had actually said 'Give me your jacket. You are getting ripped.' He was later identified as Brian Neill.

Shortly after, there was another incident. Neill approached Morris and Clive McIndoe, threatened them with a sheath knife and said he was going to 'do them with it'. This was followed by a confrontation between Neill and Devlin McIndoe, who persuaded him to put the knife away. Five of the group – Devlin McIndoe, Clive McIndoe, Curtis Briggs, Maxwell Dawson and John Morris – then made their way towards the town centre, minus Steven Taylor who had gone off to a friend's flat.

But their tormentors were determined to have a further confrontation. They drove past the group twice and on each occasion Neill hung out of the window brandishing his knife. When the car passed for a third time one of the group threw something at it and the vehicle screeched to a halt. The men in the car got out and gave chase. Morris and Clive McIndoe chose to run into a side street – a decision that may have saved their lives – while Devlin McIndoe, Curtis Briggs and Maxwell Dawson sprinted into a lane at the side of an old church. Unfortunately, the lane was a dead end.

They were followed by four men, one of whom made the chilling comment, 'We are going to cut you open'. Fearing for their lives, all three made desperate attempts to escape. Maxwell Dawson somehow managed to scramble over the eight-feet-high wall at the end of the lane, despite the fact that it was covered in barbed wire. But his two friends were not so lucky. As he made a desperate attempt to escape, Devlin McIndoe was stabbed twice through the chest by two assailants and slumped to the ground. The thugs then turned their attention to Curtis Briggs, grabbed him in a headlock and struck him in the side with a knife. Despite this Briggs managed to break free and ran into the street where he hailed a taxi. The taxi driver quickly called an ambulance and within minutes McIndoe and Briggs were being whisked to Ayr Hospital. At the hospital desperate attempts were made to save Devlin McIndoe's life. Dr Leo Murray, the head of the casualty department, immediately went to work on him by clearing his airway. When he failed to find any sign of life, he cut open Devlin's chest and massaged his heart. It was all to no avail: the second knife blow had gone right through his heart and had probably killed him within seconds. Devlin McIndoe was pronounced dead at half past four in the morning.

Despite the fact that two of the accused went into hiding they were quickly rounded up by police and put on trial for murder at the High Court in Glasgow in July 1992. The case for the prosecution lasted for six days and included evidence from police, forensic and medical experts. Then the four accused had a chance to give their side of the story. Two of them – Neill and Thomson – refused to give evidence for the defence. When Kevin Kirkland took the stand he attempted to put the blame for Devlin McIndoe's murder onto Terence McIntosh who, he claimed, had admitted the murder while they were smoking cannabis together. McIntosh denied these claims and, when he was in the witness box, put the blame on Kirkland. McIntosh was also asked why they had chased the Ayr boys and replied: 'To teach them a lesson.'

At the end of the trial the jury of ten women and five men took exactly two hours to find three of the accused guilty of the murder of Devlin McIndoe and the attempted murder of Curtis Briggs. They were Brian Neill and Kevin Kirkland, both of whom were given sentences of life imprisonment; Terence McIntosh, then aged only twenty, was ordered to be detained for life in a young offenders' institution. The fourth man, Lorne Thomson, was found guilty of two breach of the peace charges and released. Although McIntosh broke down in tears as he was led from the court, the group soon reverted to type as they were taken to a police van outside. The three killers laughed in the faces of the huge crowd of family and friends outside, as they had done throughout the trial.

The McIndoe family was clearly pleased that the three killers had received their just desserts, although they were dismayed that the fourth thug, Lorne Thomson, was able to walk free from the court. They were unhappy about the actions of Strathclyde Police on the fateful night their son was murdered. Devlin's mother, Brenda McIndoe, said shortly after the trial: 'We would like to know why the police were called three times in Troon and told there were people flashing knives and yet nothing was done. If the police had picked up this lot, Devlin would still be alive today.' Mrs McIndoe, in common with many people in Ayr at that time, was concerned about the level of violence in the town, and also took the view that drastic action was needed to make it safe for innocent people. In particular she called for more police on the streets and heavier sentences for those caught carrying knives.

41. Dennis Nilsen
Killing for company

Dennis Andrew Nilsen was born on 23 November 1945 in Fraserburgh, a fishing town in the north-east of Scotland. One of the baby-boomer generation, he was the second child of Betty and Olav Nilsen, his mother having married the Norweigan soldier in May 1942. They divorced in 1948 by which time Olav junior, Dennis and finally Sylvia had been born. Dennis Nilsen had almost no memory of his father who split from Betty while he was still a toddler. Searching for a father figure he became very attached to his grand-dad, Andrew Whyte, Betty's father. So intense was the bond that Nilsen came to believe that it was his grandfather's sudden death in 1951, and the sight of his body in its coffin, which triggered his bizarre feelings. Warped emotions that eventually turned him into a serial killer. However, like many incidents described by Nilsen these may simply have been the product of his own adult fantasies as he sought to justify the later horrific events in his life.

In fact, Nilsen's childhood seems, if not ideal, relatively stable and there were no obvious signs of a disturbed personality. His mother remarried, becoming Betty Scott, and Nilsen ended up with four more brothers and sisters. At school, not shining academically, he took the initiative to find a job and, in 1961, went straight from the classroom into the army as a 15-year-old recruit. His first posting was to the military training camp at Aldershot. Nilsen, however, was hardly SAS material and graduated to catering jobs, eventually training as a butcher. A skill he would later put to macabre use.

On the surface, content with army life, deep down Nilsen was feeling increasingly uncomfortable over his sexual feelings. He knew he was attracted to other men and had fallen in love with a fellow squaddie. In 1972, aged 27, Nilsen suddenly left the army and enrolled as a trainee constable in the Metropolitan Police. But Nilsen, who had joined the Campaign for Homosexual Equality, did not carry on past his probationary year. He applied for and was taken on as an executive officer at the Job Centre in Soho's Denmark Street interviewing job-seekers.

He was, typically, competent at work and if he did not strike his colleagues as outgoing, neither did he appear a social misfit. But Nilsen was leading a double life and something had to give. By the late 1970s, downing large quantities of his favourite white rum and cola at week-ends, and indulging in casual gay sex, he was slipping into a bizarre dreamland. Nilsen later claimed 'fantasy exploded into reality by my loss of control over it. All moral restraints loosened by alcohol. Until then my fantasy world had been an unacknowledged problem. After the first death it became ritual, a cruel medicine to sedate encroaching insanity.'

On 3 February 1983 one of the residents at 23 Cranley Gardens, Muswell Hill, where Nilsen was occupying the attic flat, noticed that the toilets weren't flushing. An examination by Dynorod of the main drain leading from the house revealed that a strange soup-like 'plug' was blocking the flow. It was too late in the evening to deal with it so it was decided to return the following morning. During the night, however, one of the residents caught sight of Dennis Nilsen in the back garden and heard the manhole cover being removed. When the plumbers returned the slurry had disappeared. This could not have happened by accident. Further prodding revealed a chunk of flesh of some kind further along the drain. Sensing something was badly wrong, the residents called in the police.

Nilsen was not surprised to find officers waiting for him on his return from work. Examination, at Charing Cross hospital by professor David Bowen, of the meat-like morsels discovered in the drain, revealed them to have come from a human body. The set-up of the sewer system at Cranley Gardens suggested that they could only have originated from Nilsen's attic flat.

From the outset Nilsen was remarkably cooperative. As soon as detectives entered his bedsit he directed them to the spots where 'cuts' of his victims had been stored. 'There are some pieces in two plastic bags in the wardrobe', he explained. As Nilsen was being driven to the police station detective inspector Stephen McCusker asked Nilsen, 'How many are we talking about, Des?' 'About sixteen', Nilsen replied coldly. 'Three at Cranley and thirteen at Melrose Avenue.'

It emerged that Nilsen's killing spree had begun five years before in December 1978. He claimed not to know the name of his first victim, a man with an Irish accent aged about eighteen. On the thirtieth of the month Nilsen murdered him in his ground-floor flat at 195 Melrose Avenue, Cricklewood.

He had a better memory of his next victim, whose disappearance attracted national interest. In December 1979 Nilsen got into conversation with Kenneth Ockenden, a Canadian student visiting London, who he then invited back to his flat. He claimed that in this short time he became very attached to the young man. Ockenden was due to fly home the following day, but Nilsen couldn't bear the thought of his new-found friend going and leaving him all alone. His solution was to wrap a wire round Ockenden's neck and strangle him. He then stripped the body, washed it and kept Ockenden beside him in bed overnight. In the morning he put the body in a cupboard and left for work.

Nilsen was now on a slippery slope. Homeless and alone in London, 16-year-old Martyn Duffey accepted Nilsen's invitation to spend the night at his flat. When Duffey went to bed, Nilsen jumped on top of him, trapping him beneath the covers and strangled him with his bare hands. He then dragged him to the kitchen sink, holding his head under water to make sure he was dead. Nilsen and the 16-year-old's corpse then ended up in a bath together in a bizarre twosome, with Nilsen talking to Duffey, saying, 'you've got the youngest looking body I've ever seen'. Aroused by the sight of dead flesh, Nilsen kissed Duffey all over then masturbated to orgasm on his stomach.

Nilsen claimed to have no recollection of murdering 27-year-old Billy Sutherland, a fellow Scot from Edinburgh, but simply of waking in the morning to discover Sutherland's body beside him. He stuffed it under the floorboards, intending to dispose of it later. Nilsen was cute enough to realise that the smell of rotting flesh would attract attention. And that flies would home in on the bodies. He sprayed a generous amount of fly killer over the corpses and splashed deodorant around the rooms to mask the pungent smell of his decaying victims.

Malcolm Barlow was another victim Nilsen could put a name to. An orphan with mental problems, Barlow hung around Nilsen's flat hoping to be invited in. Eventually Nilsen asked him inside, but soon strangled him because Barlow was getting on his nerves. Nilsen, however, was running up against a storage problem. He had two intact bodies under the floorboards and the dismembered parts of a third. He had stored chunks in the garden shed, concealed beneath wads of paper, and other parts that he stuffed into a hole beside a bush. He had a severed torso hidden inside a suitcase in the wardrobe. Pieces like hearts and lungs he'd dumped underneath the hedge believing that these would quickly be eaten up by stray animals. Whenever it was safe, or he ran out of hiding places, he burnt the bodies in the back garden, using tyres and pieces of rubber to hide the smell of cooking flesh. No one ever questioned his actions. On one occasion children came round to watch the blazing pyre. Bones that survived the bonfire, Nilsen crushed to dust.

He left clues for the forensic scientist, but nothing obvious to the casual observer. However, given the quantity of body parts concealed in his flat and garden, even Nilsen realised that the situation could not go undetected for ever. Other residents had puzzled over the strange smells drifting from his flat. He was also under pressure to move out as the owners wanted to sell. Nilsen eventually agreed to go, taking up residence at another address owned by his landlords at 23 Cranley Gardens in Muswell Hill. It was an attic flat, consisting of a small hall that served as a kitchen with a gas stove and sink, a bathroom and two other rooms, one a bedroom that came to serve as Nilsen's main living space.

Nilsen, feeling that 'a change is as good as a rest', believed that moving to a new flat might halt his killing spree. However, it proved impossible to control his murderous instincts. A few weeks after he moved, Nilsen attempted to murder Paul Nobbs and, soon after, Carl Stotter was lucky to escape alive. John Howlett and Graham Allan were less fortunate. Howlett insisted on going back with Nilsen to Cranley Gardens then refused to leave. This triggered a murderous response in Nilsen who took a strip of leather and strangled Howlett as he lay in bed. Nilsen then dragged him into the bathroom and threw him into the bath, where he was left overnight. The following morning he stuffed the body inside a closet. Nilsen realised that the only safe way to dispose of Howlett was to cut him in to little bits and flush it all down the toilet. It turned out to be a much slower task then Nilsen had expected. He decided to boil the head, hands and feet in a large aluminium pot on his cooker to remove the flesh then got rid of the bones either in the rubbish bin or by dumping them in the back garden.

But it was the murder of Stephen Sinclair, a 20-year-old from Perth, that ended Nilsen's killing spree. In Melrose Avenue, situated on the ground floor, Nilsen could hide bodies under the floorboards and had time to arrange their disposal. In his cramped attic flat at Cranley Gardens he had only cupboard space so was forced to dismember the corpses quickly. And get rid of it all. It was by acting in this hasty manner that Nilsen resorted to using the toilet, blocking the drains and bringing the police to his door.

True to his bizarre mentality, Nilsen could never understand what all the fuss was about. And he became irate at press descriptions of him as a ghoul, revelling in the dissected bodies of his victims. He calmly told police officers, 'The victim is the dirty platter after the feast and the washing-up is an ordinary clinical task.' Nilsen wanted everyone to believe that he was really a normal guy, apart from his uncontrollable urge to kill.

At the end of a ten-day trial, on 4 November 1983, Nilsen was convicted of six murders and two attempted murders on a 10–2 verdict and received a twenty-five-year sentence. The verdict shocked Nilsen's mother. Speaking to reporters she said, 'I did think they would give him the benefit of the doubt. I still think he is innocent of murder. I dread to think what he is thinking now. I will never abandon him.'

In 1994 Nilsen's sentence was changed to life and it is unlikely that he will ever be released. He has used his stay in gaol to produce an account of his life and times as a serial killer. A 400-page book that, in December 2003, the courts banned him from publishing. Though it has been seen by some as an attempt by Nilsen to come to terms with his crimes, others see it as the work of an egomaniac, filled with the uncontrollable rage of someone who wishes to bask in the notoriety of his grisly record. As one of Nilsen's surviving victims has said, 'He was a nobody, and he has become a somebody through killing. It is wrong to keep feeding the myth.'

42. The Brenda Page case

The strange double life of a scientist

Thirty-two-year-old Brenda Page was a talented scientist with a bright future. An expert in genetics she worked in the biochemistry department of Aberdeen University, which she had first joined in 1977. Tall and attractive with blue-green eyes she was far from being the typical dusty academic and cut a distinctive figure. If there was a fly in the ointment it was the breakup of her marriage to fellow scientist, Dr Christopher Harrison. He took the failure of their relationship badly and tried hard to persuade Brenda to give it another try, repeatedly phoning her at work and following her through the streets of Aberdeen.

On the day the divorce became final, in October 1977, Harrison turned up at Brenda's flat and, in a rage, broke plates, splattered tea on curtains and threatened his now ex-wife. Eventually, Brenda was forced to take out an order banning Harrison from the area around her ground-floor flat at 13 Allan Street, Aberdeen. Her nervousness was made worse by the fact that Kit, as she called Harrison, lived close by at Mile End Place, just a few minutes drive away. To Brenda's friends the breakup of her marriage did not seem to lead to a flood of suitors or wild partying. Chris Halman who lived in the top flat of 13 Allan Street said: 'Brenda was a very quiet person who kept herself to herself . . . I seldom saw her.'

Friday, 14 July 1978. A day Brenda Page was due to sign important documents in connection with a new research project into the birth of deformed babies. However, she failed to turn up for work and, unusually, had not called in to explain her absence. Around lunchtime Jessie Watt, who worked closely with Brenda, set off for Allan Street to find out if her friend needed any help. But when Brenda failed to respond to repeated knocks on the door, Mrs Elizabeth Gordon, who lived in the flat opposite, and had a key to Brenda's home, was alerted.

Brenda Page's body, fully clothed, was discovered sprawled across the bed. Badly beaten about the face she had been the subject of a sustained attack. Elizabeth Gordon recalled, 'I found her in the bedroom. I saw nothing but blood and hair.' A small window in the spare room had been forced open and it seemed at first glance that whoever had attacked Brenda had got into the flat by this means. But doubts soon emerged. Nothing had been stolen. Brenda had not been sexually abused, and why choose such a small window to force an entry? So if she had not interrupted a burglar in the middle of a crime, was someone lying in wait for her? But, if so, why would anyone want to kill Brenda Page?

The police did have some clues. The murder weapon was thought to be chisel-shaped and they judged, from an examination of Brenda's fingernails, that the killer had been scratched across the face during what they called a 'frenzied attack'. It also emerged that Brenda had been at the nearby Treetops Hotel in Springfield Street on the night of Thursday, 13 July, not arriving home till 2.30 a.m. the following morning, when she had been observed parking her beige Mini Clubman in the cobbled street outside her flat. This was the last time she was seen alive. Around two hours' later, a milkman going to work noticed a man leaving the tenement door of 13 Allan Street who he described as 'between five feet five and five feet eight inches tall, stocky, with dark medium-length hair combed to the left, wearing faded jeans and a dark jacket'. On the basis of this sighting the police issued a photofit picture of the man they wished to interview to the press.

Events then took a bizarre twist. Police investigations into Brenda's life revealed that, in her spare time, she had been working for an escort agency, calling herself 'Miss Adams'. Capital Escorts, based in Edinburgh, provided high-class female company for men visiting the Aberdeen area. William Austin, who ran the agency, spoke very highly of Brenda saying: 'The news of Brenda's murder came as a terrible shock. She was one of our very good escorts being a sociable person of some standing.' And for a brief period it seemed that there could be a link between Brenda's secret life and her death. It emerged that she had gone to the Treetops Hotel the evening before she died to meet two businessmen on a 'date' arranged through her escort employers. However, the lead turned into a dead end and the two men were quickly eliminated from the murder inquiry. Chief inspector James Ritchie, running the investigation, went out of his way to declare of Brenda's encounter with her clients, 'We have no evidence that it was anything but above board.'

However, news of Brenda Page's double life came as a shock to her workmates who knew nothing of her evening job as a paid escort. On the surface, for all her physical appeal and social charms, she appeared to have few friends. The main focus of her attention seemed to have been the three black cats that shared the Allan Street flat with her.

As the police inquiry progressed, Brenda's ex-husband, Christopher Harrison, aware of a whispering campaign, issued a statement through his solicitor. It read: 'Dr Harrison has asked me to state publicly the sincere and heartfelt grief which he feels at the death of his former wife. He hopes that the person or persons responsible will soon be apprehended. For his own part he has cooperated fully with police inquiries and has given a full account of his movements.'

On the surface, the police seemed confident that they were closing in on the murderer, and within a week of Brenda's death assured the public that they were following 'a definite line of inquiry' and had 'no fear that the killer might strike again'. Privately the police were sure that Brenda Page had been deliberately targeted and was well known to the killer. Police teams began a close search of the A92 Aberdeen to Stonehaven road for the weapon that had been used in the attack on Brenda, and for bloodstained clothing, without explaining why they were concentrating on this area. At the same time they appealed for information from anyone who had noticed a dark-green Mini Countryman on this stretch of the road from late on Thursday night, 13 July, to early Friday morning, 14 July.

And they called on any passengers who had boarded the 6.27 a.m. train from Aberdeen to Edinburgh on 14 July to get in touch. They suspected that Brenda's killer had driven to Stonehaven station and caught the train there. Detectives refused to name the man they were focussing on, but claimed that he had not given a satisfactory explanation for his journey to Edinburgh that day. Police also revealed that carriages from the train had been examined by forensic scientists and that parts of the East-Coast line had been searched for clues.

However, in spite of a good description of the man responsible for Brenda Page's death and a strong suspect, the police failed to uncover the evidence that would lead to a successful prosecution. Her mother, Mrs Florence Page, died in 1993 without seeing the person to blame for her daughter's death face justice. However, the file on the case has not been closed and, with advances in genetic fingerprinting, police are convinced that one day it will be solved.

43. Jamie Petrolini

The ultimate dare

Founded by education expert Dr Kurt Hahn in 1933 – and topping the league of Scotland's exclusive schools – Gordonstoun, close to the village of Lossiemouth on the Moray Firth, has earned a reputation that brings children from the world's wealthiest families through its gates. It can proudly claim Prince Charles and the Duke of Edinburgh among its roll of old boys, but, understandably, prefers to remain silent on the behaviour of another, rather more notorious, of its former pupils.

Jamie Petrolini was far from being downtrodden. His parents – Johnny, from an Italian background, and Vanda from Falkirk – lived in the village of Cromdale, owning first a restaurant then an ice-cream parlour in nearby Grantown-on-Spey. They worked hard and saved hard to give their son what they saw as the best education, a coveted place at Gordonstoun. And as an only child they could afford to indulge him. But Jamie, with no brothers and sisters, and only a collie dog, Jake, for close company was a loner. At Gordonstoun in the 1980s, he felt that isolation more keenly as his background couldn't compete with the kids of the super rich. He compensated by turning himself into a games 'jock'. He trained to become super-fit and excelled at contact sports, eventually captaining the school judo team. One friend commented, 'He was always an army sort of guy, and fantasised about the SAS. He wore a cammo jacket, boots and that type of outfit.' But there was nothing to suggest that anything extraordinary would happen in his life until he became friends with Richard Elsey and then a lethal cocktail was formed.

Like Petrolini, Elsey had gone to a private school, Merchant Taylor's, and was an only child. His father was an executive in the electricity industry – financial director of the National Grid – with a plush address in Buckinghamshire. Elsey was an attention seeker and made-up stories to win sympathy, even lying to friends that his sister had been killed in a car crash. He invented roles, claiming to be a second lieutenant in the Parachute Regiment on secondment to the SAS and entrusted with secret life-or-death international missions. In fact, he had only ever been a school naval cadet. The 'false-identity document' he described as having received from the SAS was in reality a railcard he had stolen from a friend and then altered. It is doubtful if many believed Elsey's fanciful tales, but Petrolini claimed that he was taken in by his new friend who he had come to idolise and described as 'an exceptional man'. The two met at a crammer's college, Modes Study Centre in Oxford, where they had gone to retake failed A levels. Both men's parents hoped that a course of intensive study might bring the qualifications to set them up in a productive career. But they were to be disappointed.

Elsey's inability to pass exams meant that he had to give up his ambition of joining Sandhurst to train as an officer. But he could not come to terms with his failure. Instead of abandoning the idea, his burning ambition to be a soldier turned into a weird fantasy. Elsey claimed that he was inspired by reading Andy McNab's book *Bravo Two Zero*, a true story of an SAS patrol behind enemy lines in Iraq. He wanted to be part of that undercover world and Petrolini enthusiastically joined in. At first their actions were at the level of childish games. They pretended to be army officers and gatecrashed a wedding party at the Royal Garden hotel. At another hotel they moved from table to table swapping menus around. They climbed tower cranes in Oxford city centre as height training. But this period of bonding, characterised by rule breaking of a juvenile nature, was leading to something more dramatic and threatening. Elsey was amassing a large collection of deadly knives and both he and Petrolini started 'patrolling' local woods at night, dressed in combat gear, acting out the role of an SAS hit squad.

These pretend games couldn't last for ever, but instead of outgrowing their fantasy the two men turned it into nightmare reality. On 14 January 1994 chef Mohammed El-Sayed (44), a married man with two children, slowed down at a give-way sign at a junction in the Bayswater district of London. He was alone and had forgotten to lock the front passenger door of his silver Audi. In that moment his fate was sealed. Elsey and Petrolini had travelled to London intending to kill a drug dealer; frustrated they seized the opportunity that presented itself. Petrolini slid into the front seat, pulled out a commando knife and waved it in front of El-Sayed's face, at the same time unlocking the vehicle's rear door for Elsey to get in. El-Sayed made a desperate attempt to defend himself and sustained cuts to his arms and shoulders as he fought for Petrolini's dagger. He even managed to open the car door in a frantic bid to escape. But Elsey leaned over and dragged him back, holding El-Sayed tight while Petrolini slashed his throat then rapidly thrust the dagger into his body fifteen times. It was the day before Petrolini's nineteenth birthday.

After the killing, the pair grinned at each other during their tube journey to Victoria coach station. Petrolini was on a high after the murderous attack and told Elsey, 'Sorry, boss, I didn't get it quite right. I will get it right next time.' Later Petrolini claimed that he was in total awe of Elsey at the time of the attack and had a homosexual crush on him. He confessed, 'I was an automaton. I stepped out of the car and walked off as if nothing had happened. It just left my mind. Richard Elsey was the murderer and I was just the knife.' But other evidence suggests that Petrolini was on a mission to prove to his friend that he could kill a man, in what was described as the 'ultimate dare'. Both boys had read books on philosophy and developed an idea that they were demigods while everyone else was expendable.

And they might well have escaped detection if Petrolini had kept quiet about the event. Maybe it was nerves, or maybe sick pride in his deed, but Petrolini could not stop talking about his involvement. To his mother he made a rambling phone call, saying that he no longer wanted to join the army: 'You don't know what they do at weekends', he told her, 'they go out and murder people.' Vanda had no idea that her son was talking about himself. To his college friends he was more direct, and told them what had happened in Bayswater.

Rumours of Petrolini's boasting reached the head of Modes, Dr Stephen Moore. He called Petrolini to his office then asked him directly, 'I understand from another student you have murdered someone – is that true?' After trying to explain his 'role' in the SAS, Petrolini broke down and admitted the killing. The police were notified and Richard Elsey arrested. At his digs officers quickly discovered the £30 commando knife that Petrolini had bought on his friend's instructions and which had been used to kill Mohammed El-Sayed. The weapon had not been cleaned and was still bloodstained. In his confession to the police, Petrolini chillingly explained that the murder was to get 'first blood' so that it would ease his way into the SAS. He added that he felt 'like a vigilante getting rid of the bad in society'. After his arrest, Petrolini was to claim to his parents that he had carried out the killing 'for Queen and country'.

As their trial came ever closer the bond between Richard Elsey and Jamie Petrolini, which had undoubtedly been strong, fell apart as each tried to blame the other for instigating events. In court Petrolini told the jury that the cross-country runs, physical training sessions and 'games' played at night while wearing camouflage gear were part of Elsey's attempts to help him get into the Paras. He added that the two had become blood brothers, cutting their hands and joining them together in a ritual bond. Petrolini argued that he was so much under the domination of his friend that he believed Elsey's claim that the killing of El-Sayed had been sanctioned by the SAS and so they would avoid punishment for what they had done.

Elsey from the witness box gave a completely different version of events, testifying that the pair, 'had gone to London to see a peep show'. He explained: 'I had no idea Jamie was going to kill someone. He had suggested hijacking a car and then suddenly jumped into one as it slowed down at a give-way sign. By the time I caught up, Jamie had already killed.'

The jury, however, gave neither man the benefit of the doubt. Both were found guilty of murder and given life sentences by the judge, Neil Denison, who, addressing the pair, told them: 'You created a world in which you were both playing out your fantasies. It started with relatively harmless pranks and progressed to criminal offences and it developed into an obsession with killing and death. This led to the brutal and senseless slaughter of a complete stranger who just happened to be in the wrong place at the wrong time.'

As Petrolini was led to the cells, fiddling nervously with his rosary, his weeping mother, supported by relatives, admitted, 'Over the past nine months we have had to live with the dreadful knowledge that our son played a part in a terrible criminal offence.' But there was little sympathy for the pair from Sue El-Sayed, the victim's widow. 'The result is excellent', she exclaimed jubilantly, 'I will never forgive them, they are evil. If I had my way they would hang. Prison is too good for them.'

44. Iain Scoular
He could have been a serial killer

The detectives who found Catherine McChord's body at three o'clock on the morning of 1 October 1982 in Braeside Place, Cambuslang knew they were dealing with a cold, calculating and brutal killer. She had been stabbed twice in the back of the head and three times in the chest, suffering what one forensic scientist described as 'extreme violence'. The corpse of the 36-year-old taxi driver from Carmyle in Glasgow had then been stuffed into the luggage compartment of her cab. In a bizarre twist her ignition key, an inhaler and a cigarette lighter had been arranged in a straight line on the driver's seat. This laying out of the victim's possessions was one of the hallmarks of a ritual murder. And it was not the only bizarre aspect of the crime; it later emerged that the killer had spent an hour alone with the corpse in her taxi.

Almost immediately, police had a significant lead to investigate. They were somewhat surprised to discover that the victim had a conviction for a serious crime. Mrs McChord had been found guilty of a £143,500 fraud involving a Spot the Ball competition in the *Scottish Daily Express* and sentenced to three years in prison. This, detectives reasoned, could mean that she had been the victim of an underworld hit. The police urgently pursued this line of inquiry, but it turned to be a complete red herring. It appeared that the McChord murder was motiveless, a fact that chilled the blood of the senior officers in charge. They knew this was a man who was likely to kill again.

At the same time that the underworld connection was being pursued, a massive murder hunt was under way in the local area. Rutherglen CID office was quickly transformed into an incident room and a police caravan was sited in Braeside Place. Appeals were published in local newspapers asking witnesses to come forward and a taxi like the one driven by Mrs McChord was parked in areas she had worked in to jog memories. In fact a number of people did remember seeing her that night, helped by her conspicuous appearance – she was always immaculately dressed, wore lots of jewellery and, invariably, a wig. Yet police were nevertheless disappointed by the response, and some officers attributed this to the victim's conviction for fraud.

Another problem was that the night of the murder was very wet and, as is the norm when it is raining heavily, cabbies have a large number of hires. It proved difficult to locate everyone that she had picked up. As time went on the number of officers involved dropped to twelve as leads were exhausted. But the men in charge of the investigation were concerned. They felt it was only a matter of time before the killer struck again.

Their fears were justified a matter of weeks later when Cambuslang – a quiet suburb to the south of Glasgow – experienced one of the most shocking murders for years. Elizabeth Walton was a nursing sister who lived in the area with her husband and children; a hard working, highly respected member of the local community. After a night-out in Glasgow with a female friend to celebrate her recovery from illness, Mrs Walton made her way home. Her train got into Cambuslang station just after eleven. Her normal practice was to phone home for a lift but this time she decided to walk to her house, which was less than half a mile from the station. She never reached her destination. An assailant, hidden by shrubbery, pounced and knocked her unconscious. He then dragged Mrs Walton into thick undergrowth next to West Coats primary school – the school attended by her 9-year-old daughter – where he strangled and savagely beat her. When she was dead the killer stripped off her clothes and mutilated the body with a knife. Still not content with his handiwork he then 'decorated' the body with the knife by slashing her wrists and cutting her thighs. The killer also tied her clothes in knots. These were the tell-tale signs of a ritual killing. It is little wonder that hard-bitten detectives later described the murder of Elizabeth Walton as one of the most sadistic they had ever encountered. This breed of murderer is often referred to today as a 'signature killer'. Often driven by violent sexual fantasies, they have a compulsion to leave their personal stamp on the victim.

With Cambuslang now in a state of shock, efforts to find the killer intensified. But as so often happens in murder cases the police got a break. A very lucky break. Only seventy-two hours after Mrs Walton was killed a local man, one of many who had called to assist, walked into the caravan with a piece of information. Information that might crack the case. Was this the breakthrough the police had been praying for? The witness, Iain Scoular, aged twenty-four, was personable and well dressed; and he came from a respectable family. This was not the profile of the crank who pesters the police with dubious information and spurious confessions during murder cases. He told detectives that at about 11 p.m. on 2 December 1982 he had been walking home from the pub when he saw a strange man acting suspiciously near the spot where Elizabeth Walton had been murdered. At the time, he said, he thought little of it and went straight home. The officer in charge instructed officers to follow this up by checking out the lead and – given that Scoular had been in the vicinity of the crime scene around the time of the murder – detectives spoke to those closest to him. It was at this stage that police discovered there was more to Scoular than met the eye.

Iain Scoular was a disappointment to his parents, despite their obvious devotion to him. His father, John, was a successful businessman and the family lived in an expensive private development in Cambuslang. But despite his background Iain was a boy with problems. At school he was described as immature, and tended to hang around with children younger than himself. He also told lies constantly and was referred to a psychiatrist as a result. Although his parents had high hopes for him he left Cathkin High School with only one O grade, in woodwork. Following a number of nondescript jobs he ended up as a forklift-truck driver.

Much of his social life centred around visiting pubs, where he frittered away large sums of money on fruit machines. Indeed the problem became so bad that he decided to hand over his pay packet to his father on a Friday night to curtail his spending. Despite his apparent lack of interest in girls, he met a young woman in a local club in July 1980, when he was twenty-two, and they fell deeply in love. The object of his affection, Irene Anderson, described Scoular as, 'the perfect gentleman . . . he was never pushy or fresh and did not try to have sex with me.' Ignoring the disapproval of Scoular's parents about Irene's background – she was brought up in a council house and worked in a factory – the couple got engaged.

Although he was an adult, Scoular's mother still kept a protective eye on him. She admitted to 'old-fashioned views' on the family and would wait up for her son and daughter if they were out for the evening. In fact, she would go out in her car to look for them if they were late home. Iain Scoular even felt it necessary to hide his collection of pornographic magazines from his mother. It is therefore ironic that an ever-vigilant and caring mother would play such a large part in convincing police that her son was a double murderer.

Following Iain Scoular's dramatic appearance in the incident caravan, detectives began to notice cracks in his story. They questioned him no less than ten times in eight weeks, which provoked his father into instructing the family solicitor to write to the chief constable to complain that his son was being harassed. But it did no good; the police team were like a dog with a bone and had no intention of letting go.

It was information provided by Jean Scoular that sealed her son's fate. She told detectives that he had not returned home until one o'clock on the night of Elizabeth Walton's murder. Indeed she remembered the time clearly because she had been out looking for him and they subsequently had a heated argument about him being out so late. Scoular, of course, told police that he got back home shortly after eleven.

Now exposed as a liar Scoular desperately changed his story. He claimed that he had not gone home at eleven but had visited a friend's house to watch a video; police discovered this was also a lie. His next claim was that he had crossed the road to avoid the 'suspicious stranger' who, he said, scared him and had then gone to a local park to sober up. This seemed unlikely because, if he was afraid, why go to a park late at night where he could have been mugged?

With a definite suspect, police could now explore other avenues. There was scientific evidence: hairs from Mrs Walton's musquash jacket were found on a pair of Scoular's trousers – along with bloodstains, grass and mud. The blood was from the victim's group and the grass was identical to that at the scene of the murder. And the draw-cord from his anorak was missing – it may well have been the ligature used to strangle Mrs Walton – and police noted that he was unable to account for its disappearance. The police also found witnesses who identified Scoular as the man seen running at full pelt through Cambuslang shopping centre not long after the murder.

Although detectives were not convinced there was any connection between the McChord and Walton murders another dramatic interview with Scoular's mother helped to change their mind. In an emotionally charged atmosphere at Rutherglen police station Jean Scoular threatened to walk out after being grilled by detectives. She accused police of lying and, clearly at the end of her tether, she made a statement that would put her son in the frame for the McChord slaying: 'It's a wonder you are not blaming him for the taxi murder. It's as well he was at home with his father and I that night.' This was at odds with Scoular's version of events and was compounded by evidence from two witnesses who identified him at an identity parade as the man they had seen running away from her taxi. It was also established that Mrs McChord had been stabbed by a left hander and Scoular was left handed. And it was surely no coincidence that Scoular lived only a few hundred yards from the scene of both murders.

The trial of Iain Scoular for the murders of Catherine McChord and Elizabeth Walton began at the High Court in Glasgow at the end of May 1983. He pleaded not guilty and lodged a special defence of alibi in both cases. During the trial the jury heard a mass of evidence and were shown horrific photographs of Mrs Walton's naked body. The proceedings had no visible effect on Scoular who exhibited a complete lack of emotion. This mirrored his behaviour when being interrogated by police, who noted that he was always polite, helpful and calm. In fact, on one occasion he even halved his sandwich and offered it to the startled officer sitting across the desk. The only time he lost his cool was during questioning by the prosecution about his sexual inadequacies. Psychiatrists who had examined him came to the conclusion that, as well as being a psychopath, he was impotent.

While the jury members were considering their verdict, Scoular sat alone in his cell reading a novel, apparently without a care in the world. When he returned to the dock he again showed no emotion as the jury brought in a guilty verdict on both charges. He even nonchalantly popped a sweet into his mouth as the verdicts were being read out. The judge, Lord Allanbridge, handed down life sentences for both murders, with a recommendation that Scoular should serve at least twenty years, describing him as an 'extremely dangerous young man'. The officers who had worked on the investigations agreed. Indeed one said of Scoular: 'He was the nearest thing we have seen to an evil, emotionless murder machine. . . . He could have been another Yorkshire Ripper.'

But there was at least one person who still cared for him at the end of the trial: fiancée Irene Anderson, who had grown close to the Scoular family in the face of adversity. She told one newspaper, 'I can't stop loving him. I wish I'd married him sooner.' The reality is that signature killers like Scoular develop a growing taste for murder and rarely stop until they are caught. Miss Anderson could well have been a victim of the man she loved.

45. Jason Simpson
Web of the black widow

Despite her subsequent notoriety, Nawal Nicol was never found guilty of murder, or of any other crime. But she became a source of endless fascination for the media when her husband, 29-year-old Stuart Nicol, was murdered by Jason Simpson and Muir Middler in Ellon, Aberdeenshire. The case had much to commend it to the tabloids: a brutal killing, infidelity, greed, jealousy and a dark-skinned woman motivated by a seemingly insatiable sexual lust. It was little wonder that the press nicknamed her the 'Black Widow'.

The basic facts of the murder are not in dispute. One night, in early June 1994, Stuart and Nawal Nicol had gone to a nightclub in Ellon with their friends, Simpson and Middler. On the surface nothing seemed amiss and the Nicols even had the last dance together. All four of them went back to the couple's home and Simpson and Middler – who had been drinking all day – stayed until Nawal Nicol went to bed. They returned half an hour later and, when Stuart Nicol answered the door, Simpson held him and Middler stabbed him four times in the chest with a survival knife. One blow pierced his heart, killing him within seconds. The killers dumped the knife and their blood-soaked clothes in a wood, where they were later found by police.

At their trial in September 1994 both men were found guilty of murder and given life sentences. There was a further bizarre twist when Frank Nicol, father of the murdered man, got a phone call offering to have Simpson and Middler murdered in Perth prison. The caller said that two cons were willing to murder both men for a fee of only £400 each – quite clearly the value of human life is not highly rated in the criminal underworld! Mr Nicol turned down the offer flat. As he explained, 'I want them to rot in jail. I want them to serve every minute of their life sentences.'

Despite the guilty verdicts against Simpson and Middler, the Crown took the view that the case was far from over. In fact prosecutors were in the process of preparing a case against Nawal Nicol for murder and incitement to murder. It was only when her trial on these charges started in the High Court in Forfar in June 1995 that the astonishing allegations against her were revealed in full. It was suggested by the prosecution that 21-year-old Simpson had been having a torrid affair with Qatar-born Nicol, a woman eight years his senior, and had been driven to kill because of his lust for her. Indeed it was claimed that Nicol had made love to Simpson only four days before the murder. It was also alleged that Nicol had offered Simpson and Middler – who was also said to be her lover – £25,000 each to murder her husband.

In the witness box Jason Simpson testified that Nawal Nicol had been plotting for some time to kill her husband. At first, he said, she had dropped hints about 'getting rid of her husband'. Initially he presumed this meant getting a divorce, but he claimed she actually meant something quite different and more chilling: 'It eventually began to dawn on us that she wanted to kill him and was asking us to help.' Simpson alleged Nawal Nicol had even devised a number of different strategies for the foul deed. One plan involved pushing him over cliffs at Slains Castle in Aberdeenshire, the setting for the Dracula stories – it was alleged that Nicol had dreamt up this plan after she had seen a television documentary about vampires. Another of Simpson's allegations was that she planned a mock burglary with her husband being murdered when he disturbed the intruders. A third scheme envisaged tampering with the brakes on his car.

Simpson denied that Nawal Nicol had offered him money to kill her husband and he also claimed that he had only gone to the house on the night of the murder to warn Mr Nicol of his wife's intentions. He went on to say that when they were in the house he turned round to see Middler stabbing Stuart Nicol with a knife. Nawal Nicol's lawyer, Donald Findlay QC, accused Simpson and Middler of being 'out-and-out liars'.

The Crown may have been persuaded by Findlay's arguments, or perhaps realised that the chances of a guilty verdict were slim. In any event, on the second day of the trial there was a dramatic, and wholly unexpected, twist. To gasps from the crowded public gallery, the prosecution dropped all charges against Nawal Nicol. She was, Lord Johnston said, free to go. At first Nicol looked bewildered but, after regaining her composure, she smiled and whispered 'thank you'.

Although the legal proceedings had reached a conclusion it was far from the end of public interest in Nawal Nicol, the so-called Black Widow. In fact there was what can only be described as a tabloid feeding-frenzy, a frenzy caused in part by her shameless behaviour. Her husband's death left her, at the age of thirty, a wealthy woman. She got more than £100,000 from the sale of the marital home in Ellon, and received tens of thousands from insurance policies. She was also paid £10,000 by the Criminal Injuries Compensation Board for the loss of her husband. She wasted no time in spending her windfall. After buying a luxury flat in Ayr and filling it with fine furniture, Nicol took expensive holidays and partied hard, telling one newspaper she had more than fifty lovers in a year.

But it was her cosmetic surgery that attracted most attention. She paid £6,000 for an operation to have her breasts enlarged from a 34A cup to a 34D cup, and had liposuction on her thighs. The results delighted her and, wearing a micro-mini skirt and a skimpy top with a plunging neckline, she told the *Daily Record*: 'I have nothing to be ashamed of. I had the operation in a Glasgow clinic. It was money well spent. I did it for me, no one else, but the guys certainly seem to approve. Yes it was money I got after Stuart died but I was entitled to it. Remember, I had nothing to do with his killing. Any other grieving widow would receive a cash payment, so why shouldn't I?'

The family of her late husband most certainly did not approve. His mother, who had been granted custody of Stuart and Nawal Nicol's son, was livid and said of her daughter-in-law, 'She's a waster. It is blood money. She's parading around having a life of luxury paid for by my son's death. I just cannot believe her and what she will do next.'

Yet by 1997, three years after the murder, Nicol's cash reserves were draining away. So, no doubt helped by her breast enhancements, she moved to Spain to begin a new career as a stripper. According to one of her close friends this new occupation suited her down to the ground, 'She's going to be a stripper and she'll be a sensation – she loves showing off her breasts.' But her new career in the Spanish sunshine proved a disappointment. After working in go-go bars she graduated to a seedy brothel in San Antonio, Ibiza where she stripped for the male clientele. This work was clearly uncongenial and in October 1995 she was back in Ayr and living in a downmarket rented flat with second-hand furniture; a far cry from her former life of luxury.

Her downward spiral continued and by 1998 she was performing in a lap-dancing pub, called the Fantasy Bar, in Edinburgh. But few customers even noticed her, and even fewer were prepared to pay the £10 charge for a lap-dance. Her best days had gone for good. As one member of staff said: 'Nawal isn't the youngest or prettiest girl we have here and she finds work hard to come by on midweek nights when the place isn't so busy. Guys tend to ignore her if there are younger girls about.' The Black Widow's fifteen minutes of fame – some would say infamy – had come and gone.

46. Angus Sinclair
No hiding place for evil

On 26 November 1978 the body of 17-year-old Mary Gallacher was discovered on waste ground near Barnhill railway station on Glasgow's Petershill Road. Mary, the eldest of six children, was naked from the waist down. Her killer, having removed her trousers, had wrapped them tightly round her neck in an almost ritualistic manner. Her throat had been brutally slashed several times. Mary, a diminutive figure less than five feet in height who dreamed of being a nurse, had last been seen alive when she left the family home in Springburn, Glasgow for a night out with friends. It was to be twenty-two years before scientific advances led the police to her killer. Semen preserved in Mary's pubic hair was the key that eventually linked the murderer to his victim. While the leads to Mary's attacker ran cold, for the next four years the man responsible, Angus Sinclair, raped and brutalised his way across central Scotland. Crimes which, police now suspect, could include bank robberies and murder. In fact, Sinclair could be Scotland's most prolific serial killer. A tag this psychopath would probably revel in. A man without remorse and a vicious child killer.

Sinclair had already served time for homicide before he attacked and murdered Mary Gallacher. His first conviction was in February 1961 when 15-year-old Sinclair was put on probation for three years for a sex attack on an 8-year-old girl. The mental dam in the disturbed teenage mind that was Angus Sinclair had been breached. Six months' later Sinclair was on trial for murder. Catherine Reehill was only seven when Sinclair tricked her into his tenement home at St Peter's Street in the St George's Cross area of Glasgow. A few minutes later she was dead, strangled with the inner tube of a bicycle tyre, her body hidden under his bed, to be dumped in the close of his tenement later. However, detectives quickly linked Sinclair to the murder because of his existing criminal record. On 25 August 1961 at the High Court in Edinburgh, Sinclair was gaoled for ten years on a lesser charge of culpable homicide. Lord Mackintosh told him, 'No young girl would be safe with you about. I cannot conceive a more wicked crime.' A medical report prepared for the trial read, 'Sinclair is obsessed by sex, and given the minimum of opportunity, he will repeat this offence.' But even the experts couldn't have imagined the depths of depravity to which the young criminal would eventually sink.

To the authorities, he presented himself as a reformed character. In Edinburgh's Saughton prison, Sinclair – a former van driver's boy – made good use of his time, training as a painter and decorator. He was released in 1967 to start work in the capital. In 1969, he married Sarah, a student nurse, who knew he had been in prison, but Sinclair hid from her the fact that he was a child killer. Years later Sarah remembered that her husband, 'was a really quiet man, but he did go out a lot. He would go out during the day and I wouldn't see him again till late at night. He would always give me a story about where he was going. He was never aggressive towards me.' The couple moved to Glasgow where, eventually, Sarah became pregnant. In 1972 a son, Gary, was born. Sinclair meanwhile had bought a van and built up a successful ice-cream business. But it was also the perfect cover for sexually assaulting young children. Sinclair was rapidly getting out of control.

By 1982 police in Glasgow were faced with a series of unsolved attacks. These had taken place in different parts of the city, but detectives were convinced they were the work of the same man. They all involved children aged between six and fourteen. And the attacker used the same trick every time. He lured the girls into a close by asking them to help him in some way then threatened them with a knife. In May three little girls were assaulted. On Saturday, 5 June, a 10-year-old girl was tricked into a tenement, but managed to escape before she was attacked. On the same day a 7-year-old girl dressed in her swimsuit was sexually assaulted in a close in Partick after she was tricked to going inside to look for a tennis ball. The victims gave a similar description of their attacker. A man with freckles, paint-splashed shoes and long 'golliwog' hair. The 10-year-old picked out Angus Sinclair's face from a collection of photographs held by the police. Police discovered that Sinclair had returned to his painting trade, which explained the paint spots remarked on by his victims.

Detectives were now on Angus Sinclair's trail and they re-opened the investigation into three brutal, but unsolved, sex assaults on children which had taken place between 1978 and 1979. The attacker, who had lured the youngsters into a tenement, had worn a distinctive tartan lumber jacket. Suspecting Sinclair because of his involvement in the attacks of 1982, police searched his house at 154 Craigflower Road, Nitshill, where a jacket matching the one described by the girls was found. Faced with this incriminating evidence, Sinclair broke down and confessed. He told police, 'I don't know how many. It could be fifty or five hundred.' He offered to help with the investigation to identify the crimes in which he had been involved. And at his trial at Edinburgh High Court made history by asking to be castrated. A request that was refused. But Sinclair's cooperation only went so far. He kept from police the fact that he had murdered Mary Gallacher. And because children had been his victims, he was not at this time linked to Mary's death. It was to be a long time before Sinclair's luck ran out. Nearly twenty years, in fact.

By 1999 advances in scientific techniques led police to reopen Mary's case. Police tested body hair kept following the post mortem. DNA from her attacker was discovered and compared to profiles kept on the national DNA database. It matched Angus Sinclair's. A witness, Barry McGonigal, confirmed that he had seen a man matching Sinclair's description running away from the scene of the crime. In March 2000, Sinclair was arrested in gaol and in June of the same year convicted of Mary's murder. Detectives now faced the shocking possibility that Sinclair, who had previously been seen as a child killer, could be involved in several unsolved adult deaths. He was linked to five killings for which no one has yet been convicted. These were the deaths of Anna Kenny in August 1977, Hilda McAuley in October 1977, Helen Scott and Christine Eadie (the so-called 'World's End' murders) in October 1977 and Agnes Cooney in December 1977.

Anna Kenny was last seen alive as she left the Hurdy Gurdy bar in Townhead, Glasgow on 6 August 1977. Her skeleton was found nearly two years' later in a shallow grave near Skipness in Kintyre. Mother of two Hilda McAuley left the Plaza ballroom in Glasgow and disappeared. Her body was found on 2 October 1977 in Langbank, Renfrewshire. Agnes Cooney was standing at the back door of a social club on the south side of Glasgow one evening in December 1977 when she vanished. Her body was later found on moorland near Caldercruix in Airdrie. She had been stabbed twenty-six times.

These shocking cases have never been solved and caused heartache to the families involved. No one murder is more tragic than another, but some do strike a particular chord. The case of the World's End murders aroused huge publicity. Partly because two young women were murdered at the same time, but also because of the brazen and public way in which the killers went about their business.

It began as a night of fun for two 17-year-olds, Helen Scott and her long-time friend Christine Eadie. On Saturday, 15 October 1977 they were enjoying a pub crawl through Edinburgh city centre up Cockburn Street and into the Royal Mile. At ten o'clock, the crawl came to a temporary halt at the World's End bar situated on the corner where St Mary's Street and the Royal Mile collide. The pub, a popular haunt, was busy. At least two hundred customers, it was later judged.

Although they had arrived with two female friends and knew others in the pub Christine and Helen took a spot by themselves at a table close to the public telephone. Christine, a size twelve, was wearing a blue, midi-length winter coat with an imitation fur collar. And underneath a denim jump-suit, also coloured blue, with a front zip-fastener, cut sleeves and flared trousers. The outfit was finished by a pair of black suede boots with stiletto heels. Helen was more casually dressed with blue jeans and black clogs. Shortly after they arrived the girls were seen talking to two men. The one who seemed to be leading the conversation was aged between 27 and 30, a good bit older than the two teenagers.

Christine and Helen had been invited to a party on the outskirts of Edinburgh and around eleven they were approached by their friends to see if they intended coming. According to one female friend, 'They said they would follow us when they had finished their drinks, and as I left I overheard Helen say to one of the men: "We don't talk to strange men in bars. Go away."' However, other reports suggest that although Christine and Helen could have headed on to the party with the rest of the crowd, they decided to stay in the pub chatting to their new acquaintances.

At two o'clock the following afternoon, Sunday, 16 October, two walkers in Gosford Bay on the Firth of Forth coastline in East Lothian made a shocking discovery. The naked body of a young woman lying among the sand dunes. This turned out to be the corpse of Christine Eadie. Police later revealed that she had been beaten, and sexually assaulted, before being strangled to death. A few hours later, at around six, Helen's body, partially clothed, was discovered lying in a cornfield at Huntington, close to the East Lothian town of Haddington. She had met her death in the same brutal way as her friend. Both girls had their hands tied behind their back and had been strangled with their own tights. Helen had been made to walk barefoot to the spot where she met her death, as mud was discovered clinging to the soles of her feet.

It was clear that the girls, dead or alive, must have been driven to the murder scene. Both bodies were in locations which would have been very difficult to get to from Edinburgh without private transport. It also seemed that the killers were familiar with this area. Only three miles separated the locations of the bodies, but to drive from Gosford Bay in the dark to Huntington requires knowledge of minor roads which a casual visitor would not have. It is unclear in which order the girls' bodies were left, but it would seem likely that the killers, having left Christine Eadie, branched off the A198, which runs past Gosford Bay, and drove down the A6137 towards Haddington, turning into an unnumbered minor road which runs between Phantassie and Upstontigg. This stretch of East Lothian runs along the slopes of a prominence known as Bangly Hill. Having left Helen's body at Huntington the two men would then have had only a short drive to join the A1 trunk road to Edinburgh.

The brutal way in which Helen and Christine met their deaths stirred the whole country. But, on the surface, it did not appear to be a hard crime to solve. The police had good descriptions of the men seen talking to the two girls. Both were in their twenties though one may have been nearer thirty, around the same height, five feet five inches, with short hair. Their hairstyles stood out at a time when longer hair was in fashion. They had local accents. Witnesses had also described their clothes, which included pinstripe trousers, worn by the older of the two, of an unfashionable style which would surely have identified him to friends and acquaintances.

The vicious nature of the crime was also a clue. It suggested that this was not a sudden one-off explosion of sexual violence, but a culmination, based on previous crimes of a violent sexual nature. Part of a pattern of sexual deviance especially in the ritualistic way the killers had carried out the murders in an almost identical fashion. It seemed only a matter of time before someone recognised the two men and brought forward the vital clue to identify them. But it was to be twenty-eight years before someone was charged with the teenagers' deaths. The police had plenty of suspects, but not enough evidence to link anyone to the murders. The name Angus Sinclair was not on their list. But his conviction for Mary Gallacher's death brought him straight into the frame. By the twenty-first century genetic fingerprinting allowed police to link suspects to their long-dead victims. Detectives began investigating known sex killers who had been active during the late 1970s. Operation Trinity was launched in a bid to finally track down Helen's and Christine's murderers.

Angus Sinclair, the convicted killer and rapist, will never be released from prison. He was handed a life sentence in 1982, for his rape of several children, and a second term of life in 2001 for the murder of Catherine Gallacher. But for the World's End killers there will be no escaping justice. On 31 March 2005 Angus Sinclair was charged at Edinburgh Sheriff Court with the murders of Christine Eadie and Helen Scott. He may yet learn that, even behind bars, there can be no hiding place for evil.

47. Robert Smith

Ex-SAS man craved excitement

He was a genuine hero, who bravely defended this country at home and abroad. He served in Northern Ireland and in some of the fiercest encounters of the Gulf War, earning the respect of the battle-hardened soldiers who fought alongside him. Such was his military prowess that he was invited to train with the SAS, and only an injury stopped him from becoming a member of the crack regiment. But he was an adrenalin junkie who found it impossible to accept the mundane realities of life away from the combat zone. It was this craving for danger that led Robert Smith to become an armed robber . . . and a murderer.

His army career in the Life Guards seemed conventional enough and during a posting to Windsor he met and married Marie Marsh, a nurse, in 1984. Following his disappointment with the SAS he rejoined the Life Guards and, by the time the Gulf War came around in 1990, he was a lance corporal in charge of a tank. His squadron leader was Major James Hewitt, the former lover of Diana, Princess of Wales. Hewitt and Smith were in the thick of a four-day land battle and Hewitt was very impressed by Smith's professionalism and coolness under fire. He even recommended him for promotion.

After the war Smith was sent back to Windsor, but found the posting dull after the excitement of the Gulf. He quickly went off the rails. As one colleague explained: 'The Army couldn't give him excitement any more, so he looked elsewhere.' In contravention of military regulations he began collecting weapons and, when he was caught in 1993, faced a court martial. Rather than go to trial he went AWOL and seemed to lose his grip on reality. To destroy the evidence against him 32-year-old Smith tried to burn down the offices of the Army investigators who had compiled files on his activities. And, around this time, it is thought he was involved in gun-running to Somalia and in recruiting mercenaries to fight in the former Yugoslavia.

While on the run Smith – always the Romeo – took up with two women: first of all Lorraine McKay, who he left after six months, and then a Scottish barmaid, Fiona Agnew, who he met in London. But it was a chance meeting with Gerald McQuade, also in London, that put Robert Smith on the rocky road. McQuade (40), from Maryhill in Glasgow, fancied himself as a criminal mastermind. The reality was that his crimes normally ended in ignominious failure; he had a string of convictions, including one for armed robbery that landed him in jail for five years. But he was still able to persuade Smith to join him in an audacious bank raid: a raid that he had meticulously planned; a raid he hoped would earn hundreds of thousands of pounds.

But first they needed a getaway man. They thought that Paul Bootland was the perfect candidate. Bootland, aged twenty-five, was from a wealthy family in Edinburgh and grew up in the lap of luxury. But he was a Walter Mitty character who craved respect and thought he could get it by becoming a gangster. In his boyhood he made a start by committing petty crimes, a process that culminated in him stabbing a nightclub bouncer. He moved to Glasgow, gradually losing touch with his family, and met Smith and McQuade in a pub. The three of them went out on drinking sessions and the naive young man from the comfortable background was impressed by the exploits of the former SAS soldier and the hardened criminal.

The die was cast and on the morning of 19 October 1994 the trio drove to the quiet town of Bonnyrigg in Midlothian in a stolen Ford Granada. Their target was a Securicor van that was delivering cash to the Bank of Scotland in the High Street. When the three security men entered the bank Smith and McQuade, both masked and armed, sprinted in after them. As terrified staff and customers looked on they snatched four bags containing £185,000 and ran towards Bootland in the getaway car, which was parked seventy yards away in a car park. They had been in the bank for less than a minute.

But the robbers reckoned without the brave men of Bonnyrigg. There was a shout of, 'the bastards have robbed the bank' and John Duffy, an off-duty detective, and his pal, Duncan 'Spike' Milliken, gave chase. Duffy caught up with McQuade and, as they grappled, the robber tried to shoot him in the chest with his Webley revolver. Fortunately the gun didn't go off. As the struggle continued, McQuade pulled the trigger again but, for a second time, the gun jammed. Amazingly, when Robert Smith tried to fire his gun it also misfired and the bullet stuck in the barrel. By this time the two have-a-go heroes had been joined by John Girdler, a former RAF policeman. Between them they managed to keep McQuade pinned down.

Meanwhile Smith had dived into the back seat of the Granada and screamed at Bootland to go. But the young man had been spooked by the robbery, panicked and stalled the car. That gave Duncan Milliken the chance to haul Bootland – who was also armed – from the driver's seat and pull the keys out of the ignition.

By this time another member of the public had arrived on the scene to tackle the robbers. Retired mining engineer Davie Dunn, a 63-year-old grandfather, had been loading groceries into his car when he saw what was going on. Instinctively he acted, yanking open the back door of the Granada and swinging his shopping bag at Smith. At point-blank range, Smith fired his pistol. The second bullet forced the jammed bullet out and both projectiles hit Mr Dunn in the chest. The bullets made only one entry wound and passed through both lungs and the two main arteries. Davie Dunn staggered against a car and then fell backwards onto the ground. He suffered torrential bleeding and, despite desperate attempts to save him, died within minutes. A witness at the scene said that, as he was trying to help him, Mr Dunn had put his hand up to his chest, looked him in the eye and smiled.

Smith ran off but was quickly spotted and surrendered rather meekly. But such was the level of concern about his fighting skills that he was kept in solitary confinement while in Saughton prison awaiting trial and was guarded by five prison officers when let out of his cell. When the case came to the High Court in Edinburgh, armed police ringed the building because it was thought that Smith had been in contact with another former soldier and might try to escape. In the witness box, Smith admitted that his gun had killed Davie Dunn, but claimed it was an accident as he believed the gun – a Glock pistol he got from an American soldier in the Gulf – would not clear itself after it had initially jammed. McQuade and Bootland elected not to give evidence in court.

Although Smith fired the shot that killed Davie Dunn the jury – after a night in a hotel – found that the robbers had acted together and brought in a guilty verdict on the murder charge against all three accused. On 1 March 1995 Lord Osborne handed down life sentences for the murder and the trio also got long, concurrent sentences for attempted murder and armed robbery. He praised the courage of those members of the public (including the Securicor guards) who so courageously intervened and especially Mr Dunn, who he said had paid with his life.

Bonnyrigg honoured Davie Dunn. He had spent his whole life in the town and the parish church was packed for his funeral. The mourners included have-a-go cop John Duffy. Hundreds more lined the streets in a silent tribute. There were accolades to Davie's bravery from the secretary of state for Scotland, Ian Lang, and the chief constable of Lothian and Borders police, Sir William Sutherland. And the *Daily Record* announced it was setting up the Davie Dunn Bravery Award, to be given annually to a Scot who shows the same level of courage and determination as the eponymous hero.

48. Gemma Valenti and Isabell Carvill
The mother-and-daughter killers

If murders by women are rare the chances of a mother and daughter committing the crime together seem almost outwith the bounds of possibility. But, in June 2003, Isabell Carvill, aged 37 of Rutherglen, and her 17-year-old daughter, Gemma Valenti from Hamilton, made legal history by becoming the first mother and daughter to be convicted on the same murder charge in Scotland. Even more astonishingly they were not the first murderers in the family. In 1993, Frances Carvill, Isabell's sister and Gemma's aunt, stabbed Daniel Currie to death in Glasgow, was convicted of his murder and given a life sentence.

The story of the mother-and-daughter murder began in a house in Blantyre, Lanarkshire in July 2002. Three women, Carvill, Valenti (then aged 16) and their close friend Isobel Black arrived at a party to celebrate a friend's win on the horses. But the mood quickly turned sour when another guest, 32-year-old Kenneth Finnie, allegedly made indecent remarks to the three women. He followed two of them to the toilet, at which point one of the women thrust a glass into his chin breaking his jaw in three places. With Finnie helpless, Gemma Valenti then grabbed a knife and plunged it deep into his heart. As he lay dying from the stab wound, he was subjected to a prolonged and frenzied attack as his assailants kicked and punched him, stamped on his head and hit him on the head with a bottle. Shortly after the attack they were seen wiping his blood off their faces.

Despite the enormity of what she had done Valenti was almost flippant when she was the subject of a medical examination to gather forensic evidence. She said to officers, 'I'm daein' nae mair murders if you've got tae go through this. I should have learned frae my Auntie Frances. She did eight years for murder.' Indeed at the trial in Edinburgh's High Court in June 2003 the judge, Lord Bracadale, took the view that Gemma Valenti was the most vicious of the three assailants and sentenced her to life imprisonment with a recommendation that she should serve at least twelve years before being eligible for parole. For her mother, Isabell Carvill, he may have taken account of the fact that she had attempted to resuscitate her victim and handed down a life sentence with a minimum term of ten years. Isobel Black was convicted of attempted murder and given seven years. The next day one tabloid newspaper spoke for many when it described Carvill and Valenti as the 'she-devil and her spawn'.

Kenneth Finnie's family was outraged at the sentences. His mother, Margaret Finnie, said, 'I am not happy. They should never get out at all.

We have still not got over Kenneth's death and probably never will.' His father, Alex, agreed, 'The sentence was pure rubbish. It doesn't matter if they are all women. Life should mean life.'

The Carvills might well be categorised as Scotland's most dysfunctional family. Three female members of the clan have been convicted of murder. And Gemma Valenti's father Bert – a man she is said to idolise – has served an astonishing total of thirty-seven years in prison for a variety of offences. Indeed did the background of these women lead inexorably to a life of crime? Is there something in the genes that predisposes them to carry out despicable acts, or can we attribute their behaviour to the way they were brought up? It is the old nature versus nurture debate in another form. Neil Murray QC, Isabell Carvill's advocate, pointed out in court that she had a background and upbringing that people would not wish on their worst enemy. Gemma Valenti had a 'hellish' family background, according to her lawyer Jock Thomson QC, and up to three weeks before the murder had been staying in a children's home, describing her time in care as the happiest period of her life. Isobel Black's lawyer noted that his client had suffered abuse and chronic depression, and also had a drug problem. Their chaotic lifestyles were even reflected during the four-week trial. Carvill turned up drunk one day and Black twice slept in.

We may never find the answer to the nature-nurture question. It may or may not be in the minds of Isabell Carvill and Gemma Valenti as they serve their sentences in Cornton Vale prison near Stirling. But there is sure to be one thought uppermost in their minds: their relative Frances Carvill hung herself in Cornton Vale after serving eight years of her sentence for murder.

49. Andrew Walker
Billy Liar

It was a routine job for the three men from Glencorse barracks. Just one of the rather mundane duties carried out by British Army personnel when they are not engaged on foreign fields in the defence of this country. However, it was not a particularly onerous task and they were in good spirits on the cold morning of 17 January 1985 as they looked forward to the forty-minute round trip to Penicuik, a small town in Midlothian. Their job was to call at the Royal Bank of Scotland and pick up £19,000, money that would be used to pay the wages of the soldiers stationed at Glencorse.

As they drove back to base over the Pentland Hills with the cash they saw a familiar figure on the road ahead. It was Andrew Walker, a corporal in the Royal Scots. He was a colleague and a man recognised as a highly experienced soldier. They were not surprised to see him; Walker had cadged a lift back to barracks in the Land Rover twice before. So private John Thompson, who was driving, pulled over and Walker jumped into the back seat, next to staff sergeant Terry Hosker.

Walker's intentions became clear within seconds. He whipped out a Sterling submachine gun from a holdall and expertly shot the sergeant twice through the chest, despite Hosker's brave attempt to wrestle the gun from his grasp. The third member of the payroll team – David Cunningham, a retired major in the Royal Pioneer Corps, who had taken up the post of civilian paymaster at Glencorse – no doubt tried desperately to reason with Walker. But Walker put a bullet through his ear and Cunningham died instantly.

Walker ordered John Thompson to drive up a deserted farm track and, as he drove, the blood of his two dead colleagues dripped onto the snow. Thompson, who must have been petrified, was told to stop and to pull the bodies out of the Land Rover. He was then forced to drag the corpses onto ground near a property known as Loganlea cottage, where Walker pumped two more bullets into Hosker. Then Walker made 25-year-old Thompson kneel down in the snow and executed him by firing a bullet into the back of his neck.

It was a ruthless yet chillingly efficient crime, no doubt helped by Walker's military training. With the three members of the payroll team now dead Walker took what he had come for; the money, which was stored in canvas bags. He hid it somewhere in the Pentland Hills – intending to come back when the heat from the robbery died down – and took away just a few hundred pounds.

It was not long before the alarm was raised. The commanding officer at Glencorse – colonel Clive Fairweather, later appointed as Her Majesty's Inspector of Prisons in Scotland – had returned to base from Edinburgh Castle and was told that the payroll escort was missing. He organised a search party that left immediately for the hills. It was flagged down by a woman who had seen bloodstains in the snow. After she gave them directions, the searchers followed the trail of blood for three miles and found the bodies at Loganlea cottage.

While a massive police investigation got under way Walker was cock-a-hoop and planning a spending spree. Within a few hours of the robbery he phoned a local garage to say that he would pay the £1,000 repair bill for his car in cash. (Not that he intended to keep the old car for long; he had ordered a brand-new factory-built car with many optional extras four days before the robbery, so confident was he of success.) Later that night, watching a television report about the murders with his wife, he boasted: 'I did that. One had a go and I had to shoot him. Then I had to shoot the other two.' He then added with a cold smile, 'No – I'm only joking.' In the evening Walker even had the gall to take his wife and two friends out for a slap-up meal at a Chinese restaurant, and paid the bill with bloodstained notes from the robbery.

His confidence stemmed from the meticulous way in which he had planned the crime, or so he thought. He had tried to make the killings look like the work of the IRA; it was, after all, a time when Republican violence was at its peak. And the modus operandi had some similarities to the IRA's; in particular the way that private Thompson was executed. But the police were not taken in for a minute and looked closer to home for an explanation. Their enquiries revealed Walker had drawn the Sterling submachine gun from the Glencorse armoury at 8.15 on the morning of 17 January, saying that he was going to train another corporal in the use of firearms. He promised he would bring the gun back by half-past ten but did not, in fact, return it until the afternoon. When a ballistics test was carried out on spent cartridges found at the scene of the crime it was found that they matched Walker's gun.

Detectives unearthed other pieces of evidence which, although circumstantial, seemed to suggest that Walker was their man. He was heavily in debt and faced court proceedings from a finance company over an outstanding loan of £3,500. Despite this he had ordered a new car costing £6,500. Then there was the fact that he had been given a lift on two previous occasions by the wages escort, and that on both occasions David Cunningham had been in charge – which must have made Cunningham more relaxed about picking him up. Nor was his alibi convincing; he claimed he had been driving to Edinburgh at the time the crime was committed but could produce no witnesses to corroborate his story.

The detectives leading the investigation were in no doubt. Walker was arrested and remanded in Saughton prison in Edinburgh. And it was while in prison that he devised a ploy that he was sure would clear him. Walker wrote a statement, purporting to be from the IRA, claiming that the killings were carried out by an active-service unit. He even attached a codeword used by the terrorists to verify that it was an IRA strike. Then he persuaded, or forced, fellow prisoner William Lowden to smuggle the document out of Saughton and deliver it to the *Daily Record*. Unfortunately for Walker, Lowden was searched and the statement was confiscated. Then a fatal flaw in his plan came to light; the IRA codeword was well out of date.

A casual observer might have concluded all of this was out of character for Andrew Walker. He was, after all, a brave and accomplished soldier. Born in Leith in 1955 he had joined the Royal Scots at the age of seventeen. He met and married Mary in 1975, just three months into their relationship, and they had two children to whom he was devoted. A keen boxer, Walker became welterweight boxing champion of his battalion. He proved more than competent as a soldier; he was a crack shot and gained special qualifications as a weapons instructor, sniper and assault pioneer. His prowess in the field was equally impressive: he had undertaken three tours of duty in Northern Ireland and was mentioned in dispatches for 'solid, dedicated work carrying out dangerous patrols' in the bandit country of South Armagh.

But, when police looked below the surface, they found much that was disturbing in the life of corporal Andrew Walker. One colleague who served in the same platoon in Northern Ireland recalled how Walker always carried his Magnum revolver when on patrol: 'He'd get young guys out of their homes and get them to kneel on the ground. Walker would stick the barrel of the Magnum in their mouths and curse at them to get information. I think he was always itching to kill.'

And Walker could be just as cruel to his comrades in arms. In 1978, during a tour of duty in Munster, West Germany he and some fellow NCOs operated a protection racket, in which new recruits had their money extorted. A soldier who had served with Walker explained how the gang mistreated the young soldiers:

> They were warned they would be given fourteen days' restriction of privileges for talking back to NCOs unless they handed over fifty marks – about £12.50. If they refused they would get a 2 a.m. rude awakening with the door kicked in and told they were for it. Other times their boots were filled with human excrement or they were hit over the head with a fire extinguisher.

Incidents like these led inevitably to his superiors losing faith in him. At the same time, his fellow soldiers began to tire of his constant boasting and lies; so much so that they nicknamed him Billy Liar. The pattern of deceit was repeated in his private life. In 1983 he met 26-year-old Patsy Stewart and they began an affair after he assured her he had left his wife. It was, of course, a lie. Mary Walker found Patsy's phone number and they met in an Edinburgh pub, where Mary delivered the devastating news that she and her husband were not separated. Patsy recalled the hurt she felt: 'I was absolutely stunned. Mary then asked: "Do you want him?" I replied: "No you have him. I never want to see him again." '

The case against Walker came to the High Court in Edinburgh in the spring of 1985. Walker's alibi defence was rejected by the jury, which took only ninety minutes to reach unanimous verdicts on all counts. He was found guilty of robbery, the three murders and of attempting to pervert the course of justice by blaming the IRA for his crimes. He was given life imprisonment, with a recommendation by the judge, Lord Grieve, that he should spend at least thirty years behind bars. The sentence matched the longest ever handed down by a Scottish court, reflecting what the judge called 'brutal, calculated and callous murders'.

The crimes perpetrated by Andrew Walker shocked the nation. Even hardened detectives still experience a shiver of emotion when they recall those terrible events. The officer in charge of the investigation, Hugh Watson – then assistant chief constable of Lothian and Borders Police – said: 'It was one of the worst murders I have ever attended.' This is hardly surprising; apart from the heartless way the victims were shot Walker widowed two women and made orphans of four children: 56-year-old David Cunningham had three of a family, while John Thompson had a son aged just two. Given the depraved nature of the offences – and his infidelities – it is perhaps surprising that Walker's wife Mary refused to testify against him, a move permitted under Scots law.

And it was all for just £19,000, a pathetically small sum for three lives. But Walker was consumed by greed so overwhelming that it drove him to extreme violence. Some police officers have taken the view that he was capable of such brutality after being desensitised to death and destruction in Northern Ireland. He has never revealed where he stashed his ill-gotten gains. Despite the best efforts of police the money has never been found and it is believed to be hidden deep in the Pentland Hills. Perhaps he expects the money will still be there when he gets out of prison.

Walker has hardly been a model prisoner. While in Peterhead jail in 1986 he took part in a violent siege and got ten years for his trouble. The only crumb of comfort for him is that, in October 2002, his sentence for the robbery and murders was reviewed by judges in the light of human rights legislation. They decided that his prison term should be cut from a minimum of thirty years to twenty-seven. It means that Walker could be a free man in 2012.

50. David Watt
The golf course Casanova

It was certainly by anyone's standards a whirlwind romance. In July 1974, 28-year-old Mrs Betty Torrance, an attractive, petite blonde and former beauty queen was playing golf with two male friends on the Clydebank and District course. At the last hole they were approached by 30-year-old David Watt. According to Betty, 'I was introduced to him and afterwards all four of us had drinks together in the clubhouse and then went to David's home. When the others left, David and I made love together. During the ten days that I knew him we made love three times. He was a fantastic man. So gentle and so kind.' But, in the short time that he knew her, David Watt had become obsessed with Betty Torrance. So intense was his passion that, at the end of ten days, Billy Torrance lay dead and David Watt had been arrested and charged with his murder.

The first inkling that tragedy had occurred came on 3 August when Betty rang Clydebank police station at 1.30 a.m. to report that her husband, was missing. He had not returned home to Carleith farm near Duntocher in Dunbartonshire, where they lived. In fact, she had not seen him for several hours. Police arrived at the farm to be greeted by Betty who was still wearing her nightdress. Searching farm buildings, including the garage, police quickly came across the body of dairy farmer Billy Torrance. Forensic investigation would later show that he had been shot in the body at close range by a .22 rifle and savagely beaten about the head. His skull had been shattered in the attack.

Police soon had a potential suspect. In a statement, Betty told detectives:

For about ten days I have been going out with a certain man with whom I became very friendly and went to bed with more than once. I told him how my husband was knocking about with other women and often beat me, and the man said he would have to do something about it. On the evening of Friday, 2 August, the man came up to Carleith farm. He knew my husband would be out. He had a gun with him and said he was going to kill Billy although I did not believe him. Around 10.30 p.m. I told him Billy would be returning soon and I went upstairs to my bedroom, leaving him outside in the yard. He had a gun with him. I got into bed and was dozing off when I heard a loud thump and then the sound of money falling. I realised that something must have happened, but didn't dare go out to see what. It couldn't have been three quarters of an hour after I went to bed. Then the man came to the door and I went down and out to the garage. He said, 'Do you want to see him?' I said, 'No'. And I knew at that time he meant my husband and realised something must have happened to him.

Betty Torrance did not directly name him in her statement, but there was no doubt that the 'certain man' she had talked about was her most recent lover, David Watt.

From early in the investigation, detectives harboured doubts over Betty's story. Her claim that on the night of the murder she had heard several thuds followed by the noise of money falling while lying down in her bed were tested in a reconstruction. Police sitting in Betty's bedroom could not hear the sounds she had described. But when they stood in the downstairs kitchen it was a different story. The sounds could quite clearly be heard. Police suspected that Mrs Torrance had not given an accurate account of the night's events in her statement.

Detectives guessed that David Watt and Betty Torrance had formed a plan to murder Billy. It all seemed to fit. David, besotted with Betty, wanted her husband out of the way. And Betty's love for Billy had long since turned into loathing. Even though Billy had died a violent death, Betty made no secret of her hatred of her husband, and made no pretence of playing the grieving widow, as she candidly admitted. Her relationship with Billy had scaled the heights and plunged the depths. As Betty explained:

> I was only seventeen, a trainee teacher at Jordanhill College in Glasgow. I had come from the country village of Killin and I suppose I was pretty raw. Billy was good looking and good to me. From the moment he was introduced to me I was captivated by him. A year later we married because we were both in love.

But by the time of the first anniversary of the marriage, their relationship had floundered. Betty was upset by Billy's involvement with other women. She claimed that he, 'started drinking heavily and the more he took the more cruel he became. I lost count of the number of times he spat on me or kicked me.' Of course, when Betty made these accusations, Billy Torrance was in no position to reply.

It also emerged that Betty had seen a lawyer about a divorce, but had decided against it because, as she put it, 'I had two children and I wanted to keep them and the lovely home that I had been used to.' She had also taken a string of lovers although, as she explained, 'I have only slept with men who have meant something to me.' According to Betty, she only embarked on her relationship with David Watt when she found out that Billy was having an affair with her best friend, schoolteacher Jean Orr (26), who often visited Carleith farm, even staying overnight. In May 1974 Betty came across a sexually explicit diary left behind, accidentally, by Jean Orr in a bedroom drawer. The diary detailed the course of Jean's passionate affair with Billy. Produced in evidence at the trial of Betty Torrance and

David Watt in November 1974 it caused a sensation. Press seized on the most lurid aspects of Jean and Billy's sex life together including her description of intercourse in the 'crab position', which mystified some and generated knowing winks from others. But Jean, embarrassed in front of the nation, remained steadfastly loyal to Billy's memory telling of her love for him and the gentle side of the man she knew. So different from the picture painted by Betty Torrance of an insensitive brute.

But throughout the police investigation and at her trial held in the High Court in Glasgow, Betty Torrance emphatically denied any part in the death of her husband. In fact, she seemed puzzled by the turn of events. She claimed, 'I had nothing to do with Billy's death. I didn't help Watt to plot his murder or lay a finger on Billy the night he died. I didn't think for a minute Watt's love was so intense that he would have killed to have me for his own!'

Although David Watt had confessed within forty-eight hours of Billy's murder that he was responsible, and told detectives that Betty had not been involved, police charged both with murder. Perhaps, as the judge was later to suggest, it was Betty's tangled love life that raised questions in police minds about her general morality. A sexual adventuress who was also capable of murder. Betty Torrance and David Watt were like Romeo and Juliet in reverse. If there was one factor which linked them it was their complex love lives.

David Watt, a heating engineer, seemed unable to control his passion for the opposite sex. Married, he was estranged from his wife of three years, Mhairi, but had a son by another woman only months before he became entangled with Betty Torrance. In the weeks before the murder he was seeing all three women. It was even thought that he and Mhairi would get back together again. In fact Mhairi worked part time in the bar at the Clydebank golf club where David first met Betty. Unlike Betty she continued to support Watt arguing that 'violence is completely out of his character'. But she also recognised the flaws in his personality that had brought him down. She explained: 'He did go out with other women when I first knew him, but I thought when we married that would all stop. It didn't.'

By the time the case came to trial, Watt was having doubts about denying Betty's involvement. And several days into the trial he accused his former lover of plotting Billy Torrance's death and said that he had only confessed to protect her. 'I felt guilty', he now claimed. 'I was in love as well.' From the witness box, Watt told the court, 'I don't intend to cover up for Betty Torrance any longer.' He claimed that ten days after their affair began Betty rang him and said, 'I am in trouble and need help. I have shot Billy and killed him.' Watt's account was that after receiving the phone call he went to Carleith farm and found Billy Torrance lying dead in a pool of blood. When the police came to interview him he admitted responsibility because he wanted to protect the woman he had fallen so passionately in love with. He was now telling the truth because he had come to suspect that Betty had been 'too quick' to name him to police as the killer.

He had responded to her late-night phone call, he explained, because:

> I felt that the trouble was caused by me. Betty had told me that Billy was going to kill me because he had found out about us. When I got to the farm she told me she had hit Billy with the gun and she wanted to get rid of it. She also said that there was a hammer left in the garage and she wanted me to take it away too.

Watt also clamed that he took away a bloodstained anorak which he believed belonged to Betty. He admitted that he had burned the clothing at Loch Long and thrown the gun and hammer into Loch Lomond.

But in spite of the police view that Betty had been in a plot with David Watt, and Watt's claim that Betty had killed Billy Torrance, the jury took Betty's side returning a not-proven verdict. Watt was found guilty and received a life sentence. As Betty left the court a crowd heckled and jeered her, shouting 'murderess' and 'you'll be next'. Was this simply jealousy? Betty Torrance may not have been a candidate for sainthood, but she obviously possessed some attractive qualities. Or why else would a man be so determined to kill to have her for his own?

51. Iain Wheldon

Death in the suburbs

Drunken brawls that leave a teenager badly injured or dead are the staple of a Saturday night in our inner cities and deprived areas. But even then no policeman would expect to have to arrest his own son on a charge of murder. Yet in November 1997 that was the stark choice facing a detective with the Lothian and Borders police when the village of Balerno – a byword for affluence and a world away from the slums of the city – was rocked by the death of 19-year-old Mark Ayton.

Mark, an apprentice mechanic working at a taxi-repair garage, was, as his mother Jean recalled, 'just a typical teenager, into records, computers and football'. His father, Malcolm, was a tax inspector from Glasgow who had moved to England where Mark and his elder brother Paul grew up. Although they had returned to Balerno, on the outskirts of Edinburgh, several years previously, Mark had kept a touch of an English accent. A feature that was to become critical to the night's events.

In the early hours of Sunday, 23 November 1997, having spent Saturday evening playing pool and drinking at Balerno's Kestrel pub, the brothers set off for home at Cherry Tree Loan where they lived with their parents. They took the decision to avoid a route which would take them through the centre of the village as, after the pubs emptied, it was a well-known trouble spot. Instead they chose to detour and avoid the neds by heading for Bridge Road and then cutting across the A70 to their own 'territory' on the other side of the main highway. Their walk would take them past the entrance to Balerno High School whose pupils had a history of rivalry with neighbouring Currie High, the school Mark and Paul had formerly attended.

As they reached Bridge Road, only a few minutes from home, the brothers encountered teenagers Iain Wheldon (16) and Graham Purves (16), who were both high on booze. Comments were made which sparked an angry reaction from Mark. Paul (21) later claimed, 'Mark said that they were singing and shouting about us being English.' The brothers confronted the pair and punches were thrown. It was the traditional 'square go', two against two, until Ross Gravestock – who had witnessed the brawl – decided to join in on the side of Wheldon and Purves. Realising that they were being overwhelmed, Paul broke free and ran home to raise the alarm. His last memory of Mark was seeing him pinned against a garden wall being punched and kicked.

Malcolm and Jean Ayton were watching television when Paul burst in. Malcolm recalled:

Paul was out of breath. He said that there had been a fight and he'd lost contact with Mark. Paul had a cut above his eye, but at that stage I didn't think it would be serious. We went out in the car to look for Mark. We thought we'd find him with a black eye and it would all blow over in a couple of days. Paul told Jean, 'Don't worry mum, he'll be all right.'

After searching the area, Paul and Malcolm found Mark in a garden opposite the grounds of Balerno High School. They thought he had simply been knocked out, as at first glance he did not seem too badly bruised, but Mark, in fact, was dying. Extensive efforts were made by paramedics to save him, but he lost the fight for life in the ambulance on the way to Edinburgh Royal Infirmary without regaining consciousness. It turned out that after Mark had stumbled and fallen in a flower bed his attackers had kicked him as he lay on the ground. 'Mark had twenty separate injuries to his head', Malcolm later recalled.

Police cordoned off the murder scene and detectives with forensic officers conducted a fingertip search of the area. But this was not a long, drawn-out investigation and those involved in the fight were quickly identified. Graham Purves went to the police station with his mother. Iain Wheldon with his father. Arrests soon followed. On 25 November, apprentice electrician Iain Wheldon, with Graham Purves, a trainee electronics engineer at British Telecom, and Ross Gravestock, a canteen assistant with Safeway, were charged with the murder of Mark Ayton and of assaulting Paul by repeatedly punching him on the head and body. All three teenagers, first offenders, were remanded in custody. But what rocked genteel Edinburgh society was the fact that the three youths charged with murder all came from well-off backgrounds. Purves's father was a director of Waddie's, the well-known Edinburgh printers. Ross Gravestock's dad was a senior civil servant in the Scottish Office and his mother was a teacher at a private school. Most disturbing of all, Iain Wheldon was the son of a serving chief inspector with Lothian and Borders police. Derek Wheldon was based at Edinburgh west end police station, the 'desk' that includes Balerno in its area of operation. Chief inspector Wheldon had the painful task of escorting his son in for questioning once he became aware that Iain might be able to help with inquiries into Mark Ayton's death. One neighbour said of Wheldon: 'He looked like he thought he was a bit of a hard case, always walking around with a cigarette hanging out of his mouth. But I never thought he would end up involved in something as terrible as this.' It must have been equally true of Graham Purves who the year before had been voted Currie Rugby Club's 'young player of the year'.

At the trial the issue of nationality was seized on by the media because it was an alleged taunt about being English that set events in motion. It turned out, however, that Mark was proud of being Scottish and wore a Scotland jersey. On the other hand, one of his killers, Ross Gravestock, was born in England and had English parents. Defence lawyer and well-known gay-rights activist, Derek Ogg, suggested that the fight had broken out because of long-standing rivalry between pupils of two different schools. Mark and Paul had been to Currie while those accused of murder went to Balerno.

Crown medical experts, meanwhile, told the court that Mark had died because blows to his head had caused bleeding in his brain. Photos shown to the jury revealed eighteen areas with injuries. A police expert testified that criss-cross markings which had left a bruise on Mark's forehead could only have been made by laces on the boots worn by Wheldon or Gravestock. But the defence contended that the teenagers had not intended Mark's death.

Malcolm Ayton commented: 'It does not matter to me if they really meant to kill Mark. There is a feeling in Balerno that it was just lads having a square go. But Mark had twenty separate injuries to his head, and he was kicked while on the ground. That is a lot more than a square go.' He was also convinced that Mark's accent was an issue: 'I believe it all started because they were taunting Mark and his brother with anti-English comments. Before this happened Mark told me other youths had made fun of his English accent.'

However, before the jury at the trial, held at the High Court in Glasgow in May 1998, had to consider a verdict the accused changed their plea and admitted 'repeatedly punching and kicking Mark Ayton to death'. Those involved in the incident, having pled guilty to culpable homicide, seemed genuinely remorseful. Ross Gravestock wrote, 'I hope one day I will be able to be forgiven by everyone involved in this horrible accident. I am very, very sorry for what happened. I would like to express my deepest apologies to the Ayton family and I know this has caused them grief and pain and upset my own family.' All three teenagers expressed the wish that 'the clock could be turned back'.

Lord Eassie, sentencing the three killers, took a balanced – some suggested too lenient – view of the night's events. In his judgement he said: 'However distasteful it may be to speak of someone who is dead, I am bound to take note of the fact that Mark and Paul Ayton were willing participants in the disorder and hostility and assaults which immediately preceded the fatal assault. After the earlier troubles the brothers had not gone home, and continued to behave in a confrontational and aggressive way.' He sentenced the killers to four years. Backdated to the date of their arrest it meant that with good behaviour Wheldon, Purves and Gravestock would be out in two. The short gaol sentences provoked an outcry with allegations that the youths' middle-class backgrounds had guaranteed them leniency.

There were many who saw Mark's tragic death as part and parcel of life on today's streets. Experienced detective Bob Bell commented, 'Young men will always find a reason to drink and flex their muscles. This death is a tragic, but predictable consequence of that.' Detectives also rejected claims of a racist killing. They believed the fight had developed out of a history of violent clashes between youths from Balerno and neighbouring Currie.

But James Clark, a close friend and former schoolmate of Mark Ayton's at Currie, probably summed up the evening's tragic events, 'Mark was a lovely guy and even though he had come up from England he made friends straight away and was accepted at school. I think drink was to blame. Mark was just in the wrong place at the wrong time.'

Mark's killers were released from Polmont young offender's institution on the second anniversary of his death, in November 1999. Malcolm Ayton said that he was resigned to their parole: 'I will probably be at the cemetery when they are released, so there will be a certain irony. I am not a vengeful father. I do not want to see capital punishment, just that they would pay their debt to society. Two years in gaol for stamping and kicking someone to death is at the lower end of expectation.'

52. Howard Wilson
Ex cop turned killer

On Wednesday, 16 July 1969, just after closing time at 3.30 p.m., three men arrived at the Williamwood branch of the British Linen bank in Giffnock. Dressed like businessmen each carried a briefcase, but as the door was opened in response to a knock, they barged inside, pulling stocking masks over their faces and spurting ammonia in the eyes of bank staff. One of the men pulled out a gun, shouting, 'This will only take a few minutes. If you keep quiet, no one will get hurt.' While the clerks – three men and a woman – were tied up, the manager was forced into his office where £20,000 in cash was removed from the safe. After ripping out phone lines, the gang then calmly left the premises pulling the door shut behind them. The robbery had taken less than ten minutes.

It seemed like the work of a professional squad, but detectives were baffled by the fact that not one of those involved appeared to be on police files. Fingerprints left at the scene did not match any on record and witnesses were unable to identify gang members from photographs of known criminals. Even normally reliable informants could not help as the crew was not part of the Glasgow underworld. The police investigation slowed down and ground to a halt. But as a weapon had been used, it was a case that could never be allowed to drop quietly into the 'unsolved' bin. However, no one could have guessed the horrific course events would eventually take.

Five months' later, at ten minutes past three on Tuesday 30 December, three men strolled into the Bridge Street branch of the Clydesdale Bank in Linwood. They claimed to be directors of a plant-hire business interested in opening an account with the branch. But once safely inside the office of assistant manager, Mr Mackin, one of the three men pulled out a pistol and another pressed a knife against his chest. Mackin's hands were tied and a pillowcase pulled over his head. When the manager came back he too was confronted by the gang and tied up. Forcing open the safe the gang put £14,000 in notes inside two suitcases then shovelled all the coins they could find into a black metal box. Leaving the staff locked in the bank, the gang drove to a flat at 51 Allison Street and around 4 p.m. started unloading the cash.

It was at this point that fate intervened. The Allison Street flat stood only a short distance from the headquarters of the Southern police division in Glasgow's Craigie Street. Police regularly passed that way and as chance would have it Andrew Hyslop, a police inspector, drove by and noticed three men struggling with a heavy suitcase into a tenement entrance at number 51. Hyslop immediately recognised one of the men as Howard Wilson. Wilson (31), a former policeman, had left the service after ten years in which he gained three commendations, frustrated at his lack of promotion. He had become a businessman and owned a fruit shop. There was no reason to suspect him of involvement in criminal activity, but something had triggered Hyslop's antennae although he did not immediately link it to the Linwood bank robbery as news of the raid was just breaking.

Accompanied by his colleague – constable John Sellars – Hyslop entered the close, noted that the flat the men had entered was on the ground floor and then went into the back court. A glance through the kitchen window revealed nothing to confirm any suspicions, but Hyslop's police instincts were aroused and he decided to call for back up. Three detective constables now joined them: John Campbell, Angus McKenzie and Edward Barnett. As they crossed back into Allison Street they came across Howard Wilson and, after exchanging a few pleasantries, Hyslop changed the tone of the conversation by telling Wilson bluntly that they wished to clear up the mystery of the black box and suitcase he had been seen taking into his flat.

Wilson claimed to have no idea what Hyslop was talking about but agreed to allow the officers to search the premises. When the police went in they encountered the two men seen entering the flat with Wilson standing in the living room and, beside them on the floor, two distinctive suitcases. The men were Wilson's close friends and identified themselves as Ian Donaldson (31), a motor mechanic, and John Sim (22), another former policeman. Both were involved in Wilson's business dealings and all three were members of a Bearsden gun club. Ignoring objections, Hyslop opened the suitcases to reveal closely packed wads of money, which had clearly originated from a branch of the Clydesdale Bank. The gang had been well and truly caught in a compromising situation from which it seemed impossible to deny their guilt. It was at this highly charged moment that the situation exploded.

Hyslop demanded to see the metal box the men had taken into the flat. But as he walked into the hall to begin the search, Wilson pointed a .22 gun towards his head. Hyslop shouted, 'Don't be a fool', but Wilson pulled the trigger only to hear a click. The gun had jammed. Wilson now had the chance to come to his senses, but instead calmly reloaded, aimed at Hyslop and fired. The bullet caught Hyslop in the left side of his face. He crashed to the floor, blood pouring from his wound. Reacting to the sound of gunfire Angus McKenzie rushed into the hallway and was immediately shot in the head. He was killed instantly. Wilson then turned on Edward Barnett, felling him with a shot to the temple then coldly firing again as he lay on the floor.

There is little doubt that Wilson would have continued his murderous campaign, but before he had time John Campbell jumped on him and struggled for control of the gun. Fortunately for Campbell, Wilson's shouts were ignored by other members of his gang and he managed to get hold of the weapon, which he pointed at Wilson. The killer made no attempt to escape and was led away when police reinforcements arrived, responding to a frantic radio call from John Sellars.

Strangely, Wilson made no attempt to defend his actions and even went so far as to admit that he was wholly responsible for the deaths of Angus McKenzie (31) and Edward Barnett (24), who died in Glasgow's Victoria infirmary two days after the shooting. He told the police that the other members of the gang were not implicated in the killings. On 13 February 1970 Wilson was sentenced at Edinburgh High Court to life imprisonment with a recommendation that he should serve at least twenty-five years. Despite the fact it was the lengthiest minimum sentence ever imposed, Wilson showed no emotion. He had apologised for the deaths of the men and the suffering he had caused their families. There were many who doubted his sincerity given the callous way his victims had met their deaths. It seemed that Wilson's fruit business was in financial difficulties and he urgently needed an injection of cash. Wilson came from a good family. He had attended a leading private school, Glasgow Academy, where he had been rated an excellent pupil.

Wilson was whisked away to begin his prison term, but the public had not heard the last of him. Though he had pled guilty to two murders and one attempted murder, he had no intention of serving his time quietly. In a strange twist of fate, Wilson found himself in the same cell block as hard man Jimmy Boyle, a vicious killer Wilson had helped to arrest as a rookie constable in the early 1960s. But Wilson had drifted far from his position as a respected member of the community and joined Boyle in the notorious 1972 Inverness gaol riots against the introduction of 'cages' – metal barriers to section off part of a cell, which had been installed to control particularly violent characters.

Moved to Peterhead, Wilson took part in organised protests against conditions at the prison, regarded by cons as the most severe in Scotland. Wilson could expect little sympathy for his actions. In 1973 he was charged, with others, for the attempted murder of six prison officers. He eventually received an additional six years after being convicted on the reduced charge of assault. In 1994, on the twenty-fifth anniversary of the killings, he again began protesting, claiming he was being held as a political prisoner. Wilson served thirty-two years before being released on 30 September 2002. He immediately left Scotland to stay with family in England.

Relatives of Wilson's victims were horrified. Alan Hyslop, Andrew Hyslop's youngest son, commented, 'It's disgusting that somebody who has gone and killed two people and attempted to murder someone else is allowed out. This was premeditated murder in cold blood.'

53. The Wood brothers
Scotland's Krays

'We're not pups anymore. We're killers.' boasted Philip Wood to a friend. So where had it all gone wrong for a family that had emigrated from Ayrshire to Canada in the 1960s with such high hopes? They were seeking a new life, and it is not hard to imagine the excitement of David, Philip and twins Douglas and Colin at the move. But somewhere along the line things went badly awry for the boys even though both parents held down good jobs. By the 1980s Douglas and Colin were notorious in the town of Guelph, Ontario having notched up over sixty criminal convictions between them. Douglas seemed to have led the way and, aged only fourteen, earned a spell in a detention centre for car theft. He ignored the warning and along with Colin and Philip, graduated to housebreaking, arson and robbery. Next the brothers made the fateful step of taking, and dealing in, drugs. It brought more money but also arrogance. A sense that somehow they were above the law. Over six foot with blonde hair, an eagle tattoo on his skull and a dagger carved on his forearm, hard man Douglas Wood cut a distinctive and feared figure.

On 15 June 1984 holidaymakers Bryan Bucher and his wife were taking an early morning stroll in Oakville's Coronation Park. As the couple wandered by the side of Lake Ontario, Bryan glanced down the short slope to the shore's edge and was stunned by the sight that greeted him. Lying face down, partly in and out of the water, was the corpse of a young woman. Her dress pulled up above her waist. When the police moved the slightly built body, blood oozed from a savage wound on the forehead. Eventually the corpse was identified as that of 21-year-old Karen Thomson, a sometime waitress. She was a friend of the Wood brothers and had last been seen in the company of their sister on the night of 14 June.

It emerged that Karen, a former girlfriend of Philip, had agreed to testify against Colin in a burglary trial. Karen had been present the night in August 1982 that Colin broke into the branch of the Royal Canadian Legion in Alton. The stolen property had been quickly traced to Philip Wood, who admitted his involvement. Meanwhile Karen had been talking to the police. To avoid being charged she agreed to testify against Colin Wood and signed a statement in November 1982 admitting that she, Philip and Colin had burgled the Legion. Karen's cooperation with the police enraged Colin who stood to lose huge drug deals if imprisoned. He confronted her in the house of David Wood's girlfriend, Rita Gabiniewicz, who said: 'He was screaming at Karen. He said she'd be hurt if she didn't change her testimony.' The incident left Thomson terrified and in tears.

Convinced they were their prime suspects for Karen Thomson's murder, police bugged the homes of the Wood brothers and their friends. On 25 September 1984 a SWAT team stopped David and Colin Wood on the motorway and, weapons at the ready, arrested both brothers. Philip Wood was taken into custody later that same day. Douglas Wood was already in jail for other offences and could not be implicated in the young woman's death.

At the trial, which did not get underway till April 1986, forensic pathologist Dr Chitra Rao testified that Karen Thomson had met a brutal death, beaten about the head with a blunt instrument, maybe a rock, before being dumped in the water, where she drowned. According to Dr Rao, the battering Karen received – at least three hard blows that had fractured her skull – would have been enough to kill her. She estimated the time of death between 4 a.m. and 8 a.m. on 15 June. And according to trial witness, Kim Battersea (17), Karen had gone with David Wood to a flat in Guelph around one in the morning on 15 June, only hours before her lifeless body was discovered on the shore of Lake Ontario.

If true it was a damning link, but there were witnesses with a different version. Denyse Glen claimed that she had seen Karen with three quite different associates. Glen stated that she had caught sight of Karen at around 1.45 a.m. on 15 June, recognising her because she usually came to the Mr Submarine sandwich shop on Thursdays or Fridays for a roast beef sub with double cheese. Denyse remembered that Karen took the meal outside to share with two men, one of whom she recognised as a local drug dealer. Her account was backed by Michael Belcastro who claimed that he saw Karen at 1.45 a.m. outside Mr Submarine talking to a bunch of people sitting on some flowerpots. If true she could not have been, at the same time, in a flat with the Wood brothers.

Whether or not down solely to their vicious reputation, as Patricia Wood, the boys' mother believed, the Wood brothers were convicted of first-degree murder and sentenced to twenty-five years in gaol. On appeal, the charge was reduced to second-degree murder on the grounds that there was no evidence that the killing was planned in advance. But there were more twists to come.

One Sunday in February 1994 Colin Wood escaped from the open prison where he was being held, running from the gym and straight into a waiting pickup truck. Then he just disappeared. Though sightings were made of Colin, even in Guelph itself, it was not until three years' later that he emerged, discovered working at a service station in Birmingham, Alabama. He was flown back to Toronto to continue his sentence and perhaps learn for the first time of the death of his son, 11-year-old Terry, who had been found dead in mysterious circumstances, lying under a pile of leaves. It was speculated that he was a hit-and-run victim. Some suggested a more sinister motive, even revenge.

In September 2000 Philip Wood was released from gaol with shocking news for Scotland. He was still a British citizen and the Canadian authorities were determined to deport him to his homeland. As Scotland absorbed the shock, worse news followed. The gang's leader, Colin Wood, had also failed to take out Canadian citizenship and on his release would also be returned to his homeland. There was an outcry from both press and politicians at the return of a 'psychotic killer', as the Scottish media labelled him. In fact, unnoticed by the public, Douglas Wood had already been deported to Britain in 1990, sent back in shackles in a Canadian air-force jet because commercial airlines refused to take him. He had set up home in London where Philip now joined him, and where he soon hit the headlines, charged with assault after a complaint from a female companion. Colin Wood, perhaps the wildest of the brothers, has also now been released. A man who, according to Michael Prue, mayor of Toronto's East York 'made the blood run cold'.

54. Thomas Young

A danger to women

In early 1967, 17-year-old Pat McAdam took a fateful decision to spend a weekend in Glasgow, travelling up from Dumfries with her 19-year-old friend, Hazel Campbell. The girls spent the day – Saturday, 18 February – shopping then dancing, ending up at a party that lasted to the early hours. Exhausted and tired they decided to head for home even though it would be some time before train and bus services would start up again. The girls, however, thought they had the answer. They would hitch a lift from a passing motorist or lorry driver. They guessed that they would easily find a male driver more than willing to stop for two attractive young women. On this particular February morning, however, they found the going hard. No doubt the fact that it was early on a Sunday made it less likely that they would find a friendly driver heading as far south as Dumfries-shire.

Eventually a lorry pulled over. The driver told them he was heading for Hull and would drop the girls at their home addresses, Hazel in Annan, Pat at Dumfries. The driver, in his mid-thirties, soon revealed a more than passing interest in Pat and when they stopped at a service station at Lesmahagow for something to eat, paid for by the driver, he persuaded Pat into the back of the lorry where they kissed and cuddled. At two o'clock Hazel, as promised, was dropped off in Annan while Pat remained in the cab to be driven on to Dumfries. Pat, however, failed to arrive at her home. By evening with still no sign, her worried parents contacted the police.

Through the description given by Hazel of the lorry, police rapidly traced the haulage firm and then the driver. He admitted that he had given the girls a lift, but insisted that, after making love to Pat in a lay-by outside Annan, he had dropped her off as promised in Dumfries. It all, however, seemed too much of a coincidence. According to Hazel, Pat was having her period, and would not have considered having sex at that time of the month. Furthermore, although Young's lorry had not been seen in Dumfries, one similar to it had been seen speeding along roads between Annan and Lockerbie at the time he claimed to have been in Dumfries. And one very much like it had been spotted parked beside a bridge over the river Annan, which flows into the Solway Firth. One additional piece of suspicious evidence was that the lorry driver had not turned up at his digs in Hull on the evening of Pat's disappearance. The police guessed the driver was not telling the truth, but the fact that Pat's body, if she was dead, could not be found meant that in the end no charges were brought. But there seems little doubt that she was murdered. For the man who picked the teenagers up that day was Thomas Ross Young. A man notorious in Scottish criminal history.

Thomas Young had a criminal record stretching back to his teens with a conviction for sexual assault at the early age of thirteen. Astonishingly, later in 1967 – the year that Pat disappeared – Young was sentenced in England to eighteen months for rape. Then convicted again in 1969 and sentenced to eight years for the rape of a 15-year-old in the back of his lorry. Young was clearly a major danger to any woman unlucky enough to find herself alone with him. In 1975, however, he was released from his eight-year sentence, rented a flat in Glasgow at Ashely Street by St George's Cross and returned to long-distance lorry driving. He also resumed his predatory lifestyle.

On Monday, 22 June 1977, Henry Morgan was driving his tractor on a farm road running off the B804 near the village of Glenboig when he caught sight of an unusual object half-hidden by some bushes. Investigating, he was shocked to discover the body of a woman, her pants stuffed into her mouth and her hands tied behind her back. The body had started to decompose. Although the state of the corpse delayed formal identification, the police were sure from an early stage that it was that of missing bakery worker Frances Barker, who had not been seen at her Glasgow home since 10 June when a taxi driver dropped her off at her tenement flat in Maryhill Road.

Although appalled by the discovery, police suspected that the killer had given away more than he had intended. In April of that same year a prostitute had been picked up by a lorry driver who drove her to the very road on which the body of Frances Barker would later be dumped. The customer had demanded oral sex and, when the prostitute refused, he had attacked her with an iron bar. Though badly beaten she managed to escape and flagged down a passing car. Fortunately, though it would not save Frances Barker, the woman concerned reported the attack to the police. Now the police had something solid to take forward as it seemed more than simple chance that one woman had been brutally attacked and another murdered so close to one another. But would there be enough evidence to link the murderer to the crime?

Police began a systematic investigation of haulage firms around the west coast, checking log and route times. Young's criminal record, coupled with his route times, soon attracted their attention. Suspecting that the police were on his tail, Young abandoned his Ashely Street flat on 1 July and disappeared. The police were sure that they had gathered a strong-enough case to charge Young with at least one count of murder, but it seemed that their suspect had escaped the net. Police guessed, however, that he had not gone too far. Young had a wife, Alice, who he had married in 1956. She had left him by 1970 because of his violent behaviour and remained, understandably, terrified of him. Especially as, in spite of his shocking criminal record and the nature of his crimes, Young was allowed to visit Alice as she had custody of their children. It was, in fact, to Alice's home that Young secretly fled, threatening to kill her unless she allowed him to hide there. Alice, frightened for her life, agreed to Young's demands, forced to watch as he built a crude hiding place beneath the bedroom floor. The police, however, had judged that the flat was a potential safe house as far as Young was concerned. Keeping watch, it was not long before Young was seen moving about. Police went in and Young was arrested. And it turned out that he was not as clever as he clearly believed himself to be. On searching his home, police discovered a number of articles that could be linked to Frances Barker, including a powder compact and lipstick. Like many serial killers, Young could not control the urges that drove his brutal nature. Could not stop himself collecting trophies from his victims. He even gave a bracelet he had taken from Frances Barker's corpse to his daughter. A daughter he apparently doted on.

Meanwhile, furious at his arrest, Young denied all the charges made against him which included, as well as murder, both rape and violent assault. His victims ranged from the age of fifteen to sixty-five. At his trial in October 1977 it emerged that Young drove round Glasgow with a false taxi sign on his car searching for potential victims. He had abducted Frances Barker in this way. Young was clearly a very dangerous man. Arrogant too in believing that, in spite of a mountain of evidence against him, he might just get away with it. But the jury, seven men and eight women, were not taken in and took less than an hour to find Thomas Young guilty of the main crimes with which he was charged. He was given two life sentences.

Young remains the prime suspect in the Pat McAdam case. But true to his cold indifference to the feelings of others he refused to admit to his involvement in her disappearance. Which means that, unless Pat's remains are discovered by chance, we will never know for sure her last resting place. Officially, Pat McAdam is still classified as a missing person. Forever to remain a carefree 17-year-old in the memories of those who knew her.